“As a former minor league catcher and, in 1964, a rookie baseball writer who went on to cover the Indians for 14 years, I very much enjoyed Tom's recollection of his experiences in the clubhouse and the bull pen. I had no idea these records were being set—I'm impressed by the analysis.”

Russell Schneider, former baseball columnist for the *Cleveland Plain Dealer*, noted Indians' historian and author of several books about the Tribe, most notably *The Cleveland Indians Encyclopedia*

“Lots of stats—I played during that era, and the book is of great interest. In the 60s, strikeouts were to be avoided. Now there's no stigma.”

Vern Fuller, former Indians' infielder and executive director of the Baseball Heritage Museum in Cleveland

“Why couldn't a team with this pitching staff—win anything? The anecdotal 'stuff' about individuals was fascinating—stories were great.”

Leo Bradley, Ed. D., Professor, Xavier University, author of *Underrated Reds: The Story of the 1939–1940 Cincinnati Reds, the Team's First Undisputed Championship*

“*Strike Three!* brings a little-known, under-appreciated baseball team into the light. As a former catcher, I relate to the joy Tom shares as he lauds the powerful Indians pitching staff. A book for diehard baseball fans, especially those with fond memories of the game in the '60s.”

Al Spector, author of *Baseball: Never Too Old to Play 'The' Game*

# Strike Three!
# My Years in the 'Pen

Thomas A. Tomsick, M.D.

# Strike Three!

# My Years in the 'Pen

**Thomas A. Tomsick, M.D.**

Jarndyce & Jarndyce Press
Cincinnati Book Publishers
www.cincybooks.com



ISBN-13: 978-0-9817269-6-0
ISBN-10: 0-9817269-6-8

Published by Jarndyce & Jarndyce Press
Cincinnati Book Publishers division of PSA Consulting, Inc.
Anthony W. Brunsman, President

Cover design: Mark Eberhard
Interior design: Mark P. Painter
Editor: Mark P. Painter

Printed in Cincinnati, USA, by The John S. Swift Company

# Contents

# Dedications

*To My Darling Judy, Lisa, Scott, Jackson, Grace, and Megan, who dot the i in my life*

*To patience: Stay focused, work hard, and the game will come to you!*

# Introduction

As might be suggested by its cover, *Strike Three! My Years in the 'Pen* is a semi-biographical recounting of events surrounding the bullpen catcher and the pitching staff of the Cleveland Indians from 1964–66. As such, it would seem to be the ho-hum story of an also-ran baseball team, one that would not for many years yet rise above the "curse" of Frank Lane's trading of Rocky Colavito to the Detroit Tigers in 1960, on the day before opening day, for Harvey Kuenn. It might, at first glance, seem that the book would focus on a number of players only a limited number of fans would be interested in, and therefore it would have similarly limited appeal.

Beneath the cover, however, is the core and major focus of the book: the impressive strikeout records of the Tribe's pitching staff of those years, admittedly led by its nucleus trio of young starting pitchers, the Big Three of Sam McDowell, Sonny Siebert, and Luis Tiant.

Here I present the hypothesis that this staff, and the Big Three, were, as a group, the top strikeout staff in the history of the American League. The Big Three enjoyed individual records as well, especially McDowell who continues to hold individual records and still remains high on the all-time strikeouts list. The accomplishments of the three collectively, all in the first five uninterrupted years of their major league careers, will likely never be repeated.

Appended to this hypothesis, and broadening its impact, is the proposal that latter-day records, some of which ultimately wiped out the individual-season record of the Tribe's staff, were achieved in the era of performance-enhancing drugs. Whereas the attention to drugs has been primarily directed at their impact on home run records, this book refocuses on the potential effect on pitching records.

Recent acknowledgements by hitters, such as by Mark McGwire on January 11, 2010, and by pitchers, such as Andy Pettitte Dec. 16, 2007, and others, that they used performance-enhancing drugs such as steroids and human growth hormone (HGH) raises the specter of a complicated interaction of their effects upon the forces of offense and defense in conflict on the field. Accusations by Ferguson Jenkins that McGwire should apologize to pitchers ignores the fact that some pitchers should apologize to hitters, and guarantees that the battle on the field will continue as a war of words for years to come.[1]

The primary hypothesis above is virtually irrefutable: the numbers speak for themselves, changes in the game over the years notwithstanding. The secondary hypothesis may be untestable: the variables taken into account are numerous and complex. Firm evidence for, and understanding of, the drug effect on strikeouts may never be accumulated.

The central theme is presented from my observations as the Indians' bullpen catcher for the years 1964–66. Wound around that central core of the staff's accomplishments are my personal experiences. These experiences offer insight into the behind-the-scenes activities of the bullpen and batting practice catcher, in the clubhouse and on the field, with comparisons afforded of the 60s to modern-day practices, as they have evolved through the years. The text is supplemented by a collection of photographs that recall people and places of those years, and also serve as a retrospective of old Cleveland Municipal Stadium, with its nooks and crannies hidden amidst its cavernous confines.

A second thread is the resolution of my personal conflict between career choice of professional ball player, first unobtainable but later becoming within reach, or medicine, and the course of events that determined the decision process. The Title *Strike Three!* recalls not only the frequent umpire's exclamation on the ball field elicited by the Tribe's pitching staff, but also my own failed swings at a career in baseball. This sphere of narrative, when ultimately stitched together, culminates in the product of a "misspent" youth pursuing the game, and an adulthood spent in intermittent reflection on the intercurrent events.

At first glance, the 40-plus year passage of time might seem to warrant a "so-what" response to this literary effort. But only through the passage of time can retrospective analysis call attention to any event, or string of events, initially taken for granted, not fully explored, or not fully appreciated at the time it was happening. It is only by comparison to the evolution of pitching and hitting standards that have been established subsequently can the story of the Tribe's staff's true place in the annals of pitching history be bound together for evaluation and appreciation.

The bullpen catcher went on to graduate from St. Louis University School of Medicine, become a Neuroradiologist and Professor of Radiology at the University of Cincinnati, where I still practice, teach, participate in stroke research, and maintain a fan's interest in baseball.[2]

# Chapter 1—The Book

I have been telling my wife for years that I was going to write a book, and I had a couple of ideas for material. No, it wouldn't be a ready-for-TV/movie drama based on my experiences in medical training in St. Louis and Cincinnati, or a comedy with irreverent behavior and raucous partying. A number of authors had long ago beaten me to that punch. Such carryings-on weren't my reality, anyway. I was a bit more of a close-to-the-vest, nose-to-the-grindstone kind of guy.

Perhaps it would be a ready-for-movie-production novel called *"Brain Man,"* the story of an autistic savant who walks around repetitively naming areas of the brain, numbered according to their structure and function (the Brodmann areas of the brain, for those in the know). "Area #4, primary movement center . . . area #44, primary speech center . . ."

I envisioned actor Dustin Hoffman as the afflicted savant, with actor Robin Williams as his doctor, who would somehow bring him from this jail of autistic perseveration of cerebral functional anatomy to a more humanistic and physical relationship with the world around him. This would perhaps include catching butterflies, studying the rotation of small round objects, determining the effect of varying pressure points or lubrication on direction of motion on same, determining the speed of sound from explosive noises 300 feet away, or preventing horsehide from abrasion/staining on dirt and grass surfaces.

Our hero-savant would go on to make his fortune at the new Cincinnati Casino, providing valet service and counting cars, while memorizing customers' license plate numbers and car models in lieu of valet tickets. Somehow, that title and general plot seemed eerily familiar also.

But one title always recurred and resonated in my ears: *"Strike Three! My Years in the 'Pen."* The title, at first hearing, might suggest a recounting of experiences during a period of incarceration after a third criminal offense, with the book cover depicting a forlorn man in jail stripes behind bars.

And I envisioned a different book jacket: a husky, smiling youth, his face behind the bars of a catcher's mask, regaled in the tools of his trade, locked in his own reality of being handcuffed to a catcher's mitt. Yes, *"My Years in the 'Pen"* focusing on the events during three seasons spent as batting practice and bullpen catcher for the Cleveland Indians: 1964, '65, and '66.

It won't be a Jim-Bouton-style *Ball Four!* baseball expose,[3] or a Jim Brosnan-style *Pennant Race* day-by-day recounting of individual queries, quotes, and quips from the author, his teammates, friends, and family during a successful pennant-winning season.[4]

Rather, it would most importantly be a delayed celebration of the accomplishments of the record-setting pitching staff of an also-ran major league baseball club. And it would also be a tapestry of recollection, reminiscence, and remembrance of some of the on- and off-the-field antics of the cast, the characters, the clowns who participated in the daily events surrounding the record-setting seasons. This mosaic is superimposed on a framework of personal involvement that not only gives structure and substance to the observation and opinion, but also offers an interwoven novelette-like story of personal conflict and resolution.

Memory of the individuals, events, and vignettes stayed with me, but I never got around to writing due to limited time, with time that was available filled with preparing lectures, writing scientific manuscripts, chapters, editorials, as well as reviewing the work of others who had the same compulsion to write.

Anyway, who would care about the experiences and the ups and downs of a fellow who toiled behind the plate and behind the scenes? The players I had come in contact with through my position had done notable things on the field, setting records along the way, but why would anyone else really find their story noteworthy now? The records had been broken . . . hadn't they? Several events converged to convince me that there was indeed merit to the effort of chronicling the events, then allowing others to evaluate their significance.

First, the Web gave me reason to reconsider. No, not the web I knew as a youth—the leather piece between the thumb and index finger portion of a catcher's mitt. The Worldwide Web; the Internet. When I logged on, and put "bullpen catcher" into the search request, curious about what might pop up, I came up with 150,000 results! I read some of the content, and found some interesting, some pedantic, some possibly more personal than I could offer. None of the content seemed even close to complete and comprehensive, however.

Second, the Web had given me an insight into how one man's non-necessities can fill another's interest, and be another man's treasure. I had a number of items of baseball-related interest (old player and team pictures, for example), and I thought I'd test the waters of EBay.

I listed originals and copies of some old photos, signed team pictures, individual signed pictures of young men in their prime, but now in their 60s, 70s, 80s, and, in many instances, deceased. Yet the items drew interest, even if copies of the originals. This barometer suggested that some people, perhaps real baseball nerds as I was as a youth, actually were interested in linking to the past. The Web served not only as a yardstick of cultural interest, but also as a ready source of information for documentation of past events: people, places, dates, statistics, and records.

Third, my dear mother, Lucille, (recently deceased, but who lived to read an early, incomplete version of this book) called my attention to an on-line web excerpt of a print book written by an old friend of mine, Dennis Kucinich.[5] The web might also provide a vehicle for dissemination of the story I had outlined in my mind.

The Congressman had written an *apologia pro vita sua* that recounted his youth, his background, hardships, and gravitation to the politics of the less fortunate. Dennis and I had been classmates at St. Peter's Grade School at 17th and Superior in Cleveland for several years, and we had been good friends.

I still have pictures of Dennis and me together on birthdays, First Communion, religious processions, events of note to Catholic families of the 50s. In Dennis's book, he actually mentions my mother and me kindly.

Dennis Kucinich (he left, me right) and I were "Angels" for a First Communion ceremony in 1953.

Although Dennis and I may have gone different ways in political ideology (he left, me quite right) and geographical localization (he north, me south), I admire his singular purpose and fidelity to his background. It was about where he's from. Dennis is to be congratulated for his career of caring service, and for his continuing crusade to serve the constituents of his congressional district and the country. This book is, in part, about where I'm from as well: an inner-city background where sports were an overriding interest, tempered somehow by a compulsion to succeed academically, and to rise above the humble but happy lifestyle my parents had provided.

Other impetus? My son Scott gave me a copy of *Moneyball,* by Michael Lewis, a book about how the Oakland As, one of the financially poorest teams in baseball, won as many games as they did, despite being a small-market, low-budget club.[6]

The answer to the question "How?" is that their general manager, Billy Bean, applied statistical analysis of player performance in decision-making about which players to draft, which to sign, and which to let go. I started to read it, and had a hard time putting it down. It was a great read and got me thinking about more deeply statistically analyzing the Tribe's staff of the mid-'60s. I knew that they had had one impressive statistic: strikeout records. In combination with my other experiences and some additional material I had to offer, perhaps there was a story there, too.

Why in the heck would *I* attempt to write such a book that had something to do with one man's association with, and observations on, baseball? Hitting a moving baseball may be only slightly higher than writing an interesting book on the hierarchy of life's most difficult pursuits, with the risk that many card-carrying sports reporters might find the effort trivial.

Bill James' "book" (*Baseball Abstract*), the basis for the statistical analysis detailed in *Moneyball*, was published in 1977 with only 75 copies sold. I can relate to that stunted success, having in 1997 written and edited a medical monograph with a very narrow focus that sold less than 400 copies, despite positive reviews. If the audience is small, the response can't be big! Yet James's book certainly proved to have value beyond its popularity. It was the seed for an explosion of statistical baseball data analysis: *sabermetrics*, as he coined the term.[7] Some of that analysis related to pitchers' success, and I had been associated with some very successful pitchers. How did they measure up? Where did they fail?

The interest and attention of others isn't the only measure of value. Sometimes there's validity in just putting something you know, but others haven't yet realized, down on paper (or on a computer screen) as an affirmation of your personal viewpoint or insight.

*Moneyball* forced me to recall some of the accomplishments and failures of the teams I was associated with, and made me analyze them in a new light. Of course, I knew at the time many of the pitchers I had caught were great pitchers. But their collective status in the panoply of minor mound gods had been, it seemed, either never fully appreciated, or subsequently lost to the ages in the inevitable advance of athletic accomplishment. It was the classic case of the former leader or record holder sliding step-by-step down, as new records push former holders to lower and lower rungs on the ladder of superlative performance.

The statistical philosophy of *Moneyball* dovetails with my interest at the juncture of record and result: should not the records set by the Tribe's staff have translated into greater success? The philosophy described in *Moneyball* may be a business success method that had yet to be totally successful on the field. Player selection based on appropriately selected statistics identifying baseball bargains by Billy Bean hadn't yet won any championships, but had won a lot of games at low cost. Containing cost was certainly an issue in the 60s as well (it almost moved the Indians to Seattle!), but not the overriding one it has become in the age of $100 million contracts.

The focus in *Strike Three!* is indeed on the *strikeout*, which may, or may not be, the most valued of pitching standards. The groundball may be valued higher by some, where there can be two outs, or occasionally three outs, with just one pitch. With the base on balls (BB), and the home run (HR), the strikeout is one of the parameters under the pitcher's control, not dependent on the players around him.[8] If the pitcher can't throw the ball over the plate in four pitches, and the batter doesn't swing at the offerings, the pitcher gives the batter a free pass to first base. It may be true that the strikeout is hardly economical, requiring a minimum of three pitches to accomplish. When a strikeout can be made, however, it is done with essentially no threat of advancing the offense. If a batter swings and doesn't hit the ball, he can't get on base, with the uncommon exception of the passed ball or wild pitch on a third strike. Nevertheless, some consider it the most overrated of baseball statistics.[9]

Insofar as the home run is the most valued play in baseball by most fans, with up to four runs scoring on one swing of the bat, every true fan is likely able to recount the top individual season and lifetime home run leaders, and many can recall team leaders from the past. On the other hand, while the strikeout may be considered the most valued single pitching statistic by the average fan, fewer fans know which team led the league in strikeouts, or which team holds records for strikeouts in a game or a season.

In 1997, Claire Smith wrote that "Numbers Tell It All: 1997 Was Impressive," recounting a myriad of individual and team records and near-records that fell or were threatened during the '97 season. Randy Johnson said, "The game is really all numbers."[10] Despite recounting a host of record performances, the article failed to note that the Seattle Mariners, led by Johnson, just set a new American League team record for strikeouts in a season that had stood for 30 years.

Finally, it became compelling to write the book when the issue of steroid-enhanced performance of pitchers in the mid-90s through 2004 gained attention through not only public accusations but also admissions of use by individuals in and close to the game, and organized baseball's investigation into those allegations and admissions.[11] The many records of the Indians' staff were broken near the turn of the century, and it seemed feasible that drug-enhanced performance somehow played a part in the evaporation of the staff's records.

Academic and scholarly pursuit dictates we take no events for granted, and subject any observation to scrutiny and analysis. Opinion from one front that an observation, finding, or hypothesis is not valid does not warrant its immediate dismissal. Observations should be recorded, hypotheses developed and tested, and then results carried through to their logical conclusion. Not to do so risks loss of discovery and invention. No topic is necessarily too small or too insignificant to subject to this process, provided there is time and energy to do so. Documenting and analyzing events of those record years is such a pursuit, and represents both a need and a willingness to share something you've come to realize does have value, allowing the baseball community to interpret, dissect, and discuss its significance to its heart content.

The tale of the limited success of the Indians during those years has been well documented, and is already part of the history of the game. The team-member protagonists have been detailed and analyzed, yet not with the fresh focus and outlook applied here. My personal link to the events of that era may merely be circumstantial, but the contemporaneous occurrence does uniquely legitimize my recounting and analysis. No one else participated in the events and activities, or can recount them, in the unique fashion that I am able.

As things have evolved, it would be a mistake to take for granted those record-breaking events of that mid-60's era, and to allow tarnish from the passage of time to diminish the accomplishments of the players involved. Whereas Bill James might look upon my effort as disregarding his admonition that "what we need is for the amateurs to clear the floor"[12] when it comes to serious baseball statistical analysis, even rudimentary evaluation, at minimum, initiates the discussion of the historical import and significance of the Tribe's staff's accomplishments and records.

The later era of performance-enhancing drugs has made it all the more important to revisit the records. The value in evaluating both these eras may not be immediately evident, but may be realized only by ongoing analysis in future years.

# Chapter 2—The Job: 1964

Bullpen catchers have been a part of baseball for at least a century. The baseball use of the word "bullpen" is popularly thought to have arisen from the "Bull Durham Chewing Tobacco" sign. That sign was on the outfield walls, usually next to the warm-up area for pitchers in many ball parks around the country just after the turn of the 20th century.[13] In 1909 there were said to be 50 signs in place, and 150 by 1910. The Bull Durham Company also paid $50 to any hitter who hit a ball off the sign, and a carton of tobacco to any player who hit a home run in a stadium with a sign. As "pen" has been a term used for any enclosure for animals, including bulls waiting to be released into a rodeo or bullfight arena, a combination of the words "bull" and "pen" may have led to the term "bullpen."

Another theory regarding the origin of the term is that relief pitchers in New York's old Polo Grounds warmed up outside the outfield fence, where a there was a fenced stockyard with bulls below Coogan's bluff. Yet another: Casey Stengel supposedly attributed the term to a manager's getting tired of the relief pitchers' shooting the bull on the bench and sending them elsewhere: the bullpen. Insofar as others, not just the relief pitchers, shoot the bull as well, that explanation is highly suspect.

The term bullpen applies to the place itself, or to the aggregate of pitchers who comprise the relief corps who hang out there. The earliest use of the term in relation to the warm-up area for the relief corps is attributed to an article in the 1924 Chicago Tribune.[14] Origin of the term "bullpen" itself, independent of baseball use, remains uncertain, but "bullpen" had been used as an enclosure for prisoners as far back as the Civil War.

Gabe Paul, who became President, Treasurer, and Director of the Indians in 1961, had been a batboy for the Rochester Red Wings of the American Association at age 11. He graduated to bullpen catcher himself in the 1920s, while also reporting high school sports for local newspapers. Paul became a correspondent for the *Sporting News*, then was invited by Warren Giles head of the Red Wings in 1928 (and who would become president of the National League in 1964), to cover the team for the local papers. As a former bullpen catcher, Paul worked his way up the ladder of the organization, and when he became President/Treasurer of the club, he saw the value of having someone in that bullpen-catcher spot, and he also hired amateur players to do the job.

In the post-war era, from 1946–60, the Indians had a bullpen catcher, Bill Lobe, a native Clevelander, whose family owned a tavern and lived on E. 47th Street, not far from my home on E. 57th. He initially was a batboy in 1927, later worked on the ground crew, and then finally was hired as bullpen and batting practice catcher. In 1939, the Tribe activated him as a minor-league player until 1941. He entered the Army in 1942, returning to the Indians for the 1946 season as batting practice and bullpen catcher.

The appearance of the bullpen catcher as coach also coincided with players' returning from the end of World War II. A glut of capable players, and relative prosperity heralded by the war's end, made adding additional coaches feasible. George Susce (who had played for the Indians from 1941–44) served as bullpen coach until 1949. He continued with 4 other clubs until 1972, at age 65. He and Benny Bengough of the Phillies (from 1946–58), were the first two bullpen coaches, in what was initially just a bullpen catcher warm-up job. As bullpen coaches assumed increasing responsibilities as coaches working in tandem with pitching coaches, additional non-roster bullpen catchers were hired. I would see Susce still catching in the Senators' bullpen in 1964 at age 57.

Bill Lobe was also elevated to bullpen coach in 1951, serving through 1956 for manager Al Lopez (another former catcher!). In 1952 Lobe said, "I couldn't hit enough to play pro ball. I could hit well enough on the sandlots, but not in the minors. Maybe it was just as well. Maybe I wouldn't have the job I've got today."[15] He was indeed the prototype predecessor of my position in the 'pen. I'd casually notice Lobe in the Indians' bullpen during games I would occasionally attend, never quite knowing, understanding, or appreciating the full spectrum of his job.

The practice of identifying and using a bullpen coach who spends his time in the bullpen continued to evolve in the 50s. The Tribe had Lobe, who had been a bullpen catcher elevated to bullpen coach, in the bullpen, and Mel Harder as pitching coach, usually in the dugout. Harder was the dean of pitching coaches, serving with team from 1948–63. This was the beginning of defining the job of bullpen coaches—overseeing the activities of the relief pitchers in the 'pen—and the different job pitching coaches, sitting on the bench near the manager, in greater proximity to the current pitcher. The job description overlapped a bit, but the bullpen coach was envisioned as an extension of the pitching coach's influence, just hundreds of feet away.

Jim Hegan, the former Indians' catcher and Harder's teammate, became bullpen coach for the Yankees after retiring in 1961, serving until 1973. In 1964, the pitching coach, Whitey Ford, who was still active as a player, was in the dugout, as Cot Deal (1965), and Jim Turner (1966–73) were later. Hegan also warmed up pitchers himself in the bullpen.

In 1962, with Harder as pitching coach in Cleveland, Gabe Paul hired Hank Izquierdo as bullpen catcher/coach as a favor to Mr. Paul's (pre-Castro) wealthy friend Bobby Maduro. Izquierdo had spent ten years in the minor leagues, with a lifetime average under .200 in the minors.[16] After his year in the 'pen, he then signed with the Twins' organization in 1963 for seven more years. He would finally reach the majors and catch in 16 games for the Twins in 1967, at age 36.

In 1963, the Indians were hurting financially due to poor attendance (562,507). There was some talk of moving the team, so saving a few dollars with an amateur, rather than former professional, who might request a higher salary, was a reasonable plan. All clubs did not necessarily handle the bullpen duties, or allow the same visibility as the Indians did. In *Sports World Magazine*'s 1964 end-of-year summary edition, of the 20 team pictures printed, only two teams included and identified "batting practice" catchers: the White Sox (Joe Heinsen) and the Indians. Six clubs identified batting practice pitchers. Teams generally had four coaches included in the photos, none identified as bullpen coaches.

Warming up pitchers in the 'pen before they enter games in relief of the current pitcher is, by definition, the bullpen catcher's primary duty. Bullpen catchers have become a more visible and vital part of the game itself. With starting pitchers progressively leaving games earlier, with fewer complete games being thrown and more relief appearances made, there's been progressively more activity in the 'pen with each passing decade.

The terms "fireman," "set-up man," and "closer" have been introduced into our lexicon in the past 50 years to describe this new group of hurlers who specialize in the late innings of the ball game. As there are more short-term changes in pitchers, occasionally on a batter-by-batter basis, the bullpen catcher has become busier.

As witness Lobe's and Izquierdo's backgrounds, bullpen catchers at the major league and higher professional levels may have had a variety of backgrounds before the job. Today, however, as we'll see in the next chapter, most current major-league bullpen catchers have been professional players (and not necessarily catchers) who never made the major leagues. Some have even been major leaguers who merely want to stay connected to the game, or use the position to be closer to and learn the decision-making processes involved in coaching. Fewer may be collegiate players with some form of team connection who just happen to be available when the opportunity arises. Whatever the background, they want to keep contact with the game they love. Some bullpen coaches who generally have a greater background for analyzing pitchers, their mechanics, and game strategy itself, may serve as a catcher in the bullpen at the same time.

Bullpen catchers are found at every level of organized professional baseball. Many colleges, independent leagues, and low-minor league teams have bullpen catchers. Chores may widen at the minor-league level to include clubhouse and even public relations duties.[17] The job description can vary from team to team even at the major-league level, depending on the needs of the team. The Seattle Mariners' strength and conditioning coaches have even doubled as bullpen catchers.[18]

The first major component of my job on a day-to-day basis was catching batting practice. It was certainly too menial a duty for roster catchers, but it's a job a bullpen catcher may do as well. In fact, it was the third-least important aspect of my job, and catching BP could have been done by an additional non-roster catcher hired specifically for that purpose. Where teams, including the Indians, did not have bullpen and batting-practice catchers travel with them, they would occasionally hire batting-practice catchers on the road.

But in 1964, there was a certain economy in having a bullpen catcher who would catch not only batting practice but also in the bullpen, rather than hiring people for each of the two jobs. Catching batting practice was a pretty cut-and-dried assignment, lasting about an hour at home, yet it's a draining and tiring hour under a hot summer sun. In 1964, the batting practice pitchers threw from the mound. I often thought the batting practice catcher's job is primarily to give a target to the pitcher, and secondarily to return not only pitches not swung at, but also foul balls lying on the ground in and around the cage after each hitter.

In batting practice in 1964, the catcher might be catching for a non-professional batting practice pitcher, a coach, or much less commonly, a roster pitcher needing a workout. The Indians had three or four non-professional BP pitchers in my tenure, including regulars right-handers Frank Keeney, Clark Grey, Paul Stephen, and lefty Bill Deutcher, in addition to several others who worked intermittently.

Deutcher would usually work the starters' round when a lefty was scheduled to start against the Tribe. Non-professionals are usually chosen who have excellent control, throw strikes with little, or at least predictable, movement on their pitches, and at medium velocity of around 60-70 mph.[19] They typically have uncomplicated, smooth deliveries, with no quirky jerks or motions that would serve to distract or disrupt a hitter's rhythm. You may have seen the type pitching in the Major League All-Star Game Home Run Hitting Contest: no wasted motion, with the ball always visible, at the "right" velocity, and the *same* velocity, right down the middle. Joe Mauer of the Twins even brought his high school coach to pitch batting practice at the contest!

Coaches commonly threw BP as well. They may have been pitchers or position players, but they too learn to have a compact delivery that serves the hitter's purpose of getting his stroke down. Pitching coach Early Wynn frequently threw batting-practice sessions, with his excellent control. Solly Hemus, a former infielder, did so in '64 and '65. Solly had a lot of energy and could throw strikes in rapid repetition, with the limited motion I described.

In addition, a staff pitcher requiring a workout after coming back from an injury, or one merely looking for a workout due to too few appearances on the mound in recent games, might also throw for five or ten minutes. This latter option isn't necessarily the batter's choice, because the pitcher doesn't usually give himself up as readily by reducing his wind-up in achieving the batter's goal, rather perhaps working on keeping the ball low, or working on some degree of movement with a new grip. There's always the temptation for them to "test" the hitter . . . it's almost irresistible. There were no simulated game sessions, where the pitcher throws his repertoire of pitches as if he were actually in a game situation, emphasizing location and number of pitches as if he were pitching consecutive innings, with rests in between.

The second major component of my job involved warming up the starting pitcher before the game. Warming up the starting pitcher is certainly more leisurely than warming up a reliever in the bullpen. Starting pitchers will warm up more slowly and systematically, typically about 12 or 15 minutes, and work on a variety of pitches, only capping off the session with several pitches near full speed. The pitcher will throw 60-80 pitches in his session, and, of course, the catcher returns an equal number. The pitcher will usually soft toss 15–20 throws in front of the rubber, moving back toward the rubber. Some continue past the rubber for another five to ten throws. Then when on the rubber using his windup, the pitcher will increase his velocity slowly for five to ten pitches, then begin to throw several change-ups with the same motion, and then curve balls, sliders, split fingers, etc. Then he will go into his stretch and throw a rotation of his repertoire for another 10-15 pitches. Finally, he will return to his windup, throwing several of each of his pitches, and working up to near-top speed for his last few fastballs.

As a catcher, I usually started the session in the standing position for the early throws, then put down a towel to rest my knee (primarily to keep the pant leg clean) once the pitcher is on the rubber. Then I would assume a standard crouch, starting to give the target more seriously with each delivery from the rubber.

Warming up the starter usually requires greater attention to giving a good target as the session progresses, thus helping the pitcher get his control down and his confidence up. For example, as a right-hander extends his arm, glove palm down, and moves it in a horizontal leftward direction, a motion that that indicates "slider coming," I would just move to his right to give a target on, or just off, the outside corner of a right-handed hitter. He should alternate from the outside to the inside corner, as well, with consideration for the line-up the pitcher will be facing that day. Of course, there's also a premium on making the pitches look as good as possible, to give the starter confidence that he's got his best control and his best stuff. The catcher should be sharp and precise in his receiving, holding the ball within the zone with each pitch, making it look like a strike, and not sloppily pushing it out of the zone, making it look like a ball. The bullpen catcher should treat the session as if catching a game, and give his best effort in his positioning and mechanics.

Before most starting or between-start warm-up sessions, the catcher should be aware if there's anything in particular the pitcher would like to work on. This is more pertinent to "work-out" sessions in the pen, as starters might do between starts, or warming up starters or long relievers, where the session may be unhurried. There's seldom time to "work on something" for short relievers, whose game appearance may be imminent. Over time a relationship of trust in the experience of the bullpen catcher in preparing the pitchers does develop, as Trevor Hoffman pointed out in 2006, and as did Barry Zito and Houston Street in 2007.[20][21]

The value and necessity of the bullpen catcher in 1964 was determined in part by the number of catchers a team was carrying on its roster, as well as the availability of utility players and emergency catchers who might be asked to catch in the 'pen. Availability of only two roster catchers demanded that both be relatively well rested—the second receiver might be forced into action at any time. Bullpen duties would only serve to tire out the second roster catcher if he were to be relegated to the 'pen.

The bullpen catcher becomes an important resource when availability of roster catchers is limited. Typically, a reserve position player, or perhaps a utility player identified as an "emergency" back up, might also be used as an additional catcher in the bullpen. In '63, Ron Hunt, a rookie second baseman with the Mets tired of being relegated to the bullpen, went to Casey Stengel, and re-introduced himself. He told Casey: "I'm not a bullpen catcher. I can play second base." Casey put him in the lineup, and Hunt ended up being second to Pete Rose in the Rookie of the Year voting.[22] The Indians' Chico Salmon, an all-around utility guy, and Chuck Hinton, an outfielder-first baseman, made rare appearances in the bullpen. In fact, both were usually starters in '65 and '66, and not available for 'pen duty. Chuck actually was finally pressed into service behind the plate in 1970, and did catch a few games that year.

I used no protective catcher's equipment warming up pitchers during my tenure, as pictures throughout this book will attest. Coach George Susce used a mask in the Washington Senators bullpen, but virtually no one else did so at the time. Nevertheless, I had only one mishap of a ball glancing off my glove and hitting me in the lip and lower face; it occurred during a pre-game starting pitcher warm-up, in the late afternoon, before the first game of a twilight doubleheader. Dick Donovan was the pitcher, and the setting sun shining from over the left field roof on the west side of the stadium reflected down onto the right field stands, making the backdrop to Dick's pitches very bright. (That's my excuse, and I'm sticking to it!) The ball sailed a bit, but I didn't navigate my mitt into position to catch it, and the ball glanced off the glove and into my face.

Whereas the bright sun led to the incident I just described, I'm a bit surprised the same did not happened during a night game, where the bullpen is less well lit than the remainder of the field, making the recognizable spin of the pitch more difficult to appreciate. Bullpens didn't differ greatly in regard to night-game darkness, and all were relatively less well lit. My ability to see the ball at night actually did seem to decrease over my three seasons in the 'pen. The following year, I would have a formal eye check-up that demonstrated myopia and astigmatism, and I've worn glasses since. (Maybe that's why I couldn't hit.)

In the bullpen, when a pitcher is called to warm up, there is often a sense of urgency, due to a change in game conditions. Late relievers are typically acclimated to heating up quickly if game conditions demand, and some may be ready to go in after 15 or 20 pitches, with eight more on the mound. I've seen Don McMahon go in after ten pitches. If you needed him, he was ready to go. If the reliever isn't going to go in until the next inning, perhaps after a pinch hitter hits for the pitcher, the bullpen warm-up is leisurely, with 20–30 pitches, a rest, then perhaps five to ten more, and another rest, then another five to ten before going in. But different pitchers, and different game circumstances, will require a greater or lesser amount of time and number of pitches.

There were a few other variations on the job theme as well. Separate bullpen sessions for pitchers trying to come off the disabled list seem more common. Occasionally there was a young pitcher or prospect in town that the front office or coaches wanted to evaluate before batting practice. In Cleveland, this workout would occur in front of the dugout, where the starting pitcher warmed up, for everyone to see and to check out the goods.

As bullpen catcher, I would also warm up with other team members in addition to the pitching staff. Position players will want to play long-toss with someone before infield practice, and may just call on the bullpen catcher. Between innings, the outfielders will warm up a bit while the pitcher is warming up. The outfielder closest to the 'pen will want to long-toss with someone from the bullpen area, while the other two outfielders throw to one another.

At Municipal Stadium, Johnny, the right field warning-track gate attendant, opened the gate where I could walk out onto the outfield track or grass, and I would toss the balls to the right fielder for the left and center fielders, and then play catch with the right fielder. In '65 and '66 Colavito and I always enjoyed throwing BB's at one another between innings in right field.

So the bullpen catcher's job will vary from day to day and from team to team. I was a batting practice, starting-pitcher warm-up, and bullpen catcher from '64–66. To catch batting practice, warm up the starter, then catch in the bullpen for a single game was a six- to eight-hour job. Doubleheaders were more common in those days, but there was no batting practice on Sunday, the usual doubleheader day, and it would frequently be cancelled on other unusually hot doubleheader days, or on occasional unusually hot single-game days.

Doing all three jobs can be hot, dirty, tiring, and to some degree dangerous. The foul balls in batting practice can be a risk, requiring that a clenched bare throwing hand be kept behind either your glove or back during the swing, to prevent foul balls from coming back and injuring fingers. Foul balls into the dirt blacken toenails, or may bounce up into the crotch area. You put your body in front of a lot of baseballs every session.

But catchers, by the very nature of their calling, relish tough assignments. You throw hundreds of baseballs every day. The corollary to a starting pitcher throwing 70 warm-up pitches is that the catcher throws 70 in return. Catching BP prior to that probably added another 75–100 throws, as most pitches are hit and not returned. Playing catch with position players before infield practice or the game add another couple dozen. Warming up three pitchers could add another 50–100 throws. Just hope it's a quiet night in the 'pen if your arm is sore!

Doing all three jobs (throwing batting practice, warming up the starting pitcher, catching in the bullpen) may shorten careers, or just make you unable to comb your hair years later. Joe Voccio of the Pawtucket Red Sox (AAA) required shoulder surgery after his first year as bullpen catcher.[23] There's nothing like having batting practice called off, warming up the starting pitcher, then having him pitch a complete game-shutout in a blowout to give your arm a rest. But despite the physical wear and tear of the job, few guys who love the game would even think of turning the job down!

# Chapter 3—The Bullpen Catcher: 2010

Over the years, the major leagues transitioned from non-professionals to professional bullpen catchers—as opposed to the non-professional status I enjoyed in 1964–66. It's difficult to tell exactly when this happened. The Indians' front office had no yearly list of bullpen catchers to share with me. Russell Schneider's *Cleveland Indians Encyclopedia* has no list of bullpen catchers, although he did include recent bullpen coaches in his compendium.[24] Bullpen catchers usually weren't included in the media guides, affirming their behind-the scenes, low-profile position, so getting a comprehensive record was challenging.

But a little detective work has allowed me to fill in the blanks in the Tribe bullpen after I left the job after the '66 season. In '67 and '68, batting-practice pitcher Frank Keeney took over the 'pen job, in addition to throwing and catching BP. In 1969, Don Smith took the job. Don was a local West High graduate, who played baseball subsequently in the Army at Fort Knox. He played in the Cleveland Plain Dealer Class A League, and subsequently the Cuyahoga Valley League, top amateur leagues in Cleveland. He worked for the Cuyahoga County Sheriff's office, and later as a detective sergeant for the City of Mayfield Heights. "Sarge," as Don was called, combined his day job with the police force with the night and weekend job in the 'pen with the team until 1991. He's currently in his 48th year in law enforcement.

Sarge caught batting practice, warmed up the starting pitcher, and caught in the bullpen, just as I did. Over time, however, the practice of moving the batting-practice pitcher off the rubber, and toward home plate evolved, and catching batting practice slowly was eliminated. In addition, the pitching coaches spent the game on the bench, unlike Early Wynn, who spent the game in the bullpen from '64–66. So the job had evolved such that Sarge became the pitching coach's right-hand man in the pen, answering the phone, charting pitchers, getting the staff ready for their assignments, and catching the relievers. Eventually, the Tribe began to hire a bullpen coach to oversee the functions in the 'pen. Don's day job allowed him to go to spring training for the last week or ten days, and to make two or three road trips a year. Don continued in the bullpen until the Tribe hired Luis Isaac as their first bullpen coach in 1987, then worked in tandem with Luis, both warming up the starting pitchers, as well as the bullpen relievers. The switch to bullpen coaches in the bullpen had officially begun. Appendix 1 outlines the bullpen catchers and coaches for the Tribe since Bill Lobe.

Teams currently list five or six coaches on their roster: pitching coach, bullpen coach, first- and third-base coaches, hitting coach, and bench coach. Major league teams averaged two coaches in 1930, three in 1946, four in 1960, five in 1982, and six from 1999 through 2007. As bullpen coach duties expanded, adding a bullpen catcher became reasonable as well. Recently, many teams have begun to list the bullpen catcher as "coach" on their roster web sites. The system is now so detailed that all teams have bullpen coaches who, with rare exceptions, have been either pitchers or catchers as players.

Having both a pitcher-bullpen coach and a bullpen catcher-coach could lead to issues of job description, and potential conflicts of opinion and direction. Of the 30 teams, 19 have former pitchers as bullpen coaches, 10 have catchers, and one is a former infielder, Jim Lett, with the Nationals. Where a pitcher is the bullpen coach, and not helping warming up and working with pitchers himself, the bullpen catcher is busier doing so. The Chicago Cubs, with former pitcher Lester Strode as bullpen coach, have two bullpen catchers, Edgar Tovar and Cory Miller, to warm up the relievers in the 'pen.

Mike Stefanski of the Reds notes the decision to have a bullpen coach who is a former pitcher or catcher is up to each individual pitching coach. Pitching people understand mechanics better and catchers understand how to apply a pitcher's stuff to get hitters out. Conflicts between the pitching and bullpen coaches should never really happen.

There seems to be no uniformity or convention among Major League clubs in identifying their bullpen catcher on their official websites. The Indians note David Wallace as a Coach, although his official title is "Assistant to Major League

Coaching Staff." The Rangers list Josh Frasier as "Video Coordinator and Bullpen Catcher" under their Front Office tab. The Mariners list Jason Phillips in their Front Office Directory, under Baseball Operations, as "Bullpen Catcher." The Reds do not currently include Mike Stefanski anywhere on their site, even though he's been with the club seven years.

A few bullpen catchers with no professional experience are currently active in the major leagues.[25] Dave Racaniello has been bullpen catcher (coach!) for the New York Mets since 2000. He fell into the job through a mutual acquaintance of manager Bobby Valentine. Racaniello had played at a local community college, but had no professional experience.[26] When the bullpen catcher couldn't make a game in 1997, Dave filled in, and then took the job in 2000 when a permanent opening occurred.

Brandon Buckley caught in the bullpen for the Oakland As while studying for his bachelor's degree on line. He lugged his books, computer, and printer onto the road with him during the season.[27] Scott Pickens, the bullpen catcher for the Detroit Tigers, joined the organization in 2005, after graduating from Central Michigan and playing three years in Independent Leagues. Pickens is so valued by the Tigers' hitters for his skill in throwing pregame batting practice that two of the team's All-Stars invited him to pitch to them in the Homerun Derby Competition: Magglio Ordonez in 2007, and Brandon Inge in 2009.[28]

Pierre Arsenault is an interesting story of the modern bullpen. Pierre parlayed one season as a catcher in the Rookie Gulf Coast League in '86 into a batting practice pitching job with the Expos in '87, followed by a full-time bullpen catcher gig in '88 and '89, followed by promotion to Expo's bullpen coach in '91.[29] He experienced more than the average number of bullpen ups and downs between bullpen catcher, coach, and now bullpen coordinator in 2009, through the Expo's move to Florida.

A number of bullpen catchers have just recently retired from professional careers, which included some time spent in the majors. Tim Gradoville became the Phillies bullpen catcher in December 2008. He had been a 37th-round draft pick in 2002, and had a brief stay with the Phillies in '06. He had been playing at Triple-A Fresno before retiring to take the bullpen job[30] Jason Phillips first reached the majors in 2001 with the Mets, and played parts of six seasons in the majors. He went to the 2009 Seattle Mariners' spring training trying to earn a job on the Mariners' roster. When he didn't make the club, and was asked him to serve as bullpen catcher, he decided to retire from playing and take the position. He recently acknowledged a difference in playing the game versus viewing it from a coaching and front office administrative perspective.[31]

Others have been in their positions for many years. Rick Stelmaszek is the current dean of bullpen catchers/coaches.[32] He has been with the Twins for 30 years, longest such tenure in major league history. He was drafted in '67 at age 18, and had brief appearances in the majors from '71–74, before retiring as a player in '78. He managed in the Midwest League through 1980, before joining the Twins' 'pen.

Gary Tuck of the Red Sox caught three years in the Expos' farm system, then became a coach at Notre Dame and Arizona State, and then managed six years at AA or below. He is the only bullpen coach to win the World Series with two different teams: the Yankees in 1998–99, and Boston in 2007.

The politics of the bullpen may be no more evident than in the recent history of the Indians. Luis Isaac caught in the Indians' bullpen as coach from 1987 to 1991, and again from 1994 to 2008. Luis replaced former major-league catcher Doc Edwards as bullpen coach when Edwards took over the club's reins following the firing of Pat Corrales. Isaac was born in Rio Piedres, Puerto Rico, June 19, 1946, and signed his first professional contract at age 16, playing at Kingsport in the Appalachian League in 1962. He made it to Portland (AAA) in 1967, and would play for 16 minor-league teams before retiring in 1980 to begin his coaching career, culminating in joining the Tribe's bullpen.

Dan Williams replaced Isaac as bullpen coach in 2009. Williams had signed as the 37th Indians' draft choice in 1988, played in the minors until 1991, then coached until 1993, when he took the Tribe bullpen catcher job under Isaac and manager Doc Edwards. When Isaac was released and Williams named coach, the Indians hired David Wallace, 29, as the new bullpen catcher. Wallace, who "retired" as a player to assume the job in the Tribe 'pen,[33] replaced Dennis Malaave, who joined the coaching staff of the Indians' Kinston Arizona League team. Williams and Wallace both warmed up pitchers during the season.

Though the bullpen catcher job does frequently go to an individual with team connections, including a relationship or connection to the manager, it goes without saying the job is tenuous, and dependent on the manager's keeping his job. Williams and Wallace both lost their jobs when manager Eric Wedge was fired at the end of the season. The new manager, Manny Acta, hired Tim Belcher as pitching coach, and a pitcher, Scott Radinsky, as bullpen coach, and David Wallace was subsequently rehired. It's clear the position can be one of stability—or a revolving door of uncertainty and comings and goings on the other.

Mike Stefanski had been with the Cincinnati Reds since 2004, after 13 seasons in the minors, including his last two years with the Louisville Bats, a Reds' farm club. When Dick Pole, the Reds' pitching coach, was replaced recently by Bryan Price, Stefanski's position was potentially in jeopardy. But the club retained both Stefanski and bullpen coach Juan Lopez to lend stability to the pitching staff, which had made great progress and showed considerable promise. Although in spring training now with the Reds, Mike is not even listed on the Reds web site as catcher/coach.

Other former major leaguers have been in the bullpen for years after retiring. Mark Salas, White Sox' bullpen catcher, played eight seasons in the majors, retiring in 1991.[34] Orlando Mercado of the Angels played eight years in the majors, last with Montreal in 1990.[35] Randy Knorr of the Cardinals played 11 years in the majors, retiring in 2001, before moving to the 'pen.

Other non-major leaguers have been in their positions for a number of years as well. Steve Soliz played nine seasons in the minors, and has been the Angels' bullpen catcher for seven years. He has even filled in as bullpen coach for Orlando Mercado. He has pointed out that the catcher has to have the pitcher's confidence, knowing the catcher knows what he's talking about.[36]

Ronnie Deck played six years in the minor leagues before taking his job in the Baltimore Orioles' bullpen.[37] Bill Duplissea played five years in the Dodgers' farm system before retiring to the bullpen.[38] Mark Strittmatter of the Rockies had played in the organization for eight years, and retired for two years, before accepting Clint Hurdle's offer to return as bullpen catcher.[39] A list of bullpen catchers and coaches, identified from team web sites, follows. Some positions remain unfilled due to the usual changes in coaching staffs that occur yearly.

**Teams' Bullpen Catchers and Bullpen Coaches, 2009–2010**

| Team | Bullpen Catcher | Bullpen Coach |
|---|---|---|
| Arizona Diamondbacks | Jeff Motuzas | Glenn Sherlock (c) |
| Atlanta Braves | Chino Cadahla | Eduardo Perez (c) |
| Baltimore Orioles | Ronnie Deck (2) | Alan Dunn (3) (p) |
| Boston Red Sox | *N/A* | Gary Tuck (c) |
| Chicago Cubs | Edgar Tovar<br>Cory Miller | Lester Strode (p) |
| Chicago White Sox | Mark Salas | Juan Nieves (p) |
| Cincinnati Reds | Mike Stefanski (6) | Juan Lopez (c) |
| Cleveland Indians | David Wallace | Scott Radinsky (p) |
| Colorado Rockies | Mark Strittmatter | Jim Wright (p) |
| Detroit Tigers | Scott Pickens | Jeff Jones (p) |
| Florida Marlins | Pierre Arsenault | Reid Cornelius (p) |
| Houston Astros | N/A | Jamie Quirk (c) |
| Kansas City Royals | Bill Duplissea | Steve Foster (p) |
| Los Angeles Angels | Steve Soliz | Orlando Mercado (c) |
| Los Angeles Dodgers | Mike Borzello (2) | Ken Howell (2) (p) |
| Milwaukee Brewers | Marcus Hanel | Stan Kyles (p) |
| Minnesota Twins | Nate Dammann | Rick Stelmaszek (c) |
| New York Mets | Dave Racaniello | Harold Niemann (p) |
| New York Yankees | Roman Rodriguez | Mike Harkey (p) |

| | | |
|---|---|---|
| Oakland A's | Casey Chavez (2) | Ron Romanick (2) (p) |
| Philadelphia Phillies | Mick Billmeyer | Tim Gradoville (c) |
| Pittsburgh Pirates | Herberto Andrade (6) | Luis Dorante (2) (c) |
| San Diego Padres | Justin Hatcher (2) | Darrell Akerfelds (p) |
| San Francisco Giants | Bill Hayes | Mark Gardner (p) |
| Seattle Mariners | Jason Phillips | John Wetteland (p) (1) |
| St. Louis Cardinals | Jeff Murphy | Marty Mason (p) |
| Tampa Bay Devilrays | Scott Cursi | Bobby Ramos (c) |
| Texas Rangers | Josh Frasier | Andy Hawkins (p) |
| Toronto Blue Jays | Alex Andreopoulos | Bruce Walton (p) |
| Washington Nationals | N/A | Jim Lett (1) (inf) |

(c) catcher (p) pitcher
Number of years with club in parentheses.

As might be expected, some bullpen catchers have developed friendships with players that go beyond the duties on the field and in the clubhouse. Mike Borzello, who played four years in the St. Louis organization, and served as bullpen catcher for the Yankees from '96–07, was a close friend and confidant of Alex Rodriguez, spending most workout days, and days on the road, with A-Rod. "Nobody in the last four years . . . spent more time with Alex than I did."[40] [41] Borzello caught the Yankee staff during their strikeout-record-breaking season of '01, with Clemens and Pettitte on the staff. Borzello left the Yankees and joined the Dodgers as bullpen catcher in 2008.

Bullpen catchers may work behind the scenes, but they are not necessarily without notoriety. Everyone now knows that Brian McNamee fingered Roger Clemens and Andy Pettitte for steroid use while they were Yankees. Fewer know that McNamee, a college catcher at St. John's University, was the bullpen catcher for the Yankees from 1993–95, hired by his former St. John's school mate, Tim McCleary, who was assistant General Manager of the Yankees.

McNamee later moved to personal training. He was rehired by McCleary as strength coach in Toronto, where his close relationships with players may have facilitated involvement in the performance-enhancing drug use that has been outlined in the Mitchell report. Luis Perez, a Montreal Expos bullpen catcher in 1992, admitted that he supplied steroids to players in 1998–2001 while he was bullpen catcher for the Florida Marlins.

On the other hand, bullpen catchers have made it to the top, even been named major League managers. John Gibbons, who was hired by his former minor-league roommate, General Manager J. P. Ricciardi, as the Toronto Blue Jays' bullpen catcher in 2002, was named manager in 2004. Of course, he had been a player, drafted in 1980, playing small parts of two seasons in the majors, with the Mets in '84 and '86, before retiring in '90. [42] Doc Edwards, a former major leaguer and coach, was elevated from the bullpen to replace Pat Corrales as manager in Cleveland in '93.

So what's the chance of the bullpen catcher ever getting in a game? Never at the major league level in 2010. I had always hoped I might get in to catch during the Tribe's yearly exhibition game with the Reds or Pirates, but I guess that would have been too much to expect. The team usually brought up a minor-league farmhand for that game, anyway. Back in 1918, during the influenza epidemic, the Indians bullpen catcher was activated for opening day when the roster was reduced by hospitalized players. The bullpen catcher named Williams was activated and played first base![43] With the recent H1N1 virus pandemic threat, who knows what could happen in future years?

There are many stories in the bullpen, the vast, overwhelming majority of which will remain untold. The stories I tell about mischief, mishaps, and mayhem may be occasionally comical, but the stories of hopes unmet and aspirations unfulfilled by the bullpen catcher reflect the disappointing side of not only sports and baseball, but also life in general. Few grab the golden ring, win the Silver Bat or the Gold Glove Award.

# Chapter 4—The Job: 2010

Whereas my day at the office in 1964–66 began with batting practice, having someone catch BP has all but disappeared today at the major league level, for a variety of reasons I'll describe. But batting practice remains a vehicle in the less common circumstance when a roster pitcher, perhaps coming off an injury, needs a workout off the mound, with a catcher. In 2010, this usually takes the form of simulated games.

According to Dave Wallace of the Indians, the "sim" is designed to be as close to game-like conditions as possible. Live hitters (usually bench players who haven't been getting much playing time) stand in and take their swings against the pitcher on the mound who is taking signs, and mixing up his pitches, just as he might in a game. The sim usually occurs before batting practice, where teams have times set aside and designated for early workouts, both at home and on the road. David had just caught a sim for Kerry Wood, coming off the disabled list in Minneapolis. The session started at 2:30 pm, well before the 5:00 batting practice.

A variety of changes in the conduct of batting practice has led to relative obsolescence of the batting-practice catcher. In 1964, batting-practice pitchers threw from the rubber, behind a net attached to a frame designed to protect them from ground balls or line drives.

The practice has evolved that currently BP pitchers throw from behind the net from a movable platform wedge in front of the pitcher's mound, perhaps only 45–50 feet away from the plate. Being closer to the plate makes it easier to throw strikes, even without a catcher's glove as target. Thus there are fewer non-strikes, leading to more balls hit, and hence less need for a catcher. Today 80–90% of pitches are put into play, with some pop-ups hitting the net above the plate, and falling around home plate. I often thought the batting practice catcher's job is primarily to give a target to the pitcher, and secondarily to return not only the pitches not swung at, but also the foul balls lying on the ground in and around the cage after each hitter.

Since catching BP has essentially disappeared, some bullpen catchers throw batting practice as well at the major league level. The uncomplicated body rotation and movement of the typical catcher's throw does lend itself to throwing a lot of balls in a short period of time.[44] [45] Certainly, coaches continue to throw BP as well, and non-professionals are still hired to do the job, just as in the 60s.

In BP, each pitcher typically throws about 125–150 pitches in about 15 minutes: a rapid-fire, effective method to get in more swings than the 60s method. Balls are placed in a wheeled basket that holds about 150 balls, with the basket at waist height, precluding the necessity to bend over constantly for a new supply.

Balls that aren't swung at, or foul balls, may be returned to the pitcher, but are usually just left on the ground, or cast aside temporarily. Balls hit out to the field are collected in a container behind second base, and then brought in with each pitcher rotation, or as needed as BP progresses. The balls on the ground are then gathered after each pitcher's session as well, to resupply the basket with a fresh 150 balls. The pitcher is currently protected by a screen that is cut out on its upper half on the side of the pitcher's throwing hand, so that his upper body and face and non-throwing arm are protected by the screen, but his arm is free to throw. The screen does present an obstacle when a catchers or on-deck hitters are returning balls to the pitcher: the target is much smaller without the screen.

The bullpen catcher may shag balls in the outfield during BP, or collect balls as they are returned to the infield behind the screen on the outfield side of second base, and then carry them in to the mound to keep the basket supply fresh. In general, the bullpen catcher just goes with the flow, and does whatever job needs to be done to keep the session running smoothly. He may catch balls being returned to fungo hitters during BP or infield practice. Performing such mundane tasks associated with baseball is an age-old tradition. It even got George Susce the nickname "Good Kid" three generations ago!

Mike Stefanski of the Reds recently synopsized his duties in 2010. He's responsible for all pitcher preparation, long toss, simulated games, and bullpen organization. He organizes work on catching fundamentals, both in spring training and during the season. He prepares the baseballs for batting practice, and is responsible for rubbing them up for the pitchers' warm-ups. He never catches BP, but will take a rotation of pitching BP, and hits fungoes to infielders during BP, or takes return throws while someone else is hitting fungoes. Some starting pitchers will take their between-start work outs in the pen during BP as well. He occasionally warms up the starting pitcher before games, depending on the starting catcher's preference. Stefanski prepares and watches film with the pitchers. He even repairs gloves, tightening, loosening, or relacing as needed."

Today the job of warming up the starter at the major league level has increasingly fallen to the starting catcher, allowing him to loosen up as well before the game, in the absence of infield practice. This job may default to a second or third roster catcher, or in some instances a bullpen coach. But it's a job the bullpen catcher may be called upon to do as well. In 2009, the starting pitcher warms up primarily in the bullpen, which is behind the outfield fence or wall in the vast majority of parks. Catchers currently warm up starting and relief pitchers in protective gear: catcher's mask and shin protectors at the minimum, with or without their chest protector. These pieces of equipment have been known as the "tools of ignorance," although nothing could be further from the truth: catchers are valued for their intelligence, perhaps more than mechanical skill in some circles. The bullpen catcher may not be using his intelligence to direct a game, but is trying to optimize the pitcher's preparation to perform his job.

Of course, the *sine qua non* of the bullpen job is catching in the bullpen, and the job hasn't changed much, in and of itself, in 40 years. The members of the pitching staff have changed, however, a point for more in-depth discussion later.

The 26 members of the Tribe staff of '64–66 were 6' ¾" tall and weighed 196 pounds, on average. The 29 members of the 2009 Indians staff were significantly taller at 6' 2 ¼", and tended to weigh more at 201.3 pounds. Pitchers are bigger, and presumably stronger, and appear to throw harder, than former staffs.

The members of the 'pen, the relief pitchers, have perfected the art of specialization. There's the closer, who will take over when the team is ahead in the ninth, or possibly the eighth inning of a close game and the set-up man, who will pitch the seventh or eighth innings of a close or tied game. These "late" men are conditioned to pitch two or three days in a row, but seldom will need to, or be allowed to, go four days.

The middle relievers, who will be expected to give two or three good innings in transition from the starter to the late men, are pitchers who could start if called upon, and who frequently aspire to that assignment. Their repertoire of pitches is commonly wider than that of the late men, more akin to the starter's. Of course, one of them must be prepared to enter the game early, just in case the starter has one of those unpredictable inabilities to get through the early innings. Mixed into this mosaic may be the specialty pitcher, usually a left-hander used to get one or two left-handed batters out, yet occasionally called on to continue as a middle man into the late innings.

The only assignments usually carved in stone, allowing for adjustments due to frequency of use, are the closer and set-up man.

Current members of the bullpen differ not only in their function, but in their physiognomy as well. Pitchers are generally bigger, stronger, and throw harder than was my experience in the 60s.

Catching in the 'pen remains a typically back-loaded assignment, with the action most generally telescoped toward the end of the day or night's work. It continues to be a bit like sitting around the fire station, waiting for a fire to respond to. A few hits or bases on balls early in a game don't generate the same get-ready response from the manager that they will in later innings. No manager wants to start to burn out his bullpen by initiating their activity in the early innings of a game. The starter is given time to settle down and work into a rhythm. So the bullpen catcher's job is usually easy early in the game. There's a bit of sitting around and stretching, standing up and stretching, and then sitting back down. Attention to the game and the game situation—what batter is or isn't hitting what, which pitch is being called a strike and which isn't—are just a few of the components of the game that everyone follows.

Uneventful middle innings still more commonly than not bring out a starting pitcher for a mid-rotation work out: perhaps 50–60 pitches, very similar to warming up for a start.

But there later develops a tension and a semblance to a bull in a pen at times—relievers walking from front to back, side to side, scraping a bit at the dirt with their cleat or spike. The muscles begin to tighten, the stance stiffens, the pupils dilate, and the breathing becomes deeper, as the threat appears. If it's cold, the steamy breath becomes more evident. Then it's time to spring into action when the threat comes closer, until finally the threat's finally eliminated. Perhaps we would coin the term bullpen today, if it hadn't already been applied in the past.

# Chapter 5—Preparing for the Job

As for so many other boys, sports were an obsession as I grew up on the near east side of Cleveland at E. 57th St. and Wade Park Avenue. Yes, Wade Park Ave., about two miles away from Old League Park, the predecessor of Cleveland Municipal Stadium. An episode of rheumatic fever at age five predated my true interest in baseball, but was a major factor, I'm sure, in generating an interest in medicine, and in formulating the career choice conflict I would later face.

As a youth, I became an unabashed, front-running Yankee fan (probably after seeing Mickey Mantle, a 21-year-old center-fielder, hit a home run on my grandpa's Helicrafter TV in the '53 World Series). I was a Yankee fan in spite of the Indians' winning the pennant in 1954 with a major league record of 111 wins!

The Big Four: Bob Lemon, Mike "The Big Bear" Garcia, and Bob ("Rapid Robert") Feller, and "Burly" Early Wynn. Right-hander Ray Narleski and Lefty Don Mossi were in the bullpen. How could you be a Yankee fan with *that* team in your own city? But that staff never led the AL in strikeouts, despite Feller's being one of the greatest strikeout pitchers of all time. Only in '55 and '56 would the team, with their young phenom, Herb Score, lead the AL.

My most memorable sports-related event of those years was clearly May 7, 1957. That night my brother Bill and I attended the game by virtue of several tickets I had won based on good school grades. A distant cousin, Tony Tomsic (sic), was a photographer for the Cleveland Press, and had arranged a brief photo opp before the game. My brother Bill and I were dressed in our finest pink-and-black outfits: true 50s cool.

The object of the opp: The Mick himself. This picture remains treasured to this day: the two fresh faces, and the muscular, handsome, young slugger, who had won the Major League Triple Crown (leading both leagues in all three categories):

.353 BA, 130 RBI, 52HR, and he had won the MVP award and Hickock Belt just the year before.

The autographed photo remains a reminder of the ecstasy and the agony of that evening. The agony? That night marked the beginning of the flaming burnout of one of the game's great young stars. It was the night Herb Score was hit in the face by a line drive off the bat of right-hand hitting Gil McDougald. The ball smashed his facial bones, threatened his vision, and he would never be the same.

May 7, 1957. The Mick, my brother Bill (right), and I the evening Herb Score would be injured by a line drive.

"Crack . . . crack!"

We heard the split-second repeat of the ball off McDougald's bat, followed by its impact on Herb's face from our seats 180 feet away in the third-base-side upper deck. In truth, an arm injury in the rehab process probably was a more proximate cause of his shortened career. He had led the league in strikeouts in his first two years in the majors ('55 and '56), and had been Rookie of the Year in '55. His hits per nine innings of 5.847 is 15th on the all-time list.

Who ever thought I would get to know Herb Score seven years later, after he had retired and joined the Indians' TV broadcasting team. We would both be "rookies" in 1964. Sadly, Herb died in 2009 with the lingering effects of a stroke.

Little St. Peter School had a baseball team, and I played in the fifth grade, along with others up to three years older. It was the classic situation of the worst player (me) put out in right field and batting ninth! In the summertime there was Wilson School playground, just six houses down the street from my home, and then amateur baseball. We'd play baseball at the playground from morning 'till night. So much, you'd think I'd have been a better hitter.

We had this game called "Strikeouts": a pitcher would stand at the base of a large wall, approximately 70 feet wide and 40–50 feet high, a baseball-sized rubber ball or tennis ball in hand. The batter would stand against a fence, maybe 40 feet away. Then the pitcher would typically throw as hard as he could, in order to "strike out" the hitter. If the ball were hit, and bounced off the wall but was caught before it hit the ground, it was an out. If it wasn't caught, the value of the hit would be determined by what section of the wall the ball had hit, with no direct relation to whether it was a line drive or a pop-up. The best hit balls caromed directly off the wall; pop-ups frequently landed on the roof—game over—at least until the janitor could be cajoled into throwing the balls down. Wilson's close distance, the high pitch velocity, and the use of bats far too long and heavy, necessitated the batter begin his swing almost before the ball left the pitcher's hand. Thinking back on that situation, I think this engendered bad habits that I never overcame.

Once again, I batted against fellows several years older than myself, and I was frequently overwhelmed, but never overwrought. Even as I progressed though low amateur ball, somehow I never got out of the bad habit of stepping in and starting that swing too soon, jamming myself by proximity to the plate, not to mention not learning to hit the curve ball. You couldn't make a ball curve within 50 feet at Wilson School yard!

But amateur ball at the 12-year-old level was a big turning point. My family moved to the 'burbs in Parma, south of Cleveland, and I pitched, played shortstop, and third base in the Parma Class F League. I had a rifle arm, and that's where young arms played.

But I can't express the frustration I'd have when I'd walk a guy, or someone would get a hit, and they were automatically on third base—steal second and steal third. Not that my slidestep stretch off the mound was the greatest, but I thought my catchers couldn't throw their grandmothers out. I got tired of people taking something that wasn't theirs. So one game, I just said, "Give me the equipment!" I put it on, and was a catcher thereafter.

After all, the catcher is the pivot on which the game revolves. He positions and informs the other eight players, reminding them of game situations. The catcher gives the pitcher signs, every pitch is thrown to the catcher, every run is scored in front of the catcher, and he is prepared to stand and challenge bravely each one, where it is possible. Peter Morris recently wrote that the catcher "stands as the embodiment of such virtues as stoic fortitude, leadership, teamwork, and courage."[46]

Somehow, at a young age, I had a similar broad but less well-annunciated vision, and relished assuming that mantle. As a post-World War II product, I saw the actors' portrayal of soldiers stooping in foxholes, dressed in battle gear, as characters to emulate. In high school, a student of Greek literature, I saw Odysseus as a strong and resourceful hero, prepared to battle the forces of heaven and hell, long and hard. Somehow I saw catchers in the same light, just as Morris described, and decided I enjoyed being one. Perhaps I was just kidding myself, and should have subscribed to a less idealistic view of catchers, as articulated by Jim "The Professor" Brosnan: "Catchers, of course, have underdeveloped brains . . . x-rays of their heads would probably be useless. Masochists are what they are."[47] Among the various assignments that fall to the catcher, nothing gave me more satisfaction than throwing runners out stealing, or picking runners off base.

The next season, I played for the Parma Class F "Francona's" team, not worried about ever pitching another inning. Four seasons later, I'd be on the field and in the same locker room on a daily basis with *the* Tito Francona, who fell just short of the 1959 AL batting crown only because he did not have enough at-bats.

Self-help books may be primarily a latter-day innovation, but I picked up a few valuable tips from the first edition of the Sports Illustrated Book of Baseball, given to me by a neighbor in June 1960. The catching section was written by Milwaukee Braves' All-Star catcher Del Crandall. Del's overriding principle was: "The pitcher-catcher relationship has to be based on confidence—confidence the pitcher has in his catcher. The more confidence he has in you, the better job he's going to do."[48]

The book illustrated a number of techniques, including blocking pitches; catching balls forward, or back, depending on where it looks like it will be over the plate; how to catch foul pops behind the plate, etc.

Speaking of the latter, one of my most embarrassing mishaps occurred in 1963, the first year I played a night game on fields with deep backstops behind home plate, as opposed to tight quarters with an overhang fence behind the plate that eliminated catching many foul balls. The incident was at Brookside Park, with a lengthy distance behind home plate to the backstop with its concrete seating steps carved into a huge hillside, where the Cleveland semi-pro teams used to play, and where the highest amateur-level teams played. A pop-up behind home plate during a night game went up, started off behind the plate with its reverse spin, as I turned away from the field toward the backstop to get under it. Reverse spin became over spin, forcing the ball to spin back toward the playing field, and over my head as I backpedaled and fell on my rear.

Del Crandall's chapter didn't tell me that would happen! Once, again, life can be stranger than fiction: Del would join the Tribe in '66, near the end of his career, and he would prove a good bullpen and clubhouse friend as well, with advice about school, careers, catching, and the game of baseball.

Gil McDougald's chapter on fielding in the SI book emphasized the right way to execute the run-down. I only wish the SI chapter on hitting, by the Senators' Roy Sievers, had helped me as much as Del's chapter did. Sievers' chapter made hitting look so easy. I gave the book to my son Scott when he showed an inclination and facility for the game. The SI book still is on our bookshelf 50 years later.

In 1960 and '61, American Legion ball offered the opportunity for more games, and a bit of travel around town. I was asked to play for the Excelsior Post team, coached by Mike Carrick, a former semi-pro catcher with gnarled fingers, who had coached championship Legion teams in the past. Carrick taught me quite a bit about the game inside the game. No championships in two years, but lots of wins and plenty of fun.

In Mr. Carrick's unwritten book, chapter one taught that the catcher was a receiver: he is smooth, measured, balanced, and stable in his movements. Receive the ball as if you're bringing it toward your body. Maybe Mr. Carrick was taking that line from Charlie Fox, a former major-league catcher turned manager: "A good catcher is actually a receiver. He receives the ball rather than catches it. The good ones always take the ball in; the poorer ones go for it."[49] Mr. Carrick reiterated what Del had said in his book: "If a catcher is sloppy behind the plate, it's going to undermine the pitcher's confidence in him."

One of the individual lessons in Mr. Carrick's unwritten chapter became ingrained in my mechanics, but seemingly has been lost to the ages. He taught me to frame low pitches; no, not that exaggerated movement of pulling the ball back over the plate in a poorly veiled attempt to fool the umpire into thinking a ball was a strike. It was a method to make the pitch look better by orienting the open face of the mitt to the strike zone, so that strikes aren't called balls. If the ball were inside to a right-hander, catch it with your palm turned toward the plate, never with your palm turned toward the batter. If the ball were low, turn your palm up to catch it. If it were high turn the palm down (which, of course, you virtually can't help doing). This accomplishes two things: you give the umpire a look at the white of the ball, and make it look "better" than it might really be, and in doing so not push the ball from the strike zone as you catch it, thereby potentially losing strikes that you deserve.

This was a skill that members of the Indians' staff would appreciate years later while warming up before the game, or in the 'pen. It's a lesson I would teach my son and other young catchers 30 years later. The age of the hinged glove, and the one-handed method of "pickin' it," has made catching the low pitch palm up virtually extinct, however. Please don't misunderstand, I picked my share of pitches out of the dirt, backhanded and glove face down as well with no one on base, but those pitches were already clearly balls, so framing wasn't an issue.

At St. Ignatius High School, we had no freshman team, and I didn't make the team as a tall, skinny sophomore catcher. Tryouts were on an asphalt field with rubber-coated baseballs, typically in the damp cold of late March and early April! But I made it as a junior, and was on the all-city team as a senior. But I wasn't that good a hitter, still bothered by some old Wilson-schoolyard bad habits. As John Braucher, our coach told me more than once: “Tom, glove men are dime a dozen.” The Cleveland Plain Dealer reported, in reporting my only scholastic home run, that I “blasted a home run” in the 9–7 win, conjuring up the vision of a Ruthian drive and a slow trot around the bases. In truth, it was a line drive on a fenceless field that fell in front of the left fielder, who failed to make a shoestring catch, allowing me to go all the way around.

But I had good hands (more than great mobility), and I had the proverbial hose (or cannon, or rifle) for throwing. We had a good team, going far in the district tournament. Steve Huntz, our shortstop–pitcher, would sign with the Orioles. First and third, double steal? Forget it. Steve and I would cut them down almost every time. Years later, I would join him again in St. Louis when he came up with the Cardinals. He had a six-year career with a number of teams. Great glove, great arm, great guy.

Pictured here in 1963 in a “Radiarts” uniform with the Cincinnati Reds logo beneath. Ten years later I'd be a “Rad” in Cincinnati. Go figure.

After graduation in the summer of ’63, I played National Amateur Baseball Federation (NABF) ball, and we had a decent team against good competition of 17-18 year-olds. I played on a team called the Radiarts, named for a radio manufacturing company sponsor. Apparently the Radiart Co. was in the same radio/antenna manufacturing business as Crosley, Inc., owners of the WLW Broadcasting and of the Cincinnati Reds. We called ourselves the Rads, for short. I mention it only as a weird coincidence: below the script on the front of the jersey, was the team emblem of the Cincinnati Reds. I would, years later, be a “Rad,” or radiologist, in Cincinnati. True life *is* stranger than fiction!

At the end of the season, I was “drafted” by the NABF-league champs, a team simply named “GO,” to go to the *national* tournament–in Youngstown, Ohio! GO was coached by a mathematics professor from Arizona State University, Rich Liskovec. And the team had one interesting practice that I hadn't seen before, and haven't since: they used flashcards for signs, given from the bench, for the hitter and base runners, as well as for the pitcher and catcher. Each flashcard was a complex of three vertically oriented squares, top to bottom, with varying designs in black and white in each square. The cards were connected by rings, so that different patterns could be selected by paging through the cards. It would take a math professor to figure that one out. When I caught against them, I'd watch those signs, trying to find the pattern and the clue as to what was coming. No luck.

Bob Feller's sons Marty and Steve later played for GO, and Bob would act as assistant coach. Steve Stone, who would one day pitch for the Chicago Cubs, played for them later as well. Teamed with fellows I had played against in high school, we had a good team with a several players who eventually played professionally, including Jim Rittwage, from Bedford, Ohio, later to have a cup of coffee with the Tribe in 1970. As a defensive draftee, I caught Jim in our first tournament game, against the Detroit team. During that game, I had a passed ball, allowing a runner to go from first to second. He scored on a single, and we lost 1-0. So much for the defensive specialist! We then lost the elimination game to Akron 2-1, and went home. Mercifully, it was a short bus ride.

As the son of a Cleveland police detective, I was eligible for the Cleveland Police Foundation Scholarship, which was awarded every year to the daughter or son of a police officer. I was awarded the scholarship and attended John Carroll University in Cleveland. I hadn't been offered any baseball scholarship elsewhere, so I had little choice but to accept it. JCU didn't have a baseball team, and I had pretty well decided to try to excel in academics, and then hopefully go to medical school. JCU was better known for its pre-med program getting students into med schools than for turning out professional athletes. But a few have come out of JCU: most notably Don Shula, a defensive back with the Blue Streaks and the Browns, and successful NFL coach of the Dolphins, and more recently London Fletcher, NFL linebacker. Josh McDaniels, the Denver Bronco's head coach and the youngest head coach in the history of the NFL, is a 1998 JCU graduate. Mike Hegan, who had a 12-year major league career, and current Indians TV play-by play broadcaster, and also a graduate of Ignatius, attended JCU in the offseason after signing his major league contract. JCU's most famous graduate is likely Tim Russert, the recently-deceased television newsman, known almost as well as a big Buffalo Bills fan.

After my first year of college in 1964, I was invited to play for the Lyon Tailors team in the Cleveland *Plain Dealer* Class A amateur league. It was the top amateur league in Cleveland, mostly former high-school stars, college players, including many journeymen who had played in the league for years. The season started in April, and I was hitting about four for 1964 in June. One of the teams we played against was the Wenham Truckers, a perennial league power. Frank Keeney, one of their pitchers, happened to throw batting practice for the Indians. Frank was a 40-ish, friendly, veteran inveterate, a good old boy, southern drawl, chaw-in-cheek, more junk than that in an attic, with a rubber arm and pinpoint control. He was known as "Country" in the clubhouse. Frank was the baseball equivalent of the basketball gym rat; he was always at amateur games, behind the fence, checking out the action. As it turns out, Frank and I always joked around a bit, but had a friendly opponents' relationship. After all, we both loved baseball. Frank was a key to the next three years.

# Chapter 6—The Job Interview

In June '64, the Indians' batting practice/bullpen catcher was called up to Army reserve duty, and the team needed a replacement. Mr. Paul again approved hiring of an amateur player to fill the job. Frank Keeney, my sandlot friend, in charge of the batting practice pitchers, recommended me for the job. I'm surprised he recommended me, insofar as I was a pretty easy out for him in the Class A league. Frank arranged a job interview on Tuesday, June 23.

The season had already started, and the Indians had two catchers on the roster: the "Immortal" Joe Azcue, and John "Honey" Romano, a native of Hoboken, New Jersey, who had come from the White Sox in 1960. Joe was so-named because of a fantastic three months he had in 1963 after he came over from the A's. I still don't know why John was "Honey." Duane "Duke" Sims, a can't-miss rookie, would join the team in September, after the minor league season ended and major league rosters were expanded.

With two roster catchers, it would be mandatory to have someone to catch batting practice, warm up the starting pitcher, and then catch in the bullpen. None of the Indians coaches were catchers: George Strickland and Solly Hemus (a former National League manager) were both infielders; Elmer Valo, an outfielder, and Early Wynn, in his first full post-retirement year, was pitching coach.

There was no "bullpen coach" at the time, although Wynn stayed in the bullpen during games. George "Birdie" Tebbetts, an old catcher himself, would be Paul's manager once again, just as he had managed for Paul in Cincinnati 1954–1958. Tebbetts suffered a heart attack April 1, '64, and would return to the dugout July 5.

The interview had two parts: first, I warmed up a young pitching prospect working out at Cleveland Stadium. I had no problem managing his stuff, though it was generally a cut better than what I was accustomed to.

The second part was actually taking batting practice myself. I think Paul O'Dea, the chief local scout, whom I knew from his perch behind the fence at my sandlot games, and Hoot Evers, the director of player personnel, somehow still wanted to make sure I hadn't come around and become a hitter. If I took the job, my playing career would be essentially over, with no prospect of progressing as a player. So Keeney pitched, and I hit . . . er . . . swung. Frank fed me the fattest 60-mph batting practice pitches you could ask for. Nevertheless, my swing and a few weak fly balls that almost made the warning track convinced O'Dea and Evers that there was little risk of taking a future major league hitter out of circulation. And they hadn't even seen me against *good* pitching, where my stride opened up and I still managed to jam myself on inside stuff, while my rear end stuck out toward the third-base dugout while my arms stretched to make contact with outside pitches!

My father Adolph had stopped by the stadium, not far from his office at Central Police Station, probably hoping I would somehow have been transformed by the opportunity into something of a larger presence at the plate than I really was. But it didn't; O'Dea offered me the job on the spot: get this guy off the streets—he's giving hitting a bad name! I accepted the position: catch batting practice, warm up the starting pitcher, and catch in the bullpen. A dream come true for a young buck 18-year-old who couldn't hit.

The pay would be $15 per day, $25 for doubleheaders, with $15 per day meal money on the road. That was better than $1.91 an hour I was making as a stock-boy/bagger at Fisher Foods. Not a bad gig, but probably more ups and downs! As it turned out, the annualized salary of approximately $2,500 was about 40% of the major league minimum salary for rookies at the time: about $6,000 for the season (up to $400,000 in 2009!). In 1964, established veterans were making $20-25,000, and my boyhood hero Mickey Mantle was making $100,000, compared to an *average* salary in 2009 of $3.26 million. A recent estimate puts current major league bullpen catchers' salaries at $20-35,000.[50] The Oklahoma City Red Hawks, AAA affiliate of the Texas Rangers, pay their bullpen catcher $40/ day currently.[51] In addition to the pay, I was eligible to sign up for two free passes per game for family and friends. And I could always ask other players or personnel if they weren't using their tickets, so that I might use them. So occasionally I could give away four or six seats to friends or family. Other benefits included post-game snacks, sandwiches, and drinks in the clubhouse, supplied by the club. However, a nice gratuity for the clubhouse attendants from the players was expected at the end of the year.

Was I resigned to give up the opportunity to play ball as a career? Well, my hitting wasn't going to capture any professional contracts. As I said, I envisioned I'd finish college, and then go to medical school. Combine the two? Well, no one had really done it recently. I was well aware that Bobby Brown had done it a few years previous, studying for his degree while a third baseman with the Yankees from 1946–54.

"Doc" Medich, (whose name strikes me as an interesting form of synonism ("doc medic") would debut in '72 with the Yankees by facing four batters, walking two, while giving up two hits and two runs without an out, and was in the process of combining the two careers, unbeknownst to me. Nine others have been identified going back to 1898.[52] I learned later that a medical student from St. Louis, Joe Evans, played for the Indians in 1916.[53] Somehow, the uncertainty of being able to be successful in doing both left me uneasy about planning on doing it now. I had taken my swing at baseball and missed, now deciding, in effect, to forego any hope of a professional baseball career, however remote. *Strike One!*

# Chapter 7—The Staff

The Tribe pitching staff was a bit unsettled early in the '64 season. The '63 staff had led the AL in strikeouts with 1018, the first time the 1000-strikeout mark had been reached.

Staff members Jim "Mudcat" Grant, Barry Latman, and Jerry Walker had been traded by the time I joined the club. New strikeout records in both raw numbers and as strikeouts/9 innings had been set virtually yearly in the AL since 1948. The raw numbers increased with the expansion from eight to ten teams in 1961, and the increase in the regular season schedule from 154 to 162 games. The strikeout rate had been increasing from 3.5 to 4.9 strikeouts/9 innings, or by approximately 0.11 per year, from 1948 through 1960. At that rate, the average strikeout rate would have been 9.3/9 innings by year 2000. Both leagues had expanded their strike zones in 1963, expanding it to the shoulders above, and bottom of the knees below.[54] [55] The rules change was prompted by a sentiment that runs and home runs had become too easy to come by.

A constant upward trend was in place both prior to expansion from eight to ten teams in 1961, and enlargement of the strike zone in 1963. An increase in average strikeouts, and decrease in average team HR, shows after expansion. But other such periods of unlinking can be seen in previous years; 1961 was a record year for team home runs, and a later decrease may merely be an adjustment to the average from that record.

Home runs as a percentage of hits had indeed been increasing, hitting 10% for the first time in 1960, the last year of the eight-team original American League. This home run trend continued until 1964, the third year after expansion in 1961. The larger strike zone of 1963 was associated with an increase in strikeouts/9 innings slightly above its trendline, but not dramatically so, culminating in the Tribe's record performance, where they struck out a record 6.3 batters/9 innings in '63. It is unclear this new peak represented any significant alteration in an otherwise inexorable upward trend. The larger zone was one of the few rules changes in recent memory to favor the pitcher.

**AL average Strikeouts/9 innings and HR/season from 1947-1963.**

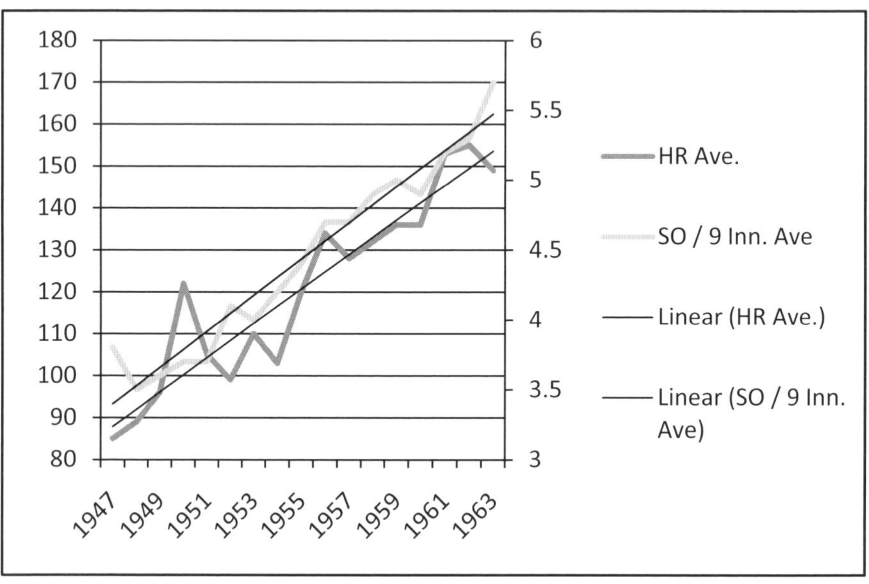


In '64, the Tribe staff had three promising young pitchers (Sam McDowell, Sonny Siebert, and Tommy John) and a number of established veterans expected to pick up the slack of losing the three key starters from 1963. McDowell was a 21-year-old 6' 5", 195-pounder who signed for $75,000 as a ballyhooed free agent out of high school in 1960. He had long arms, broad shoulders, and an imposing figure at 60' 6" away, 15" above the ground. With a slight chest concavity, he didn't have the thick, cut, muscled, barrel-chested appearance seen so often on the mound today, though.

Sam had been up first in 1961 before he was 19 years old, striking out nine in six innings in his debut. He would then be up for brief parts of the next two seasons, winning six, losing 12, striking out 0.88 per inning in 152 innings, but also walking 0.75 per inning. He would start the '64 season in AAA at Portland, and win his first eight decisions with a 1.18 ERA. Sam had pitched 76 innings for the Beavers, striking out 102, before coming up. He had won three of his first four decisions before I joined the club. He "arrived" in '64 and started 24 games, beginning a strikeout per inning streak that would become record setting.

Sam was said to throw over 100 mph, but it's not well documented when he was first measured at that speed with modern radar gun technology. I never saw any radar guns around the stadium. Nolan Ryan is widely acclaimed as the first pitcher measured at 101 mph in 1974. Steve Dalkowski of the Orioles is said to have thrown at 103 mph at about the same time. Sam also had a great slider and a curve ball that you would think was going to be shoulder high, but would then drop to almost ground level. He was known to be wild, and it was always a challenge warming him up, especially the last fastball, where he would throw near top speed, with seemingly little definite notion exactly where it was headed. With no mask on, my heart always beat a little faster before that final pitch!

Sonny Siebert was a former University of Missouri basketball player and All-American outfielder-first baseman. He converted to pitching due to injuries in the minors, and required four additional years prior to making the Tribe Staff in '64 as a 27-year-old rookie. He had been 4-10 at AAA Jacksonville the previous season, with en ERA approaching 5, hindered by some elbow trouble. He would relieve and work his way into the starting rotation in '64, and become the surprise of this first year group. Sonny had a great fastball, curve ball, and a tight slider, which broke very sharply just as it got to the plate. The latter was really his "out" pitch to right-handers, and got in on and jammed left-handers very effectively.

Sonny loved to hit as much as to pitch, and he would average almost .200 over his career, with 18 career HRs, including eight in 1971, two in one game. At 6' 3" and 190 lbs, he was solid with good power at the plate, if, like Sam, not muscular in build. Sieb and I would usually play gin rummy together on the airplanes when I traveled with the team. We would become close friends, maintaining our friendship after I later moved to his hometown of St. Louis in 1966.

Tommy John was a poised, lanky 21-year-old rookie left-hander who had been up briefly in September '63, with six appearances, a 2.25 ERA in 20 innings, but no wins. The '64 Official Indians' Sketchbook said TJ was "on his way to being one of the best in the business" and was "headed for greatness." He threw a sinking fastball at less than 90 m.p.h., and a curve ball at various speeds and angles. But 1964 would not yet be his year.

Three veteran starters promised to hold the fort until the newcomers could establish themselves. Pete Ramos had had a pretty good year in '63, appearing in 36 games with 22 starts, winning nine and losing eight with a 3.12 ERA, leading the team with 169 strikeouts in 184 2/3 innings.

Jack Kralick was a fidgety, 6' 2" 180-pound (dripping wet before a haircut) lefty starter who was always picking at his hat, his shirt, glove off, glove on, etc. He had great control, and very good stuff. He didn't throw super-hard, but his repertoire of pitches, kept hitters off balance and allowed him to dictate the proceedings. He had come to the team in '63 from the Twins in a trade for Jim Perry, and was 13-9 with a 2.92 ERA, 116 strikeouts, in 27 starts, with ten complete games. Kralick, Ramos, Grant, and Latman all had struck out more than 100 batters in '63.

Dick Donovan (aka "Tricky Dick") was a 6' 3", 205 lb. veteran starter with excellent control (2.4 walks/9 innings over his career), who had pitched with pitching coach Early Wynn on the 1959 White Sox AL champions. His ERA in '62 was lowest in the majors at 2.40. He had been the Sporting News AL Pitcher of the Year in '62, winning 20 games, but dropped to 11 wins in '63. He would go 7–9 in '64, before retiring in '65 after a 15-year career. He is listed #9 on Rob Neyer's list of the best sliders of all time.[56] The native Bostonian was a soft-spoken gentleman with a dry sense of humor. Though he was old enough to be my father, he and I would get along great until he was released in June, '65.

Gary Bell had been a starter early in his career, where he averaged 12 wins from '58–61. He had a great sinker and slider, and a tumbling, slip-pitch change-up. The right-hander moved to the 'pen in '62, and had been 8–5 with a 2.95 ERA in '63, striking out 98 in 119 innings, mostly in relief. In '64, "Ding Dong" Bell would throw a lot of middle and long relief, before moving to late relief in '65, and back to starting in '66.

Ted Abernathy was a 6' 4", 205-lb. right-handed reliever with an under-hand delivery, the only such AL pitcher in 1964. An injury in 1957 led him to adopt the unorthodox pitching method, where his knuckles almost scraped the mound as he delivered. The motion led to his fastball sinking, and his curveball usually rising. He threw an occasional knuckleball as well. He had a North Carolina drawl and a ready smile. He had had a good year in the Indians 'pen in the previous season with seven wins, 12 saves, and a 2.88 ERA in 59 innings. He would be the designated closer early in the '64 season, with five saves in the first 22 games. He would stumble later, and lose that role to Don McMahon before season's end. Abby would be traded to the Cubs after the '64 season, and become the first reliever in history to save 30 games in a season in 1965. He would have a 14-year career with 63 wins, 148 saves, and an ERA of 3.46.

Don McMahon was a Brooklyn-born, 6' 1", 222 lb. barrel-chested, redheaded veteran right-hand reliever who wanted the ball when the game was on the line. He threw a rising across-the-seams fastball, usually up and in that challenged hitters successfully. He would run a two-seamer in on right-handers. He also had a variable-breaking flat curve/slider, and a sinking with-the-seams fastball that he would use to set up the fastball. He had had a solid career with the Braves and Colt .45s before coming to the Tribe, and he was in his first of 2 1/2 seasons in Cleveland. He, too, was a stabilizing veteran force. He pitched early relief early in the season, but would take over as closer in mid-season. The Rolaids Man of the Year award wouldn't be instituted until 1976, but Don McMahon would have been a legitimate candidate, the '64 season would be the best of an 18-year career.

Lee Stange had just recently come over from the Twins in the trade for Mudcat Grant, an attempt on Gabe Paul's part to pare down the Indians' payroll. A sometime-starter, sometime long reliever, the 5' 9", 170-lb. "Stinger" had been 12–5 with a 2.62 ERA in '63, but was off to a slow start in '64 before the trade.

Luis Tiant would soon join the staff. A native of Marianao, Cuba, and the son of a famous pitcher in the Mexican League, "Looie" had been purchased from the Mexico City Tigers in 1962. Luis was 15–1 at Portland, and his call-up was certainly expected at the time I joined the club.

The clubhouse and bullpen did not include a left-handed reliever. John, Kralick, and McDowell all made a few appearances in relief, but the 'pen had no proven, reliable lefty to bring in to face a left-handed line-up or one or two lefty hitters in a tight situation.

Early Wynn was in his first full year as pitching coach. He had just won his 300th game as an Indian July 13, 1963, and then retired Sept. 13. Gus, as he was known, had a remarkable career, pitching in four decades, debuting for the Washington Senators on Sept. 13, 1939. He pitched for Washington for 10 years, winning 72, losing 87 , for a team whose average finish was 6th place. Washington: first in war, first in peace, and almost last in the American League!

Wynn became one of "The Big Four" starting pitchers for the Indians' when traded in 1949. He was part of the '54 pennant-winning team that had set the AL win record with 111, only to lose to the Giants in the Series, best remembered for Willie Mays' over-the-head catch of Vic Wertz's blast to center field. Gus led the White Sox to the AL championship in 1959, and received the Cy Young Award, and was the Major League Player of the Year. He played in ten All-Star games. He led the league in strikeouts twice ('57–8), and was second three times ('51, '52, '54). He struck out more AL batters in the 1950s than any other pitcher. He led the AL in ERA in 1950 (3.20), and was third three times, finishing with a career ERA of 3.54. On the all-time list, he is 21st in shutouts (49), 22nd in innings pitched (4,564), 48th in complete games (290). He was elected to the Hall of Fame in 1972.

Burly Early has been described as scowling, intimidating, grim, and fierce. He was actually a pretty quiet guy; described by Russell Schneider, the former Cleveland *Plain Dealer* sportswriter, and Indians' historian, as "gruff and tough." All business on the field, which he called his office, Gus was fun loving in the clubhouse, and his humor frequently broke through that tough John Wayne exterior throughout my time with the club. When Al Salerno, a retired ump, visited the dugout one day, Gus kidded him about Al's bright red sweater. When Al told him it was Italian burgundy, Gus said, "Put it in a bottle, and then I'll recognize it."

On Friday July 24, 1965, against the Yankees with 30,000 in attendance, the Indians' concession stands sold plastic horns about two feet long, orange with trumpeted ends, to the fans: "Horn Night," as it was called. We were sitting in the bullpen, and we had never seen these things before, and assumed they were some sort of give-away. The horns kept getting more numerous in the stands, and louder as the game progressed, and increasingly annoying. Early's patience melted away eventually, and he stood up, walked out from under our bullpen awning, looked up at the stands and blurted out loudly : "What mental midget decided to give these f----- horns away?! They should take their horns and shove them up their-----!" Apparently the front office heard him, and ordered sales of the horns to cease after the sixth inning. Horn night was second only to five-cent beer night in 1974 as a bad marketing idea.

Gus called on unique visuals to make his point as well, as evidenced by the time he pointed out that his pitch control was so good that, "I could pitch to the inside and to the outside of an ant's ass." That certainly gives new meaning to "pitching on the black." In looking out at vast Municipal Stadium and seeing all the empty seats, he'd occasionally straight face that "a fat lady must have gotten herself caught in the turnstile." Political correctness had not yet swept across America, much less its bullpens. I occasionally find myself unable to resist a unisex variation of the latter line, even to this day, when I find one of my lectures poorly attended.

Wynn was a competitor. Of course, there are the many variations of the story that he would throw at his own mother or grandmother in the batter's box, because "she could really hit the curveball." It's almost out of character to think of him as nervous taking the mound, but discussing opening days, he once said it's always great to win the first game, because then you know you can't lose them all!

Gus had been in the game so long he had a lot of great stories that he told, usually not spontaneously, but rather when some specific event evoked some recollection of a similar event in his mind. He recalled pitching years earlier with Luke Easter playing first base when a line drive toward first hit Luke square on the knee, dropping him to the ground in pain. Gus ran over, and asked if he was OK, and Easter looked up, smiled, and said, "It took a bad bounce!" Another Easter story: One of the Tribe, Al Rosen, I think, had hit a home run, and when he got to the dugout, no one was greeting him: they were all circled around Easter on the bench. Luke had been dozing off, and the crowd noise with Rosen's dinger awakened him, and he jumped up and knocked himself out on the dugout roof!

Gus was in charge of a pitching staff that, with minor additions and subtractions, would lead the league in strikeouts for five consecutive years from 1964 through 1968, setting records along the way. It may be no accident that the Staff's dominance coincided with a higher strike zone. Gus was a proponent of the high inside pitch, even to his mother. It was great to be a small part of this history in the making. The Tribe's staff's five-year string of leading the league with over 1100 strikeouts over each of those years was unprecedented.

# Chapter 8—The Clubhouse

I never expected to be in this position: headed for the clubhouse of a major league ball club, having given up any reasonable hope of a baseball career.

When I was in grade school, the Cleveland Press Straight A's program offered two tickets to about six games per season to Straight-A students. In the previous five years, I had gone to only one or two games per year, primarily the yearly exhibition between the Indians and the Reds, played as a benefit for amateur baseball. Amateur players received free tickets, and I usually went to the game, even if annually disappointed by cameo appearances by the starters, with the game played mostly by second-stringers needing some work, or by minor leaguers called up for the experience.

I'm not sure I could have named all the players on the roster as I pulled into the players' parking area at the stadium, perpendicular to a fence, along a roadway that ringed the stadium on its west ($3^{rd}$ base) side. From the players' entrance, you entered the stadium at a guarded roll-gate entrance, usually past fans waiting for autographs, then walked along the dark, damp, dank concourse, under the lower-deck stands, around to Section 15 on the first-base side, to the main clubhouse entrance . I always imagined the history of Lakeside Stadium, as it was originally known, as a landfill projection into Lake Erie contributed greatly to its moist, chilly character. It was later nicknamed "The Mistake on the Lake."

Opening the main clubhouse door from the concourse, you entered a small anteroom with steps immediately to the left leading down to the dugout. Straight ahead was a second door, beyond which the trainer's room was to the right. Wally "Doc" Bock was the trainer, preliminarily administering to the discomforts and injuries of the players, but quick to turn more serious problems over to the medical staff.

The trainer's room was relatively Spartan: a training table, two cabinets with supplies and medications, and a desk. There was a single large whirlpool machine. The room had no training or strength equipment to speak of. At that time a bias existed that weight training limited flexibility, and players weren't known to be as muscular and bulky as we see many today. Nautilus equipment would not be introduced until 1970.

Turning to the left away from the training room, you walked past the shower on the right, and the toilet and sink area on the left, and then into the main clubhouse room straight ahead. The entrance to Birdie Tebbetts's office was to the immediate left beyond that doorway. The clubhouse lockers were open wooded structures about three feet square, with chairs or stools in front. The four coaches' lockers were to the left on the wall adjacent to the entrance to Tebbetts's office. There were nine lockers on the left-side wall, eight lockers on the back wall straight ahead, and nine on the right-side wall. When the roster was expanded at season's end, the minor leaguers dressed in an adjacent locker room where Keeney and the BP pitchers dressed.

My locker was on the far left-side-wall corner as you entered the room. As I sat in front of my locker facing the room, Sonny Siebert was to my right, then Bell, Donovan, and Kralick. Immediately to my left there was a corner space with an exit door, used mostly by Frank Keeney to come and go from the locker room before and after BP. To the left of this space was Don McMahon. I think it was no accident that next to him was Sam McDowell, arguably the most talented left-hander ever to throw for the Indians. "48: Sudden Sam" was printed on the name card above his locker. Then there was outfielder Leon Wagner, then Tommy John, Lee Stange, catcher Joe Azcue, Pedro Ramos, catcher John Romano, then Ted Abernathy.

I was in the apex of the pitcher/catcher corner, so to speak. It wasn't a spot for group meetings, however. In fact, there were actually very few staff or group meetings that I attended, or was asked to attend. I guess they went on mostly before I got to the park, usually on the first day of a series, or in Birdie's office, where Birdie, Gus, and the pitchers would go over how they were going to throw to different hitters, or during BP. Maybe they had heard I had been a Yankee fan.

The clubhouse was an experience in itself. Billy Malone, the chief clubhouse attendant, a young Californian in his early 20s, who could talk a bulldog off of a meat wagon, was in charge of seeing to it that the uniforms were clean, the laundry was done, the sanitary socks were available, there was bubble gum and chewing tobacco on the shelf, the shower room was supplied with soap and shampoo, soft drinks were in the cooler, the shoes were shined, etc., etc., etc. He had been an assistant with the Angels previously. Bill had an outwardly seemingly gruff way of running the show, but usually with tongue-in cheek and cigar in corner of mouth. He called me "Kid" or "Rookie." The latter was a bit of a promotion, considering there were a number of real rookies in the room, including Sonny Siebert, and soon, Luis Tiant.

Billy and I got along great: two peripherals connected to the mainframe that was major league baseball. He had been a catcher himself in amateur ball, and so we had a natural link to my daily activity through his background. He probably could have gone out and done my job. Billy had an entrepreneurial sideline as an Amway home products salesman, with his free time when the team was out of town. It probably allowed him to be his own middleman for sales of products used in the clubhouse, including laundry detergent. He even tried to get me involved with Amway, and I made a few brief forays into sales. One sample I distributed, in hope of a sale, was to Mike Garcia, former Tribe pitcher, who owned "Big Bear" Dry Cleaners. Mike wrote me "the soap is very bad." I bought some of the spray shoe polish myself, and used it for my ROTC shoes at JCU. Sure made them look like glass, until the glass-like coating began to shatter and crack over time! So much for a sales career.

Billy had three assistants in the clubhouse. Cy Buynak was assistant #1, a cheerful, rotund Lou Costello to Malone's acerbic Bud Abbott. Cy was as pleasant and friendly as can be. Cy also helped out in the visitors' clubhouse. Mickey Coyne, the Indians' batboy, and Paul Gadke, visiting club batboy who would move up to become the Indians' batboy in '65, both served as clubhouse assistants as well when not on the field. Bill would leave the club after the '65 season, and Cy would take over as the boss.

On the first day, I found a uniform that fit: number 23, size 42 shirt, 34 waist pants, a woolen uniform made by Wilson Sporting Goods. The sleeveless, vest-type shirt played a bit bigger than size suggested, worn over heavy woolen jerseys with long or short red sleeves. The long-sleeve red woolen shirts presented a dilemma on hot, sunny days: they were like ovens, yet they kept arms free from excessive exposure. You couldn't wear greasy sun protection on the skin, or balls might get slick. The uniform included a blue hat with a red "C," blue stirrup stockings, and red leather belt. There would be a switch to red hats and stirrups in '65, and '66.

There were no "warm-up" shirts or uniforms as seen today: players went on to the field for batting practice in their uniforms. Most players had two or three. The road uniform was a gray blend material different from the home woolen white, cooler and more comfortable.

The players and coaches had their names in block print letters on the back of their uniforms, but I did not. I would later wear uniform #13 in '65, when Chuck Hinton joined the Indians and wanted to retain the same #23 he had worn with the Washington Senators. The numbers I wore were never included on the scorecard, confirming the anonymity the bullpen catcher toils in. Team pictures were included in some printed programs, with the names below. Eventually, in '66, I would not wear a number at all, with some pronouncement from on high that non-professionals (batboy, bullpen and batting practice catcher, batting practice pitchers) would not wear numbered unis.

But the #23 of 1964 was not lost to the ages with that pronouncement. An Indians' team picture for '64 was taken early in the year, prior to Mudcat Grant, Jerry Walker, and Jerry Kindall being traded, and before Sam McDowell and Luis Tiant joined the club. So it was repeated in July after I joined the club, and I was therefore included in the official picture. I stood in the back row, upper right of the picture, wearing #23.

The '64 picture was later used by Topps baseball cards for their 1965 team baseball card, insofar as cards usually were printed in the spring before teams were finalized, and before final official team pictures were taken. Typically, on the front you had the team from the previous year, and on the back you had team records from the previous year. So the '65 card was a picture of the '64 team with the '64 records on the back, for example.

Well, not only is the official '64 team pic on the '65 Topps card, but it's also been immortalized on the '66 card and the '67 card as well! How economical. I'd wear #13 on the official team pic in '65. My daughter Lisa still displays a '65 card in a plastic frame on her dresser. You can buy the '64 and '65 cards on EBay for about a dollar each. For some reason, the '67 card usually sells for $10 minimum, and occasionally as much as $50. As it turns out this triplicate isn't a record for most uses of a single team picture in consecutive years. Topps used the same Indians' team pic, probably the '59 team pic, from '60–64, five consecutive years.

I wanted to illustrate the Topps cards from those years, but Topps refused permission. But of course you can see them on EBay.

Someone doing my laundry in the clubhouse? No problem. I always had two clean uniform shirts and pants, and fresh washed underwear and jock, every day in my locker. It was a communal wash: everyone had their name or uniform number on their belongings, and the laundry was separated and distributed accordingly. Clean sanitary socks were kept in a communal bag, for everyone to take a pair.

Someone shining <u>my</u> shoes? Coyne and Gadke were responsible for the shoes, and they did a great job, even though I was an employee just as they were. My shoes were always beautifully black when I walked into the clubhouse, without the coating from the dusty sandlot fields I was accustomed to as an amateur.

Situated in my corner of the locker room was a wide support post with a table built around it, approximately five feet square, where players would congregate, sitting on the table, talking to the players lockered adjacent. Mailboxes were attached to the wide side of the post facing toward the center of the room. Shelves were attached above the table level, where bubble gum, chewing tobacco, and other miscellaneous items were available. A footlocker with a lock box for valuables was on the floor near the table. Occasionally boxes of baseballs would be put out on the table by management for the players to sign. "Sign the balls!" Billy Malone or Cy Buynak would call out, and everybody would loudly repeat it immediately, or just shout it out themselves as they would be walking by. "Sign the *beisbols,* sign the *pellotas*" was the Spanish command from infielder/outfielder Chico Salmon and Luis Tiant. I didn't sign my name on any of those balls, but I did sign a few outside the locker room, and on the road, "Tom Tomsick BPC," when the answer "I'm not a player, I'm just the bullpen catcher" just didn't satisfy the question "Would you please sign my ball?"

After the official team pictures were taken in July, then reproduced on 14 x 20 cardboard mount, they would be spread out on the table for signatures as well. Most importantly, the after-game snack and sandwich spread was put out on that table. A lighter spread would be put out between the games of doubleheaders. A buzz of activity went on right in front of my locker.

Some guys were just great guys to have around. The clubhouse camaraderie was easily identified: guys liked doing what they were doing, and liked doing it together. Of course, it was better when the club was winning. Leon Wagner ("Daddy Wags") was known for his positive attitude and good humor. Gary Bell was a clubhouse cut-up, the smilingest, laughingest guy on the club. "Ding-Dong" was a fun loving, clubhouse comedian and crooner, sitting and singing his country-western tunes. He had a long repertoire of songs, but the one that sticks with me to this day is "Act Naturally" by Buck Owens. It was also a cut on the Beatles' "Help" album, where I actually played it often enough to finally learn the words. I remember them even now, singing the catchy tune to my grandchildren, perhaps without the twang that Gary "brang" when he sang:

*I'll bet you I'm gonna' be a big star,*
*Might win an Oscar, you can never tell.*
*The movies gonna' make me a big star,*
*'Cause I can play the part so well.*
*Well, I hope you come and see me in the movies,*
*Then I know you will plainly see:*
*The biggest fool to ever hit the big time;*
*And all I gotta' do is, Act Naturally.*[57]

Oscar? Gold Glove or Silver Bat? Substitute "baseball" for "movies and you have the perspective of many young men who played the game. Gary made it big time, if not in the movies: he was an All-Star in 1960, and he would have a 12-year career as both starter, middle, and late reliever.

"Meat' was Bell's greeting for almost everybody. He called Siebert "Lips," I guess because of the full appearance of Sieb's lips, or perhaps in contrast to Sonny's bullpen designation of "Eyes," due to their light blue hue and sparkle. (I don't think an article was ever written about Sonny without calling him "the handsome hurler.") When Tebbetts/Strickland would signal to the pen for Sonny to warm up, they'd connect their thumb and index finger tips, encircling their "Eyes" with them. I would see Gary at an Old-Timers' Game in Cincinnati years later, and his greeting was no surprise: "Hey, Meat, what's happening?"

Bell lockered one locker down from Luis Tiant after the latter was promoted from Portland, and that block was usually comedy central. The Cuban-born Tiant was said to be 24 years old, but Bell would accuse him of doctoring his birth certificate, being 24 going on 40, talking about his bad body, little paunch, thinning top of his head: a real "mullion," which is baseballese for a creature on the lowest rung of male handsomeness or female pulchritude. There was an element of truth to Gary's opinion: Luis was older in baseball years. Luis Sr. had been a famous Cuban pitcher for the New York Cubans of the Negro League, and Luis junior had learned at his side, pitching at high amateur levels prior to signing a contract with the Mexico City Tigers. On the advice of former Tribe second baseman Bobby Avila, the Indians signed him in 1961. Luis Jr. would not be allowed to return to Castro's Cuba to see his family until 2007 after 46 years of exile. The documentary "The Lost Son of Havana" recounts Luis's story.[58]

Luis Jr. usually had a cigar in his mouth in the clubhouse, and Bell a cigarette. Smoking was certainly common in the clubhouse, with about a third of the players smoking. Of course, 1964 was the peak of adult cigarette use in the US at 42% (currently down to 20%). The Surgeon General's report on health hazards of smoking was published that year. Looie, as Tiant became know, also chewed tobacco, and had a peculiar habit that could be considered a metaphor for the game of baseball itself: he would wrap his chaw of tobacco with bubble gum, symbolizing baseball's ability to get a man wrapped up in a boy's game.

Looie had a voice that broke into a particularly squeaky high pitch at times. Hardly a day passed when Looie would not comment on the sharp outfit of a players as they were walking to their lockers. "Loookiiiieeee goooood!" was his protracted approval, delivered in near-falsetto.

Ballplayers weren't paid near as well as they are today, but they generally dressed sharp. There were a number of clothes stores around the league that catered to players, and sold to them at sharp discounts. I even purchased a few items at the York Haberdashery on our Washington-Baltimore trips. I bought a few alpaca sweaters: V-neck and button up, with wide sleeves, but tight cuffs that could be raised up the forearm a bit, as well as a black and white wool plaid and a blue pin stripe cotton sport coat, pieces of clothing I would wear for years to come. Even a poor bullpen catcher/student couldn't pass up a bargain, shopping where the stars received preferential treatment. The rhetorical "How are you feeling?" became "Feeellliiiee gooood?" usually eliciting the parallel response "Feeeeelliiiieee Goooooodd!" from Looie. It became the universal answer to any casual greeting, or to any genuine check on someone's condition. It seems to me this clubhouse lexicon probably derived from the Gillette razorblade commercial admonition to "Look sharp, feel sharp, be sharp!"

Poor Dick Donovan was stuck lockered beside Tiant and Bell. A stock broker in the off-season, much of his time between starts in the clubhouse was spent trying to read financial journalism. His dry proper Bostonian deportment may have been tested by the two good-humor guys, but he was a great clubhouse presence and sport. Bad humor and long faces just don't belong or survive in the locker room. The disappointments are too frequent, the season is too long, the proximity of colleagues too close.

Clubhouse cut-ups are a part of baseball life. Bell's sense of humor was exceptional. As the author's roommate, Gary's humor would be featured a few years later in Jim Bouton's *Ball Four*. If Gary were active today, he'd be singing in the clubhouse: "Mommies, don't let your daughters grow up to date ballplay'rs..." The phenomenon of baseball comedy is a bit difficult to understand and explain. The numbers of individuals with the knack for hilarious stories, quick quips, and funny retorts may be no greater than in the general population. Some players are humorless, just as in other walks of life. But it may be that the atmosphere of 25 men, enclosed for hours within 4 walls, or on long bus rides, or during games on the bench and in the bullpen, for months on end, has allowed humor to seed, sprout, grow and then expand exponentially as it bounces from one locker to another over time. It may bypass the less witty, but then be amplified among those whose brain, throwing arm, and funny bone are inextricably connected in a way da Vinci never depicted.

But clubhouse humor could be, irreverent, slapstick, but occasionally inappropriate and out of place. One such latter incident involved one of the players wrapping his penis in a hot dog bun, then parading around the locker room as if he were a vendor in the stands. Some truly were boys of summer.

Unlike “Ding Dong” and his song, I wouldn’t make it “big time” in baseball. But it seemed like time well spent.

# Chapter 9—The Job: Day 1

So I walked into the team clubhouse for the first time June 29, 1964, the 70th game of the season, after the team returned from a long road trip. Keeney , who was known as "Country" in the clubhouse, told me when to show up, where to meet him, then took me to intro me to none other than Early Wynn.

Early looked at me with suspicion, insofar as I didn't have the prototypical physiognomy of a catcher. At 6' 4" and 200, I was taller and thinner than any catcher in the AL at the time. In 2009, the average catcher height was 6' ¾", with Joe Mauer and Colt Morton at 6' 5". Jim Hegan at 6' 2" had been Wynn's battery-mate with the Tribe for years in the 50s. Bill Freehan, at 6' 3" and 200 lbs. at 24 years of age, was about the tallest starter around in 1964, and was rated by Birdie Tebbetts in a scouting report as the best catcher in the American League at the time. Paul Casanova of the Senators at 6' 4" and around 200, would join the Senators in '65. Phil Roof, at 6' 4" and 210 lbs. would join the Indians in 1965. Phil was the "Duke o' Paducah," a strapping build, good-glove, .215 lifetime BA guy himself.

Gus, as Early was known, wasn't a spontaneously talkative guy on the field, to say the least. But if Gus got angry, or was in a particularly good mood, then he'd open up. He never did tell me I did a good job, or a great job, or an average job, or a terrible job. I was just doing my job, and in my mind, silence meant approval and assent, and we got along just fine for three seasons. As previously noted, Gus had a reputation for being tough and crusty, as witnesses his statement he'd knock down his grandmother with a pitch if it would help him win, or if she dug in too deeply at the plate. So, I had a healthy concern for raising his ire, and admittedly went out of my way not to do so.

Initially, I knew I was to be seen and not heard, and I stuck to that maxim. As a fly on the wall, though, I would, over time, work my way into the fabric of the clubhouse, and earn the respect and trust of the Staff, learn quite a bit about catching and pitching, and became one of the guys, if not one of the players.

Author's photo taken during June, '65 batting practice. (Reproduced with permission Scripps-Howard Publications.)

For home games, I had to be at the stadium about three and a half hours before game time to get dressed and warmed up for batting practice.[59] There was typically no BP on Sundays, or for afternoon games following a night game. BP for the home team for a 7:30 game began at 4:55. BP at home consisted of pitchers first (except the starter, who would hit with the other starting eight players), followed by utility players (the "irregulars," or the "scrubbini's," as the non-starters liked to call themselves) at 5:15, followed by the starting line-up (the eight "regulars," plus the starting pitcher) at 5:45. BP consists of a bunt to each side, then seven swings in the first round, five swings in the second, then one swing in the third, and then one pitch (ball or strike!), until the bell rings. Then the visitors take over. The pitchers usually had fun, then it got a bit more serious for the utility guys, and more serious yet for the starters.

After BP there was 45 minutes before going back onto the field. I'd shower quickly to get the catcher's mask dirt and grime off my face and out of my hair, change into a dry, clean uniform, and sit around for a few minutes, getting ready to go out for long toss before infield practice, while ready to warm up the starter when he came down.

In 1964, it was customary to take ten minutes of infield practice following batting practice. After the visiting team was done with BP, the batting cage would be moved out, and they would take infield practice first for about 10-15 minutes. Then the Tribe takes the field for another 10-15 minutes.

Several times in my tenure I actually did take infield practice with the team. Strickland would hit the ball around, and we would really get that ball moving around the infield. I think I understandably had more enthusiasm than the regs, and it was like old times to fire the ball down to second, as if there were some imaginary runner daring to test my arm. Infield practice was a great way for everyone to show off their arms. Major-league infield practice during the season has generally gone the way of the batting practice catcher, however. In 2007, Jerry Narron, the Reds manager, said it disappeared in the mid-1990s.[60] Apparently the thought process had evolved that batting practice afforded the opportunity for infielders to take plenty of ground balls, and make plenty of throws, while hitters were hitting. But BP doesn't necessarily allow the starting catcher to warm up before the game. Therefore, catchers now do some tossing and long throws in the outfield, near the bullpen, prior to warming up the starting pitcher to get ready for the game. Some teams continue to take infield practice early in the season, or when too many errors get the manager irked.[61] [62]

David Wallace pointed out that the Indians have been taking formal infield practice early this season under new manager Manny Acta, usually before the first or second game of each series, in hopes of overcoming some of the fundamental fielding problems that plagued them in '09. "Infield" has been occurring prior to batting practice, not immediately before the game as it did in the 60s.

Occasionally I would go into the outfield and shag fly balls, or be a middleman on balls returned to the outfield by fungo hitters during infield practice. I remember one session in Cleveland, when Sam McDowell, who actually was a decent hitter and who loved to hit fungos to the outfielders on days he wasn't starting, was doing so from the right field foul line area, hitting toward left field. While the ball was being hit around the infield by one of the coaches, I would occasionally shag for Sam, positioning myself between the outfielders in left-center, and about 60 feet in front of Sam. Every now and then he'd hit one straight up for me to catch.

I thought it was a pretty safe spot to position myself, until one day when Sam didn't catch one of the balls square, hit over the top of the ball, and caused it to topspin off like a sinking line drive. Just as I was turning away from the outfield back toward Sam to return a ball to him, the sinking liner hit me just above the hair line in the middle of my head. Maybe "tools of ignorance" does pertain in this instance. It knocked some sense into me: I never positioned myself there again. The bigger question was: what's a multi-million dollar player doing hitting fungos?

A new ball for warming up the starting pitcher would appear in my locker after batting practice, dropped off by Wynn. The starting pitcher would also get one in his locker that he could rub up a bit before we went back out to warm up. I'd go back out onto the field a bit early, and, if time allowed, frequently play long-toss with Vic Davalillo or Rocky Colavito before infield practice started. Colavito, of course, was known for his strong throwing arm, a real cannon. He actually pitched five and two-thirds innings in the majors, giving up no runs on one hit. Davalillo had a great arm, too, having started in pro ball as a pitcher, and I think he still liked throwing to a catcher. He didn't fare so well in a brief two innings pitching in '69, walking two and giving up two hits in the four batters he faced. Lengthening our throws, stepping back with each one, we would end up firing BB's at one another from around 100 to 120 feet by the time we were done.

In '64-'66, the starting pitcher warmed up between the dugout and area behind home plate. A ball getting by would bounce and roll around the back wall to the visiting team warm-up area.

Then I would be ready to go out with the starting pitcher for about 15-20 minutes before game time to warm him up: five minutes earlier at home to allow for some rest before the first pitch of the game, a little later on the road so that he didn't get cold waiting after warming up. In Municipal Stadium, the starting pitcher warmed up between the dugout and the backstop behind home plate, a situation duplicated only at Yankee Stadium.

After warming up the starter, I'd go back to the clubhouse to rest for a few minutes and have a drink, before going out to the 'pen. I would take those two balls from warming up the starter to the bullpen (and Gus would bring a couple more). On my way up the clubhouse steps from the dugout, I'd frequently run into Birdie, who'd ask me "How's he throwing?" To me they were always throwing well, and I told him so. There were a few instances where it quickly proved not to be the case, but nothing I had seen from the warm-up sessions would have predicted it.

Sam McDowell was starting that first night, but I did not warm him up. I guess someone feared I'd be overmatched on my first assignment—including me. Sam would go nine innings, strike out seven, and leave with the score tied 1-1. I did warm up McMahon and Siebert in the bullpen, both of whom gave up two runs in the loss. So after that first game at home, it was a couple of soft drinks, a shower, a sandwich, then home, joining some friends who had come to see my debut. Walking past the waiting lineup of wives, girlfriends, other friends, and fans for the first time was quite an experience. I was in the Bigs, even if a playing a very small part.

The next night (June 30), I warmed up my first starting pitcher, Jack Kralick, who was in the midst of a good year as the number one starter, going 8–2 into this game. He didn't throw really hard, but had great control and good movement. Warming Jack up was also like sitting in a rocking chair, not a great challenge, and was a great way for me to get off on the right foot. He gave up six runs in four and two-thirds innings, while striking out seven, and the Indians lost 12–3. Was it something I did? Time would tell.

# Chapter 10—The First Road Trip

Those were the only two games of a short homestand. The plan was that as long as the team had only two catchers, I would travel on all charter flights. John Romano and Joe Azcue were the two catchers in '64. Trips to LA weren't charter, but paid by the head, and the front office didn't think my head was worth the cost. So the team would arrange for a local to catch BP, and the back-up catcher would warm up the starter, and catch in the bullpen, aided by a utility player.

The first trip was a Wednesday morning flight to Detroit for a two-game series with the Tigers. The team had given me a brown metal suitcase, with a sticker of Chief Wahoo on it. We all had similar, uniform luggage. There was a dress code: sport coats, and I wore a light tan wool blazer with dark brown striped tie. We took a charter plane DC-7, my first air flight ever! We deplaned before I knew it, and took a team bus to the luxurious Sheraton Cadillac Hotel, in downtown Detroit.

My roommate on the road for the season was Vern Fuller, a 20-year old slick-fielding rookie infielder from Canoga Park, CA, who had signed a professional contract the year before, had spent one year at Dubuque in Class A ball, but was now in the majors due to the rule that bonus players would be subject to the Rule 5 draft after their first year in organized baseball unless they were kept on the 40-man major-league roster. Paul Dicken, a 21-year-old outfielder, was the other rookie so designated. Fuller, known as "Blade" for his 6' 1" frame on 165 pounds, would eventually play six years in the majors, Dicken small parts of two. Vern would have one at-bat in '64, a story unto itself later.

A free-agent draft would only be voted in by the owners in '64, and would do away with the bonus baby and free agent signee rules that had placed such young, untested players on major-league rosters long before they were truly ready, risking that their skills might dull or be further delayed in development. In the final June free agent signing period of 1964, the Tribe would sign Fran Healy, a catcher I met when he worked out in Cleveland after his signing. Fran, at 6' 5" and 215, would eventually make it to the majors with Kansas City in 1969.

As it turned out, the first free-agent draft of 1965 would be a memorable one for the Indians from the catching standpoint. They would draft Ray Fosse, who would eventually make it permanently to the big club in 1969, and have a fine 12-year career, remembered best here in my adopted home of Cincinnati for his home plate collision with Pete Rose in the '70 All Star Game.

Several days before road trips, Charley Morris, the traveling secretary, would pass out the meal money checks, along with an itinerary for plane times, bus times to the parks, BP times, etc. We took team buses from airports to the hotel where we were staying. On the first trip to Detroit, I went to my room, unpacked, then went downstairs for late lunch in the sandwich shop. I had a hamburger and a shake, which cost more than the dollar I was accustomed to paying back home. $15 per day for meals seemed like a lot, but could easily be swallowed up in the restaurants at the hotels. On occasion, though, I could find cheaper meals and occasionally pocket some of the money. There would usually be a team bus to the ballpark everywhere but in Detroit, where the park was a short cab drive away downtown. The Tribe lost the first game 3-1 as TJ gave up three hits, two earned runs in seven innings, and the second 9-1 as Pete Ramos lasted one inning.

We left Detroit after the Thursday-night game on United Airlines Charter, arriving in Chicago well after 1 AM and checking into the Conrad Hilton Hotel on Michigan Avenue, about a mile and a half from the main shopping district. We slept in late Friday, in preparation for the 5:30 PM bus to Comiskey Park. We would again take BP second, after the home team, as remains the custom. In the Friday-night game, Dick Donovan again returned to the scene of his '59 pennant win. He threw ten innings, in a 2-1 win, with Bell getting the save. Donovan was a decent hitter, which did keep him in close games, and the tall, slow-footed hurler, walked in the top of the 11th. There's no way a starter in 2009 would still be in the game after pitching ten innings, and, after getting on base, would not be replaced by a pinch runner. At any rate, he scored on a triple by Tito Francona. I can still picture Dick's long, loping stride in profile racing around second base.

I point out this event in detail, primarily because it shows that pitching was different in '64, for a variety of reasons, compared to today. Of interest, Tito passed up an opportunity to make the record books with his triple: he had doubled three times earlier in the game. If he had stayed at second, as he probably should have with no one out, he would have had four doubles in the game, a club record. There's something about Donovan and Chicago. Later in the year on September 6th, Birdie would let him pitch 12 1/3 innings, giving up 16 hits and three runs, but losing 3-2, with no relievers brought in as the Sox scored in the 13th on a drag bunt by Tom McCraw, who stole second, was sacrificed to third, and who scored on a sacrifice fly: typical White Sox small ball.

July 4, 1964, Dugout, Comiskey Park. The first road trip. Photo by George Brace. His daughter, Mary, would tell me in 2009: "You looked like a 12-year-old!" (Reproduced with permission, George Brace Photo)

Saturday July 4's game was a day game, as were virtually all Saturday games at the time. I remember the day by a memento I have until this day. Before batting practice, immediately after I had come from the clubhouse, a local Chicago photographer asked to take my picture, sitting on the bench. I told him I was just the bullpen catcher, but he said, "That's OK, you'll make it to the majors some day." I knew I had already made it, and this was probably as far as I was going to go. But I humored him, and let him snap what I thought was a meaningless photo.

The Tribe would then get shut out three games in a row on July 4th and in a doubleheader, Sunday July 5th, for a total of three runs in six games on the road. (Maybe my hitting inability was rubbing off.) The '64 season would include 29 doubleheaders, including two doubleheaders back-to-back, and five separated by one day off.

It was still common to schedule doubleheaders at that time, but some were unscheduled and rain-related, a not-uncommon occurrence in Cleveland, where games were played on the grass field that drained and dried out less well than the artificial turf of later years. With so many doubleheaders scheduled, it's no wonder the Indians were in financial trouble: two scheduled games for the price of one. The practice has now disappeared, with the last scheduled DH played June 7, 1996 at the Metrodome. Sure, Ernie Banks had said "Let's play two!" but 29 DH was beyond enthusiasm for the game!

The Chicago photographer was George Brace, and he subsequently sent copies of his photo to my house, and they document that first road trip in '64—the baby-faced #23, sitting on the bench in his road uniform in the dugout at Comiskey Park. I would have sat up a bit straighter, and tucked in my shirt, if I had any inkling of the use I would make of the photo in 2010. Brace is deceased, but his company and a web site remains active today (www.bracephoto.com), run by his daughter, Mary. The site claims to have hundreds of thousands of photos, with negatives of over 10,000 players, and at least one bullpen catcher, listed in the group list "A3. Cleveland Indians," name spelled "Tom Tomasik." In response to my request for permission to publish the photo in this book, Mary looked up the picture and told me, "You look like a 12-year-old." Just a boy of summer, I guess.

Author on the way to Detroit and Chicago, June, '64.

# Chapter 11—Bullpens around the League

The wide variation in stadium construction dictated that the bullpens would be placed in different locations in the different ballparks around the league. The "cookie cutter" trend of the 60s–70s, where stadiums were symmetric and round or barely oblong, was just beginning. Stadiums, in general, had variety and character. Cleveland Municipal Stadium may well be looked upon as the prototype of a symmetric cookie-cutter, though built in 1932. The original design had no outfield fence, just the wall of the stands in left and right (320 feet from the plate) and the center field bleachers (473 feet from the plate). A fence was added in 1947, at the suggestion of Franklin "Whitey" Lewis, a columnist for the *Cleveland Press.*[63]

In 1964, the visiting team bullpen was behind the left-field fence at Municipal Stadium, oriented parallel to the fence itself, a mirror image to the Indians' bullpen in right field. The bullpen corps would usually walk out to the 'pen from the dugout, through a wide gate where the fence joined the right-field stands near the foul line at the 320 foot marker. It was 367 feet to the fence where the bullpen was located, and then 410 feet to straight-away center field.

The space behind the fence was quite wide, and grass-covered with the pitcher's mound and home plate/catcher's box carved into the grass. In Cleveland, both the home team and visitors' catcher's box was toward center field, with the pitcher's mound closer to the foul poles. I'm not aware of any good reason that the boxes should have been laid out in that fashion. In the 'pen, the left-hander usually warmed up on the right rubber, as seen from the catcher's perspective, and the right-hander on the left. This allows the pitch to be coming from the outside of the mound area when two relievers are warming up, as opposed to both coming from the middle of the area, creating a bit of a traffic jam. It might seem they could take turns in timing their throws, but when relievers have to get up quickly, distractions about taking turns could be an annoyance. Both pitchers throwing from the outside can create a theoretical traffic jam for the catchers, when curve balls can converge in the middle of the catchers' box. This issue would be almost a moot point for the '64 Indians, who didn't have any left-handed relievers.

The bullpen from '64—'65 was behind the right field fence. The wide grassy space, surrounded by a cinder track, then a hill to the bullpen seating area, is in front of the right field stands. On opening day, 1965, Sam McDowell (left) is taking off his blue jacket to warm up prior to the game, as I walk toward the catcher's box. Festivities on the field, including a band, precluded warming up in front of the dugout

A cinder track separated the pitching area from a grassy hill that then led up to an elevated cinder-covered plateau in front of the center-field bleacher wall.

The cinder track was used for the "bullpen car" to drive the pitcher into the dugout, before going to the mound in relief. A small red jeep-like car was first introduced by the Tribe's innovative GM Bill Veeck in 1950, presumably necessitated by the distance from the bullpen, and facilitated by the cinder track, and the parking space and access afforded by the ramp between the stands and bleachers. Bullpen cars became more popular elsewhere into the 60s, finally morphing into the bullpen golf cart decorated with the home team insignia, with a big home team cap on top. This same vehicle ramp connected the field and the grandstand promenade, allowing one to walk from the clubhouse to the 'pen without going onto the field.

The bullpen area was attractive, expansive, almost park-like. The bullpen's seating area, covered with an awning, was on the elevated cinder area, immediately in front of the bleacher wall, 465 feet from home plate. In general, pitchers liked to come out to the bullpen to get away from the intensity and tension of the game, and the scrutiny and the madness of the dugout, and they still do.[64] Usually, the bullpen is a relatively loose location in the early innings, with some memorable exceptions of early uprisings by the opposition. The pitchers are intent on the game early: who's hitting what pitch where, what's the umpire's strike zone today, etc, and not much about the game is escaping their notice. The 'pen begins to quiet down as the game proceeds, and then finally tightens up as the potential for a call for relief help in the late innings increases.

The driveway between the right-field stands (on left), and center field bleachers (not seen to right) in 1965. The "Bullpen Car" is in the background, at the foot of the access ramp

No one ever homered into the center-field bleachers, and the longest HR in Municipal Stadium history was attributed to Luke Easter (whom I would meet at Old Timers' Games over these years) at 477 ft. in 1952: into the upper deck in right field, on a 3-0 change-up. No one ever hit a HR onto the right-field upper cinder area, in my three years, although a few got close by hitting the incline just in front. Three home runs to left field, hit by Mantle, Colavito, and Frank Howard, almost made the bleachers.

When one would fall just short of the Tribe bullpen, Early Wynn would take the ball, hold it up to look at it to see if it had gotten lopsided with the impact of the bat, then show it around for everyone to see. The most lop-sided ball I can remember was hit into our bullpen by Boog Powell of the Orioles. The most prodigious home run I recall in Municipal Stadium was hit by Jim Gentile well into the right-field upper deck above us and to our left. The blast broke a slat of the wooden seat on impact. That ball must have been double-lop-sided: one from the bat, another from the slat! The science of estimating distances of home runs was not yet instantly and routinely applied as it is today, so I don't know how far that ball would have traveled. Gentile would join the Tribe for a brief period

July 19, 1966, in his last season in the majors, and locker just to my left after Don McMahon was traded. Jim was always among the league leaders in strikeouts himself, too, but at the plate.

The flimsy appearing outfield fence, covered only on top by a protective canvas, balanced the absence of a warning track as a safety measure. "Cleveland Indians" is chalked into the side of the hill in center field, just in front of an awning where a band or organist would usually play on weekends. The visitors' bullpen is in background in left field, with an awning over the seating area.

As pitching coach, Gus spent the game in the bullpen. There was no bullpen coach, as all teams have today, allowing the pitching coach to remain in the dugout. Gus didn't seem to mind being so far from the action, though. He kept his eyes on the mound, as if he were an Indian scouting the cavalry from a bluff above their position. But while he may have liked being in the 'pen rather than the dugout, he hated the large public address loud speaker that was just to the left of our bullpen seating area. If he cursed out the horns on "Horn Night," you should have heard him after the between-innings music started up.

One thing I frequently thought about while sitting in the 'pen, as probably every other bullpen catcher has, was "What would I do if a bench-clearing brawl broke out?"[65] I was not a professional, but merely an employee. I might not be viewed any differently than an usher who ran in to jump into a melee. I thought that there must be some obscure rule that would forfeit the game or somehow otherwise unduly penalize the team if I jumped the fence to run the 300 feet to the mound area. Luckily, it never really happened. One knock-down incident did lead to some 'pen members running to join one of those bear-hug-skirmishes that occasionally occur, but Gus held his location in the 'pen, so I keyed off of him and stayed put.

Gus seldom made any fast moves. Personally, I think he thought it was much ado about nothing: it's the pitcher's right to knock down a hitter, so what's the big deal? He'd explain further, deadpanning, "I'm a lover, not a fighter."

Being in the 'pen does afford a good bit of time to check out the action in the stands, to see which fair young things were sporting short shorts and tube tops, just as Brosnan reported in his book. The only difference was about 25,000 fans: the stands were 90% full during the Brosnan and the Reds' pennant race. In Cleveland, the stands were usually 90% empty, so we generally kept our heads in the game and not in the stands.

In Detroit's Tiger Stadium, the bullpen was along the right-field foul line, and that's where the starting pitcher warmed up, and where I spent the evening. It had a dugout feel with several steps going down to a below-field level, with player seating in a covered enclosure. Bullpens such as this that are on the field, along the foul line, present unique dangers. Line drives could hit pitchers warming up. For that reason, another pitcher would generally put on his glove, and stand between the pitcher/catcher warming up and home plate, to protect them from line drives. In addition, the elevated mound (though not as high as the field mound) presented a hazard to an outfielder coming in, or an infielder going out, to chase down a pop-up or fly ball. Right out in front of me in right field was Al Kaline, who had actually been the youngest hitter to win the AL batting championship (1955) at age 21.

In Chicago, the visitors' bullpen was behind the outfield field fence in deep right-center field, parallel to the fence. Starting pitchers warmed up in the pen here as well. The home team's bullpen was in mirror-image position in left-center. Bill Veeck had installed the first-ever exploding scoreboard behind the center field bleachers, and I was surprised when it was first set off after Mike Hershberger hit a HR on July 5.

My second road trip was to Kansas City, New York, and Baltimore, July 14–July 23. The Kansas City Municipal Stadium visiting bullpen was along the left-field foul line. The KC Stadium had some unique features, including a picnic area/zoo behind the right field fence, where "Charlie-O," the team donkey mascot grazed. In addition, an electronic rabbit rose out of the ground with new baseballs for the home-plate umpire. We stayed at the venerable, old Muehlebach Hotel in KC, and could usually find a good place to have a "Kansas City steak" after the games.

In Yankee Stadium, the bullpen was behind the left field fence, in an open space between the left-field stands and center-field bleachers, oriented perpendicular to the fence. We could look from the bullpen left toward the center-field bleacher area where the monuments to Babe Ruth, Lou Gehrig, and Miller Huggins were located under the flagpole. My first visit to Yankee Stadium was almost a religious experience for a childhood Yankee fan. To look up and see the monuments and the scalloped façade of the roof, where Mantle had hit a 10$^{th}$-inning, walk-off 734-foot home run off Bill Fischer in 1963 in right-center field, was a real thrill. Staying at the Biltmore Hotel in NYC was an eye-opener for the Midwest hayseed. "How you gonna keep 'em down on the farm, after they've seen Par-ee?"

After Tiant's first win in New York, we flew to Baltimore, arriving after 10 PM to the Lord Baltimore Hotel on near Howard Street. The harbor area was mostly bars and strip clubs at the time, or at least, that's where our limited sight-seeing seemed to show; development as an entertainment destination hadn't yet begun. In Baltimore Memorial Stadium, the visitors' bullpen was behind the right field fence, very similar to the Tribe's 'pen in Cleveland. Memorial Stadium was unusual to me in that there was no roof for the upper deck. I was never there in the rain to see if the birds flew the coop in the rain.

After a brief home stand, we had a short road trip to DC Stadium in Washington (later named Robert F. Kennedy Stadium after his death in 1969), which was the first modern AL cookie-cutter stadium: round, symmetric, and relatively featureless. The bullpen was located behind the left-field fence as well, in a small, confined location, in front of a tall grandstand wall. We stayed at the Shoreham Hotel (now the Omni Shoreham) on Calvert Street. My daughter Lisa would live just blocks away on Connecticut Avenue 30 years later.

I didn't make it to Minneapolis in '64, with trips being combined with flights to LA, but made it there on an early road trip in June of '65. In Minneapolis Metropolitan Stadium, the 'pen was also behind the right field fence. The stadium only seated about 40,000, about half the capacity of Cleveland Municipal Stadium. Once again, I had a ring-side seat near '64 Rookie of the Year Tony Oliva in right field. I enjoyed it when bullpens were in right field. The strongest outfield throwing arms are usually in right field, and I relished seeing them in action. Rocky Colavito of the Athletics was certainly among the strongest.

I did not travel to Los Angeles or to Boston to check out their bullpens in '64, either. Trips to LA were not charter flights, and Tribe finances dictated my value didn't overcome the individual airfare. Road trips to Boston occurred either before I joined the club, or after I went back to school, or were associated with trips to California on which I didn't go. The bullpen in Boston was, and still remains, behind the right field fence, parallel to the field, and adjacent to the home team bullpen, end to end.

The bullpens all had water fountains, or water bottles with paper cups for drinking. There was usually telephone communication to the dugout where Tebbetts could call Early Wynn to get someone heated up. No food, no snacks allowed, although some players were known to get an usher or attendant to go buy a hot dog or drink from time to time. Even police have been known to bring pizza to the 'pen![66]

Officially, there was no smoking in the bullpen, but some of the pens had hidden corners, or walkways, where a player could catch a few drags on a cigarette. In Cleveland, the small driveway between the right field stands and bleachers allowed players to sneak off for a smoke. Of course, there were always matches in the bullpen for lighting up, or for giving a hotfoot to someone dozing off. A hotfoot? That was the prankster's wake-up call: the head of one match is wedged, base-side out, into the space of the shoe between the sole and the shoe leather, ideally in the mid-foot region, where leather is thinnest. The base is then lit with a second match. The first burns down to the leather, leading to a hot foot, and a pissed-off 'penner!

Rest rooms? In Cleveland, you could run into the dugout between innings, go up the ramp and under the right field stands to a rest rooms the fans used, or go into the clubhouse either from the field, or under the stands. If you chose the latter two options you seldom were bothered by fans, attendance being as poor as it usually was.

None of the bullpens had a Bull Durham Tobacco sign, although there was a good bit of chewing going on! I even tried chewing tobacco myself: Red Man Chewing Tobacco, however. There was always a supply in the Indians' clubhouse on a shelf above the table across from my locker. As a light smoker, I guess it replaced the nicotine need, but chewing and expectorating indiscriminately was, in retrospect, a bad idea, just as smoking was. And maybe throwing over 300 baseballs a day doesn't sound like such a good idea, either.

Of the stadiums I've just described, Fenway Park in Boston is the only one of these ballparks still in use today. Plenty of changes have occurred in stadiums and bullpens in the majors since then.

In the late 60s, stadium construction turned to a design with limited room behind the outfield fence in front of high symmetric outfield walls, much like RFK Stadium in Washington (1962). Riverfront Stadium in Cincinnati (1971), Three Rivers Stadium in Pittsburgh (1970), St. Louis Busch Stadium (1966), and Veterans' Stadium in Philadelphia (1971) were of the round cookie-cutter, copy-cat variety. Riverfront Stadium had little room for pens behind the fence or wall, so the bullpens were located along the outfield foul lines, with benches for players to sit on, on the same side as the team's dugout. Some pitchers/catchers would sit in the dugout, then just walk out to the pen after the first few innings, or when told to warm up.

The recent trend for smaller, more intimate parks (such as Comerica Park in Detroit, or Jacobs Field (now Progressive Field) in Cleveland, with fans closer to the field and with less foul territory, then reversed the on-the-field bullpen trend back to the behind-the-fence locations, either perpendicular or parallel to the outfield fence/wall. The home bullpen will usually be behind the fence closer to the home team dugout, with some exceptions. For instance, in Cincinnati Great American Ballpark, the home dugout is on the first base side, while the home team pen is center-left field, farther than the home dugout than the visitors' bullpen, which is behind the right field fence, closer to the home dugout. Currently, 24 parks have both bullpens behind the outfield fence in various locations and configurations, while there are only 4 parks with bullpens still on the field, adjacent to the outfield foul lines.

Tampa Bay has a 'pen parallel to the foul lines, but behind a fence. Petco Stadium is the only park with one bullpen behind the fence and the other outside the foul line. The Padres' bullpen is behind the left-center field wall, and the visitors' is in foul territory in right field.

Many current and past stadium and bullpen facts, locations, and details can be found in Appendix 2.

Only the visitors' bullpen at Houston's domed Minutemaid Stadium is totally indoors, behind the left field wall, with fenced openings for looking out onto the field. It's bad enough to be playing indoors under domes, but playing under the stands while indoors under the dome seems to violate the age-old principle of going out and playing ball! Rob Flippo of the Dodgers recently commented on 'pens on the field, and the catacomb-like Houston location, expressing dislike for both.[67]

Bullpen locations occasionally may seem to take little planning or thought. The Tigers recently moved their bullpens from the right field foul line, a prime spot for fans trying to snag home run balls, to a new location behind the left field fence. It's been said they forgot to build a bullpen in San Francisco, just putting in a bench and a patch of dirt. Stay tuned for the next innovation in bullpen location. Maybe a virtual bullpen, with a Wii for warming up, would save space and allow a few more seats in the stands.

Starting pitchers warming up at Great American Park, Cincinnati. The visitors Bullpen (Left) is beyond the fence near the right field line, and Reds' bullpen, is in left-center field (right)

The author and his 'pen pals, 1964. Indian Gus standing and surveying the play'n from his mesa-like 'pen perch.

# Chapter 12—The Season: 1964

In 1963, the Tribe had gone 79–83, and 1964 would prove to be just another run-of-the-mill year for the Tribe: an identical 79–83 record, and a tie for sixth place with Minnesota (in the ten-team AL). The team's longest winning streak was eight games, and the longest losing streak seven games. There was some wheat among the chaff however, and some golden memories both off and on the field for the '64 Indians and me.

1964 Team Picture, taken after Luis Tiant joined the team in July: Front: Batboy Mike Coyne, Clubhouse attendant Billy Malone. 1st Row: Larry Brown, Vic Davalillo, Dick Howser, Coach George Strickland, Manager Birdie Tebbets, Pitching Coach Early Wynn, Coach Solly Hemus, Coach Elmer Valo, Chico Salmon, Lee Stange. 2nd Row: Travelling Secretary Charlie Morris, Woodie Held, Max Alvis, Tito Francona, Fred Whitfield, Gary Bell, Billy Moran, John Romano, Luis Tiant, Joe Azcue, Trainer Wally Bock. Back Row: Bob Chance, Vern Fuller, Don McMahon, Sonny Siebert, Paul Dicken, Dick Donovan, Sam McDowell, Ted Abernathy, Jack Kralick, Leon Wagner, Bullpen/Batting Practice Catcher (the author). (Reprinted with permission from Cleveland Indians Baseball Co.). This is the same team picture used for the 1965-66-67 Topps baseball cards.

Minnesota led the league in home runs (221), on-base percentage (.324), runs (737), and slugging average (.427). New York would win the AL championship, leading the league only in hits (1,442). The only offensive category the Tribe would lead in was stolen bases (79). Chicago would come in second by one game, leading the league in the pitching departments of bases on balls (401), fewest hits allowed (1,216), ERA (2.73), and tied with New York in saves (45). The Angels led the league in fewest home runs allowed (100). The Tribe would lead the league in most strikeouts by pitchers, with 1,162, a new league record. The staff would strikeout 7.0 batters/9 innings, the first year that figure had ever been achieved in the AL.

All the memorable moments on the field were not necessarily good ones. One most closely remembers the best and worst of games and events, but the vast majority of contests are merely average ball games, one much like the next, seemingly with little individual significance to a club in the middle of the pack, yet every one critical for those in contention. The former merely blend together into coalescent obscurity. But two of the most memorable games happened within days of one another, and were closely interrelated.

July 16 was a very hot, sunny day in Kansas City, almost 90 before 1:15 PM game time. It was a Thursday get-away afternoon game after two night games, always a bit tiring. Thankfully, there was no batting practice, due not only to the early afternoon game time following a night game, but also because of the heat. Tommy John, the starting pitcher that day, had gotten off to a great start on the season with a three-hit shutout of Baltimore on May 3, generating great hopes for his season. He had stumbled thereafter, however, and had fallen to 2–9 before July 16.

The Tribe got off to an early lead in this game, scoring seven runs in the top of the first inning. That's usually great news for the bullpen, an early lead on a sweltering day, with plenty of time to increase the lead. There was plenty of the usual light-hearted conversation and joking. There were a few hot feet, which might have been attributed to spontaneous combustion on such a hot day. I was relieved that I wasn't likely to be up early warming up in the heat in this blow-out.

No such luck. John allowed the A's back into the game immediately. I was up in the first inning, as the A's scored five runs; 7–5 after one inning! TJ's line was: two-thirds of an inning, three hits, three bases on balls, five earned runs. I was up repeatedly for the rest of the game. Five Indians pitched in the game, finally won by the Indians 12–9, in ten innings, with Don McMahon striking out the side in the tenth to end it. TJ would be sent back down to Portland after the game, to be immediately replaced by Luis Tiant on the roster.

Luis Tiant had been 15–1 at Portland, and his call-up had been a foregone conclusion, but eagerly anticipated. He flew to New York for his debut three days later in the second game of a doubleheader on July 19 against Hall of Famer Whitey Ford, who was 12–2 with a 2.14 ERA at the time. It was a thrill to be the first person to catch him and warm him up in Yankee Stadium, where starting pitchers warmed up near their dugouts, much like in Cleveland. He had a great fastball, sinker, slider, curve, and a palmball. No trick deliveries in his first warm-up. Tiant's line? Nine innings, four hits, four BB, zero runs—a complete game shutout in his first major league appearance! He would also throw a complete game in his home debut on July 24, beating Boston 6–1.

At about 5' 10", 190 lbs., Looie wasn't the physical specimen Sudden Sam and Sonny were, but he was thick through the thighs and core. Luis would go 10–4, with a 2.83 ERA in 19 games (completing 9 of 16 starts), striking out 105 in 127 innings (7.4/9 innings).

Years later, "El Tiante" would become known not only for a great fastball, but for his motion, where he would rotate his back to the hitter, bob his head, turn his head, look away from the hitter, while even stopping his motion as his left heel hit the ground, delaying his arm in its forward movement, occasionally followed by an blooper pitch-like toss at 60 mph, or varying combinations of the above. This was the "hesitation pitch," which was legal with no runners on base. He would throw side-arm, underhand, over-the-top. Joe Azcue, who would become Looie's favorite catcher, in part because they could speak Spanish together, years later said Looie threw about 95 m.p.h. His fastball was rated as the seventh best in the majors from 1965–1969.[68] Yet Russell Schneider of the *Plain Dealer* also described him as crafty and cunning. Quite a combination! So the Indians sent down a future lifetime 288-game winner in TJ, and brought up a future lifetime 229-game winner in Looie, even if no one would have predicted their cumulative success at the time! I've not researched if that is some kind of record in itself.

Sam McDowell finally came into his own in '64. He came up from Portland for good on May 31, pitching three and a third innings with six strikeouts in relief of soon-to-be-departed Mudcat Grant. In his first start two days later, he gave up two runs and struck out 14 in 9 innings. Sieb had only one appearance before May 10, coming out of spring training with arm trouble. He was used primarily in relief early in the season, but worked his way into the starting rotation through the course of the season as Donovan and Ramos faded.

By August, the question of the starting staff had been settled, and was comprised by Kralick, McDowell, Siebert, and Tiant. Lee Stange was a spot starter. Sudden Sam won 11 with a 2.70 ERA in 24 starts and 173 innings, striking out 177 (9.2 strikeouts/9 innings, leading the league), and giving up 0.4 HR/9 inning (near the league lead), but walking 5.2 batters per 9 innings. Combined with his strikeout numbers at Portland before coming up in late May, he struck out 279 batters that year. Sonny started 14 games, with three complete, winning seven, losing nine overall, but with a 3.23 ERA. He would strike out 144 in 156 innings (8.3 strikeouts/9 innings).

Kralick would be the only Indian named to the All-Star team, going 12–7 with a 3.21 ERA, striking out 119 (5.6 strikeouts/9 innings). Don McMahon would make 70 appearances in '64, the highest in his 18-year career, as well as a team career high, and would be voted Indians' "Man of the Year" by the "Wahoo Club," with a 6–4 record, 16 saves, a 2.41 ERA, and 91 strikeouts in 101 innings (8.2 strikeouts /9 Innings). Others jumped on the K-bandwagon as well. Lee Stange would average a 10-year career high with 7.7 K's per 9 innings, Bell 7.6, Abernathy 7.1, Ramos 6.6. Tommy John contributed 6.2 strikeouts/9 innings in his 94 innings pitched.

Pete Ramos would have a sub-par season, going 7–10 with a 5.14 ERA. I think he was just around the plate too much, with few bases on balls again attesting to his excellent control, but thereby risking too many HR allowed as well. He would be traded on September 5 to the New York Yankees, who were in need of bullpen help for their final pennant push, in exchange for pitchers Ralph Terry and Bud Daley.

After the trade, on Sept. 22 in Cleveland, Pete would save the first game of a doubleheader for his third save since the trade. The next day, he would save both ends of another doubleheader against the Indians: five saves in 18 days, three against his former team in two days. Before season's end he would save eight games, win one, with a 1.25 ERA. Talk about changes in scenery and the magic of Yankee pinstripes! This trade did nothing to endear Gabe Paul to the White Sox and Orioles, who were trying to overcome the Yankees in the pennant race, and who finished one and two games, respectively, behind the Yankees.

The strikeout totals and other individual and staff statistics are summarized for the statistically-minded in below. Despite leading the league in strikeouts, the Tribe's staff was very average in other individual statistics. Almost unbelievably, the staff had no left-handed reliever contributing, even after John was recalled after the minor league season ended in September. Kralick made one relief appearance, and McDowell seven. Sam's relief appearances were typically between-starts workouts, occurring two or three days after a start, with two or three days until his next start.

**Cleveland Pitching Staff Statistics 1964**

| 1964 Staff | IP | GS | ERA | K | K/9 | BB/9 | HR/9 | CG | SO |
|---|---|---|---|---|---|---|---|---|---|
| McDowell | 173.1 | 24 | 2.70 | 177 | 9.2(1) | 5.2(30) | 0.4(2) | 6(23) | 2(14) |
| Siebert | 156 | 14 | 3.23 | 144 | 8.3 | 3.3(21) | 0.9(13) | 3(33) | 1 |
| Kralick | 190.2 | 29 | 3.21 | 119 | 5.6(20) | 2.4(11) | 0.8(10) | 8(17) | 3(9) |
| Tiant | 127 | 16 | 2.83 | 105 | 7.4 | 3.3 | 0.9 | 9(15) | 3(9) |
| Ramos | 133 | 19 | 5.14 | 98 | 6.6 | 1.8 | 1.2 | 3 | 1 |
| McMahon | 101 | 0 | 2.41 | 92 | 8.2 | 4.6 | 0.6 | 0 | 0 |

| Bell | 106 | 2 | 4.33 | 89 | 7.6 | 4.5 | 1.3 | 0 | 0 |
|---|---|---|---|---|---|---|---|---|---|
| Donovan | 158.1 | 23 | 4.55 | 93 | 4.7 | 1.6 | 1.1 | 5 | 0 |
| Stange | 91.2 | 14 | 4.12 | 78 | 7.7 | 3.0 | 1.4 | 0 | 0 |
| John | 94.1 | 14 | 3.91 | 65 | 6.2 | 3.3 | 1.0 | 2 | 1 |
| Abernathy | 72.2 | 0 | 4.33 | 57 | 7.1 | 5.7 | 0.6 | 0 | 0 |
| Grant | 62 | 9 | 5.95 | 43 | 6.2 | 3.6 | 1.6 | 1 | 0 |
| Kelley | 9.2 | 0 | 5.59 | 7 | 6.5 | 8.4 | 0.9 | 0 | 0 |
| Walker | 9.2 | 6 | 4.66 | 5 | 4.7 | 3.7 | 0.9 | 0 | 0 |
| Team Totals | 1487.2 | 162 | 3.75(6) | 1162* | 7.0*(1) | 3.4(8) | 0.9(5) | 37(6) | 11(5) |

Innings pitched, strikeouts, strikeouts / 9 innings, complete games, and shutouts for the 1964 Staff. The 1161 strikeouts was an AL record. IP: Innings pitched; K: Strikeouts; ERA = Earned run average; GS: Games started; CG: Complete Games; SO: Shutouts. * = AL Record. Individual K, BB, HR / 9 innings, rank (parentheses) based on minimum of 1 IP / team game.

A pattern had been set, but I certainly did not realize that something unprecedented was occurring. The '64 staff set an American League record for team strikeouts with 1162: the first staff to strike out over 1100. The record elicited very little fanfare or attention at the time. This was the first of five consecutive years this nucleus of pitchers would lead the AL in K's with record, or near-record, numbers. The staff averaged 6.2 strikeouts/9 innings prior to McDowell and Tiant joining the team, and 7.4 after. The latter figure would project to over 1200 strikeouts for a 162-game season!

Another memorable personal moment from the season was my roomie Vern Fuller's first major league at bat. We were in Chicago for a week-end series September 4–6, my final series of the season before school resumed. He had a date with a friend from his hometown after the game on Friday night, and was quite tired the next day. Birdie called on him to pinch hit for Ted Abernathy in the seventh inning, down 8–0. He grounded weakly back to the pitcher, Joel Horlen, who easily threw him out. It was his only AB of the season. He would be back in the minors in '65, then return to the Tribe in '66, and finish a six-year career, all with the Tribe, in 1970.

Of course, there were a few season highlights offensively as well, but not enough to elevate the team higher than sixth in the standings. Daddy Wags hit 31 HR (8th in AL), with 100 RBI (6th), playing in all 163 games. He would hit his 23rd homer in Tiant's first win (the Tribe's 91st game). He would hit only eight more in the next 71 games, and come in second to McMahon as the Indians' Man of the Year. Dick Howser would play in 162 games, and would be fourth in AB, tenth in hits with 163, tenth in BB with 76, and second in at bat/strikeout ratio at 16.33, behind only Bobby Richardson at 18.86. Vic Davalillo would be third in steals with 21, followed by Howser fourth (20), and Wags seventh (14). Overall, however, the offense was sub-par. The team would be fourth in HR (164), sixth in 2B (208), seventh in BA (.247), seventh in OBP (.312), fourth in runs (689) and fourth in fielding (.981).

Mr. Paul came up with a solution to the offensive and attendance/financial problems: bring Rocky Colavito back to Cleveland from Kansas City!

The failure of Tommy John to produce so early in his career, with the emergence of McDowell, Tiant, and Siebert, gave an opportunity to undo Trader Frank Lane's much-cursed 1959 trade of The Rock to the Tigers. A winter three-way trade would bring Rocky home, with TJ, promising center-fielder Tommy Agee, and catcher John Romano going to the White Sox, with Jim Landis, Mike Hershberger, and Dave Talbot, going to Kansas City, and catcher Camillo Carreon to the Indians from Chicago.

But it becomes near mindboggling to think what keeping John might have meant to the Indians' staff over the next four years and beyond, teamed with McDowell, Siebert, and Tiant as a genuine "Big Four." Nevertheless, the Indians generally lacked offensive punch, and the trade worked out short-term for the club in increased attendance and offensive output. But TJ would enjoy a much longer career than the Rock, accumulating 288 career wins, and an ERA of 3.34, with

2.4 walks/9 innings. In January 2009, he was passed over for the 15th (and final) time for the Hall of Fame, the winningest pitcher not to be enshrined. Once again, only by retrospective analysis can the significance of some events be fully understood and appreciated. If trading the Rock for Harvey Kuenn in 1960 was a bad move, it was magnified to a disastrous move when they were forced to give up TJ and the promising Indian rookie, Tommy Agee, to get Rocky back five years later.

# Chapter 13—The Popper

I do owe a debt of gratitude to the departed Senor Pedro Ramos. He was a suave, sharp dresser, with a bit of a reputation as a ladies' man, deserved or not. He was a nice guy, friendly, but somehow his sly grin suggested I was a form of amusement to him, seen as something of a pretender with counterfeit credentials who didn't belong around the big boys. It was similar to the grin he would produce when someone suggested his Cuban palm ball was a spitball: a sly, knowing, noncommittal look indicating only he knows for sure.

He had a healthy ego as one of the league's top strikeout pitchers 1961–1963, with one of the best strikeout/walk ratios. The talk about the spitball prompted me to check his sinking, toppling pitches for a foreign substance, but I never detected one loaded up in warm ups. If he threw it, I caught it. Apparently, he admitted some years later that he indeed threw the spitter.[69]

After I joined the club, Pistol-Pete soon became irritated by my inability to generate enough explosive sound as his fastballs hit my glove. Hearing an explosion every time ball hit glove massaged his ego as it evoked the acoustic equivalent of a jet breaking the sound barrier. I wonder if his getting bombed and knocked out in the first inning in Detroit July 1 just after I joined the team was related to his dissatisfaction. My limited ability to generate the expected reverberation was due to the nature of the pocket of the glove I was using, a double-hinged model glove with a relatively large pocket, with plenty of room for the sound to be absorbed without percussive force.

I used a small sponge inside to absorb some of the impact to the index finger and thumb side of my palm. The combination of wide pocket and padding didn't lend itself to the explosive sound Pete liked to hear. Within a few warm-up sessions, he let me know it! Other pitchers made comments, too. With his inimitable toothy grin, Gary Bell said the sound generated by my glove sounded like "soft s--- in the rain." Aware of their dissatisfaction, Joe Azcue, the good-natured catcher with a Cuban background like Ramos, told me I should think of changing gloves to a model with a smaller, deeper pocket with no hinge: a "popper," as Joe put it. In fact, Joe had just the thing: a glove he had bought, but for whatever reason didn't like himself. He had bought a new hinged model, and thought it better to use in games.

Warming up the starting pitcher in front of the Tribe dugout in '64. The larger double-hinged catcher's mitt, with a wider pocket and a thinner "pillow" effect, did not lend itself to dependable loud pops as the ball was caught. (Reproduced with permission Scripps-Howard Publications.)

Advances in catchers' mitts and fielders' gloves are among the advances that had tipped the balance between offense and defense in favor of the pitcher. The flexible, hinged gloves with wide webs could be seen time and time again in highlight photos stealing home runs at the base of the outfield fence, or base hits over or between the infielders. The Popper was no advance in that regard, as most catchers were moving to the hinged model that behaved more like a fielder's or first-baseman's glove rather than the pillow-like Popper. So I would be regressing, in a sense, by adopting it.

I looked at the glove, a Rawlings HOH-X model, and thought it looked like the old-time models worn by Mickey Cochrane or even a youthful Birdie Tebbetts I had seen in old photos.[70] Old-time bullpen and batting-practice catchers acknowledged the limitations of such gloves, where the ball had a tendency to pop out unless covered by the bare hand upon contact.[71] Of course, that practice has its downside when it comes to foul balls and broken fingers! I had a hard time envisioning catching every ball dead center for maximum acoustic effect, or picking every low pitch in the dirt with it, as one did easily with the hinged, wider pocket model.

But Ramos, Bell, and Azcue had thrown down the gauntlet, and I picked up the glove. Joe sold it to me, with "AZC-6" in black magic marker on the back (and still visible today) for $15.—a day's pay. But it may be the best $15.00 I ever spent. I used it in batting practice first, to get used to the feel of the glove and its operation. It was less wide than my old model at 10¼" in diameter, quite small (my hand is 9½", tip of the thumb to tip of the little finger, stretched out). The web was much smaller as well. The glove had thicker padding in the body, resembling something of a pillow, as these older models were sometimes called. When finally broken in, there would be no padding left in the center of the pocket, just two opposing leather surfaces, so I would have to wear a small sponge pad inside; thick enough to absorb the force of contact, yet not so thick as to create a trampoline effect leading to the ball popping out of the glove.

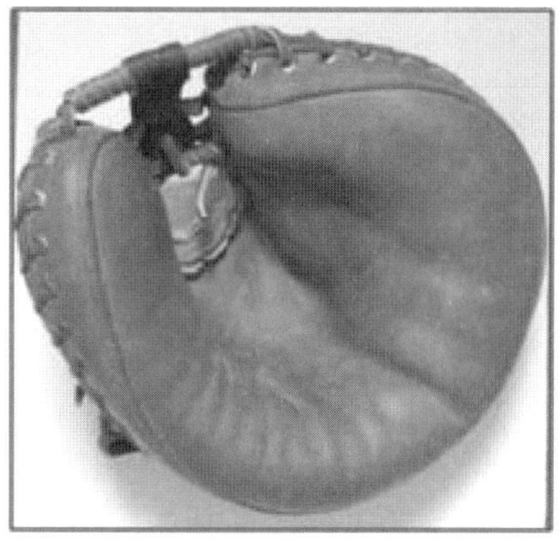

The "Popper," a 10½" wide, deep-pocket, unhinged catcher's mitt that could generate explosive sounds when balls were caught in the center sweet spot.

When a fastball hit the pocket square, the explosive "pop" echoed around cavernous Municipal Stadium. With an average of only about 9,000 bodies in the stands to absorb the sound, and 60,000 empty seats, the percussive reverberation seemed almost like a cannon at times. It catches the attention of everyone in attendance: What's that noise coming from the bullpen? Who's *that* warming up? I think it pumped up the whole pitching staff. Although Azcue may have switched to a hinged model, Duke Sims, a good receiver, continued to use a Popper-type mitt for years.

The glove forced me to be less sloppy, especially on low pitches in the dirt, which were better caught palm up, moving with the ball to keep it in front of me, so as not to let it skip past a backhanded attempt to the side. But I didn't get rid of my old hinged model. I would use it when Bob Tiefenauer, a knuckleball specialist, joined the team in late '65. Using oversized gloves had become popular to catch, or at least knock down, the butterfly pitch.

The thin sponge-rubber pad over the palm and base of my index finger diminished the sound a bit, but was a necessity to protect my hand. My catching hand would inevitably be a bit swollen after games. In fact, the chronic "abuse" led to a slight asymmetry of the index finger, including the proximal joint, in comparison to the right throwing hand, which persists to this day. This phenomenon has been identified in catchers, where the chronic swelling leads to hypertrophy (increased size) of the index finger and joints on the glove hand.[72]

It became an ingrained habit to put some padding inside the glove. This led to an embarrassing moment on November 17, 1964. Dean Chance, a local Plains Township, Ohio, native who had had a phenomenal year in 1964 with the California Angels—winning the Cy Young Award with a 20–9 record, 1.65 ERA, and 207 strikeouts—was making a television appearance on the syndicated NBC Mike Douglas Show, produced in Cleveland. The Indians were called to see if someone could come and catch him on the show, and publicity director Eddie Uhas called me at school. I had my old glove with me, so I said, sure, I'll come down. I don't know what I expected Chance to throw in a TV studio, but I instinctively put my handkerchief inside my glove for protection. After a few tosses to show the viewers Dean's stuff, Mike Douglas called me over, and wanted to take my glove to check out. When I took the glove off, and he saw the handkerchief, there was a brief, quiet hesitation, and then he thought better of it, not knowing where else the handkerchief had been. I missed the opportunity to make a joke about Chance blowing one in there! (Another coincidence: Dean would eventually be traded to the Indians in 1971 for none other than Luis Tiant.)

The Popper lasted the remainder of my three years in the 'pen, with a few repairs along the way. I would save it and use it years later, warming up pitchers on my son Scott's youth teams. Let me tell you, it was an intimidating sound to opponents to hear Mike Innis's, Mark Hindman's, Steve

McKean's, and Mike Zipf's (Scott's teammates) fastball hit that glove, even at age 11 and 12. Scott himself was an excellent receiver, strong-armed, and infinitely better hitter than Dad, but I never suggested he use the Popper. He was an all-city catcher in high school, where his coach was Jon Warden, who had pitched for the '68 Tigers staff that had the second-highest AL strikeout trio of Earl Wilson, Mickey Lolich, and Denny McLain, averaging 6.99 K/game over a consecutive four-year period from '66–69. In great part due to John's influence, Scott would be invited to walk on at Duke, but back problems prevented his playing ball there.

When I go to baseball games now, I listen for the explosion of the ball hitting the catcher's mitt. It's less frequent, less resounding, and a different pitch than it used to be with the HOH-X-type models. Current single-hinged models have become smaller and deeper than my old hinged model, so they do generate higher-pitched "crack" or "slap" noises, but less commonly the lower-pitch explosiveness of the Popper.

If you go to the Rawlings web site today to the glove images, the gloves look vastly different from the Heart-of-the-Hide Popper, with wider pockets, thinner tops, and wide hinges. I stood through a recent warm-up session at Great American Ballpark with my grandson, and heard few good explosions in 75 pitches. Yet other games I've attended and other bullpen sessions I've watched have produced a number, indicating there is clearly some variability in their occurrence: either the gloves or the catchers have variable results. The speed of the ball is not the primary determinant; it's a central, square hit of the pocket that generates the sound. You can generate a pretty good pop at 60 mph. My grandson Jackson could make it pop a bit on his seventh birthday, probably at 40 mph!

I still have the Popper today, having had some web and lacing repair done last year. Thirty-three cents per year cost, unadjusted for inflation! The Popper had exploded to the "bullets" of Colavito and Davalillo during warm-ups. It had caught Hall of Famer Early Wynn during batting practice. The Popper had warmed up Luis Tiant after he joined the Indians in Yankee Stadium July 19, 1964, warmed up Sonny Siebert before his no-hitter June, 1965, and warmed up to Sam McDowell's heat before many of his best games, including consecutive one-hitters in 1966. It had warmed up Don McMahon, Gary Bell, Steve Hargan, Ted Abernathy, Stan Williams, Floyd Weaver, Bob Allen, Dick Radatz—names that will forever spell relief in Tribal lore. It warmed up the staff during record-setting strikeout years.

# Chapter 14—The Season: 1965

With catcher Camillo Carreon coming from Chicago, the Tribe would initially once again carry two catchers (Azcue and Carreon). Duke Sims would join the club in June, and Phil Roof would come from the Angels in June, with Carreon being sent out.

I started the season while still attending classes, but did not travel until school was finished. Going to classes and studying necessitated that I would frequently have textbooks or notes with me, both in the clubhouse and the 'pen. In the clubhouse, with my locker in the corner next to the exit door, I could isolate myself, relatively speaking. With Bell and Tiant near-by, it was not necessarily quiet, however. I could move into the small open space immediately adjacent to the door for more quiet. In the 'pen, I'd frequently sit off in a corner, or in the driveway between the stands, to read and study. It wasn't tough to go to school and hold the job, but it was difficult to perform at the academic level I needed to in order to meet my educational goals.

With only two catchers on the roster, I would travel with the team after school ended. But I only made an early June road trip to Minneapolis and Kansas City, before the team added Sims and Roof. Subsequently, I didn't travel with the club. In order to earn additional money, I was able to get a second "day" job as a clerk in the Cuyahoga County Clerk's office, just a short walking distance away from Municipal Stadium. As a desk-type job, it wasn't physically taxing working from eight in the morning until 3:30 PM, then at the stadium until 10 PM. I had a great role model in holding two jobs. My father, Adolph, had worked two jobs for as long as I can remember: Cleveland Police Detective from 7AM–3 PM, then truck dispatcher at Motor Express from 3:30–11 PM.

A few other new faces joined the team in '65. Most notable, perhaps, was Ralph Terry, who came from the Yankees in exchange for Pete Ramos, and who would immediately be moved into the starting rotation. Ralph opened the season April 13 in California with a four-hit complete-game shutout, and ended the first long home stand on May 5 on a positive note, shutting out his former Yankees on three hits to up his record to 4–1. He would start 26 games, going 11–6 with a 3.69 ERA on the season. Ralph seemed to constantly have a baseball in his hand, gripping it in different ways, trying to figure out what this grip and that pressure might do to its trajectory and movement. In effect, he replaced Dick Donovan as the dean of the starting staff, bringing his experience as a winner with the Yankees to a young staff.

1965 Team Picture: Front: Malone, Paul Gadke. First Row: Ralph Gagliano, Davalillo, Howser, Brown, Wynn, Strickland, Tebbets, Hemus, Tiant, Stange, Salmon, Al Luplow, Azcue; 2nd Row: Morris, Max Alvis, Mike Hedlund, Bell, Duke Sims, Pedro Gonzales, Fred Whitfield, Kralick, Ralph Terry, Moran, Chuck Hinton, Bock; 3rd Row: Rocky Colavito, Wagner, McMahon, Siebert, Steve Hargan, McDowell, Weaver, Phil Roof, the author. (Reprinted with permission from Cleveland Indians Baseball Co.)

The promising pitching staff of '64 developed more green shoots in '65, and, with the addition of Colavito, the team would finish with their first winning season of the '60s, and a record of 87–75 (eight more wins than '64), but still in fifth place. The team was as much as 19 games over .500 by July 7 (and only 1.5 games behind the Twins), the high point of the season, and as many as 16 over as late as August 31.

Although 1965 would be a great one for McDowell overall, he got off to a sub-par start. In his first start of the season, April 15, he would strike out 10 in 4 2/3 innings against the Athletics, but give up four runs on seven hits and lose 7–3. In his second start six days later, he gave up five runs in 8 2/3 innings. One of the low-lights and most disappointing performances of the year came during that 11-game season opening home stand on April 27 against the Twins, who had tied the Tribe for sixth in '64, but who would go on to win 102 games in '65, 23 more than the previous year. Sam did not get out of the first inning, giving up three hits, with three BB, and six runs, including a grand slam HR by Camillo Pascual, his pitching opponent. After three starts, Sam's ERA was 9.00. That debacle seemed calamitous, yet modern-day computer analysis discloses that even the best get bombed more frequently than we like to think. Roger Clemens allowed seven or more runs 26 times!

In his first full season in the majors, Sudden Sam would lead the league in strikeouts with 325 in 273 innings, becoming the youngest pitcher to strike out as many batters, and the first to strike out more than 300 in fewer than 300 innings in the 20th century. Among lefthanders, only Rube Waddell has struck out more AL batters in a season since 1893.

Sam's average of 10.71 strikeouts/9 innings, was a major-league record that would stand for 19 years until finally broken by Doc Gooden. Sam also led the league in ERA at 2.18. He led the league in fewest HR (0.3) and fewest hits per nine innings (5.9)—the latter still stands as the 17th lowest total in major league history. His BB/9 innings dropped to 4.4, but he led the league in wild pitches with 17. On August 31 he would pitch the first one-hitter of his career in Kansas City with Dick Green getting the only hit, a single, on a fastball, in the fourth inning.

Donovan, Kralick, Tiant, and Siebert contended early for the third and fourth starting spots, with no one taking charge until late May when Sonny would begin to pitch more consistently. Siebert would have his break-out year, with a 16–8 record, and 2.43 ERA, beating every team in the AL. He would strike out 9.1 batters and walk 2.2 per 9 innings. Sonny and Sam were the first starting duo to average more than nine strikeouts per nine innings in AL history. *The Sporting News* had a great piece on Sonny with a cover picture August 7, featuring a smiling Sonny holding up a ball with his curve ball grip.

Tiant would pick up where he left off in '64, including a one-hitter against the Senators June 16. Woody Held, with the Tribe in '64, singled to lead off the seventh inning. Looie was 9–3 on July 29, when he gave up four hits, three BB, and four runs in the first inning in a loss to the White Sox. He went 2–8 the rest of the season, finishing a disappointing 111–11, with a 3.53 ERA, but striking out 152 in 196 1/3 innings, with ten complete games and two shutouts. He had pitched in winter ball in Ponce, Puerto Rico. I wondered if he didn't just pitch too much in '64, pitching 264 innings with Portland and the Indians, and then in winter ball, leading to a tired arm. Sonny pitched on the same team with him in Puerto Rico, but Sonny had thrown fewer innings overall during the '64 season than had Luis.

Steve Hargan joined the staff and pitched well, with a 4–3 record and 3.43 ERA in starting and relief roles. McMahon would relieve in 58 games, with 11 saves, 3–3 record, and a 3.28 ERA. Gary Bell moved to shorter relief and had 17 saves, with a 3.04 ERA, 86 K's in 103 innings.

Jack Kralick slipped considerably from his All-Star status in '65. Perhaps some frustration here led to an incident with his on-the-road roommate Gary Bell in DC on Aug. 22. Russell Schneider wrote that they had a disagreement over what TV show to watch (and over some beer and pizza) back in their room at the Shoreham Hotel, and a few punches were thrown. Jack ended up sporting a shiner when he walked into the clubhouse after the trip. Gary punched out 86 opponents, and one teammate in '65.[73]

The Tribe staff would lead the AL in strikeouts (1156), fewest hits allowed per nine innings (7.7), and finish second in complete games, fifth in shutouts, and third in saves. They struck out 7.1 batters 9 innings, breaking their own record of the previous year. Once again, the Tribe had no left-handed reliever of note to throw at left-handed hitters or lineups for the majority of the season. Jack Kralick started 16 games, and relieved in 14. Jack Spring was purchased from the Angels June 14, and pitched 21 2/3 innings in 14 relief appearances in the final year of his 8-year career. Both had WHIPs over 1.4, and 3.6 strikeouts/9 innings.

## Cleveland Pitching Staff Statistics 1965

| 1965 | IP | GS | ERA | K | K/9 | BB/9 | HR/9 | CG | SO |
|---|---|---|---|---|---|---|---|---|---|
| McDowell | 273 | 35 | 2.18 | 325 | 10.7(1) | 4.4(35) | 0.3(1) | 14(2) | 3(10) |
| Siebert | 188.2 | 27 | 2.43 | 191 | 9.1(2) | 2.2(9) | 0.7(10) | 4(31) | 1(35) |
| Tiant | 196.1 | 30 | 3.53 | 152 | 7.0(8) | 3.0(21) | 0.9(24) | 10(6) | 2(25) |
| Bell | 103.2 | 0 | 3.04 | 86 | 7.5 | n/a | n/a | 0 | 0 |
| Terry | 165.2 | 26 | 3.69 | 84 | 4.6(33) | 1.2(1) | 1.2(37) | 6(22) | 2(17) |
| Stange | 132 | 12 | 3.34 | 80 | 5.5 | n/a | n/a | 4 | 2 |
| McMahon | 85 | 0 | 3.28 | 60 | 6.4 | n/a | n/a | 0 | 0 |
| Hargan | 60.1 | 8 | 3.43 | 37 | 5.5 | n/a | n/a | 1 | 0 |
| Weaver | 61.1 | 1 | 5.43 | 37 | 5.4 | n/a | n/a | 0 | 0 |
| Kralick | 61.1 | 16 | 4.92 | 34 | 3.6 | n/a | n/a | 1 | 0 |
| Kelley | 30 | 4 | 2.40 | 31 | 9.3 | n/a | n/a | 0 | 0 |
| Tiefenauer | 22.1 | 0 | 4.84 | 13 | 5.2 | n/a | n/a | 0 | 0 |
| Donovan | 22.2 | 3 | 5.96 | 12 | 4.8 | n/a | n/a | 0 | 0 |
| Spring | 21.2 | 0 | 3.74 | 9 | 3.7 | n/a | n/a | 0 | 0 |

| | | | | | | | | | |
|---|---|---|---|---|---|---|---|---|---|
| Hedlund | 5.1 | 0 | 5.06 | 4 | 6.8 | n/a | n/a | 0 | 0 |
| Williams | 4.1 | 0 | 6.23 | 1 | 2.1 | n/a | n/a | 0 | 0 |
| Team Totals | 1458.1 | 162 | 3.30 | 1156 | 7.1* (1) | 3.1 (2) | 0.8 (4) | 40 | 10 |

IP: Innings pitched; K: Strikeouts; ERA: Earned run average; GS: Games started; CG: Complete Games; SO: Shutouts. Individual K, BB, HR/9 innings rank (parentheses) based on minimum of one IP/team game. (*: AL record)

One of the real personal bright spots of the season was getting the opportunity to catch a genuine knuckleball pitcher, Bobby Tiefenauer, who joined the team late in the season, pitching in 15 games. The success that two White Sox knuckleballers, Hoyt Wilhelm and Eddie Fisher, were having prompted Gus and Birdie to concoct a plan for Gus to come out of retirement as a knuckleball relief pitcher. He started to throw BP more frequently.

The experiment never got beyond batting practice, however, with Gabe Paul putting a rubber stopper on the test tube by purchasing Tieff from the Yankees. I brought out my old larger hinged-pocket glove for him, but didn't have the sense to put on a mask in the bullpen when he warmed up to try to protect myself from the "butterfly" pitch. The mitt wasn't as big as the 18-inch-wide "Big Bertha" manager Paul Richards of the Orioles had devised to help his catchers catch Hoyt Wilhelm's knuckler, but it was a more manageable glove. I suppose Bobby's knuckler wasn't as good as Hoyt's, either, based on a comparison of their records. Municipal Stadium's lakeside location probably affected Bobby's performance as well, with the heavier air, and cooler evenings making the knuckler less effective.

Another of the memorable aspects of the season was palling around with major-leaguers who were now actually younger than I was at 19! Redheaded, freckled Texan Mike Hedlund had signed as a free agent in '64 out of high school, and was kept on the 40-man and the big club roster for '65. He made his pitching debut at age 18 on May 8, and would pitch 5 1/3 innings on the year. Mike would be back with the Tribe in '68, then pitch four years with KC, going 15–8 with a 2.71 ERA in '71. Ralph Gagliano, an 18-year-old infielder, also signed as a free agent in '64, and also was kept on the 40-man roster. For a period, both were recuperating from injuries and didn't travel, and we would work out together while the team was away. Ralph would get in one game in the field at age 18, with no ABs. Of the four promising rookie Tribe free agents (Hedlund, Gagliano, Fuller, Dicken) that rules dictated be held on the 40-man and major-league roster in '64 and '65, only Fuller had a career that the players themselves and the front office envisioned. Baseball's a tough game, and sitting on the bench for a year is no way to keep your skills and, more importantly, improve.

Colavito proved to be a shot in the arm on the field, and one of the nicest guys you'd ever want to meet off the field. He played 162 games, led league in RBI (108) and BB (93), and was third in hits (170), fifth in HR (26), while batting .287. Daddy Wags was fourth in HR (28). Davalillo was third in BA at .301. The offense picked up in league rankings as well: sixth in doubles (198), third in HR (156) and BA (.250), fourth in OBP (.315) and runs (663), and first in fielding (.981). But the Tribe would still finish fifth in the AL, despite being above average in most offensive and pitching categories.

Other memorable game-day on-field events occurred at the stadium, if not game-related. Before game and between game ceremonies and events were becoming common occurrences. Old-Timers' Games were always an event, although I was usually too busy to be much of a spectator or to hobnob with the former stars. I met quite a few, but just in passing.

Some events were memorable, however. On August 17, 1965, Robert Manry, a *Cleveland Plain Dealer* copy editor, completed a 78-day non-stop trans-Atlantic sailing in a 13 ½ foot sailboat from Falmouth, Massachusetts, to Falmouth, England. The Indians honored him during a brief ceremony between games of a doubleheader in September. He was driven around the cinder track, sitting up on the back seat of a Pontiac Bonneville convertible, with his wife Virginia, towing his tiny sailboat "Tinkerbelle" behind.[74]

Another Sunday game attraction, though I can't pinpoint the date, and it may even have occurred after my tenure with the team on a day I visited the clubhouse, was an appearance by the "Rocket Man," the early predecessor of the same jet-pack propulsion system that helped James Bond escape in

"Thunderball," and later starred in the opening ceremonies of the 1984 Olympics. With a backpack of compressed gas, the helmeted Rocket Man took off from behind the pitcher's mound, circled the infield for about 30 seconds, about 30 feet in the air, before landing. I wondered if he could catch a baseball headed for the seats at the base of the outfield fence: a performance-enhancing assistance for the vertically challenged. "Tinkerbelle," who could sprinkle fairy dust and fly, and "Rocket Man": what if humans could truly do something to develop almost-super-human powers of flight—or to enhance any other performance by artificial means, such as catching, hitting, or even throwing a baseball?

"Strike Three!" was a resounding call around Municipal Stadium once again in 1965. The pitching staff led the league in strikeouts once again, falling only six strikeouts short of breaking their own AL record set the previous year. They would also allow the fewest hits in the AL. With this progress over the previous year on the mound and at the plate, I could hardly wait for the '66 season.

# Chapter 15—The Season: 1966

In 1966, the team again carried three catchers from the start of the season: Azcue, Sims, and the veteran, Del Crandall, the latter signed as a free agent in the off-season. Del would become Sam McDowell's personal catcher due to Del's ability to effectively handle pitchers who tended to be a little wild.

New additions would also include John O'Donaghue, a veteran left-hander with a good sinking fastball who was 9–18 in Kansas City in '65, obtained in return for Ralph Terry, who refused Gabe Paul's contract offers. Bob Allen, a lefty reliever, and Tom Kelley, the hard-throwing right-hander with an off-the-table curve ball, who had been 16–3 at Portland in '65, and 2–1 at the end of the season with the Tribe, averaging 9.3 strikeouts/9 innings, also joined the club.

1966 Team Picture. Front Row: Brown, Davalillo, Howser, Coach Reggie Otero, Wynn, Tebbets, Strickland, Tiant, Buddy Booker, Salmon, Azcue. 2nd Row: Morris, Alvis, Bell, Tony Curry, Kralick, Gonzales, Tom Kelley, Hinton, Jim Landis, Sims, Whitfield, Bock. 3rd Row: Wagner, Siebert, Hargan, McDowell, Radatz, Colavito, Del Crandall, John O'Donaghue, Allen. No riff-raff clubhouse attendants, batboys, or part-time bullpen catchers!

Bob Lemon, manager of the Angel's Seattle AAA farm team, said Tom had looked better than McDowell or Tiant in the Pacific Coast League in '65. For the first time in my tenure, the Tribe had two lefties in the 'pen: Allen and O'Donoghue, who would have 55 appearances between them.

In 1966, the Indians moved the 'pen along the right field foul line, with a small dugout to sit in. Being on the field placed a priority on keeping the ball in front of you, to avoid embarrassing delays of game to retrieve the loose bullpen ball that had gotten onto the field. The large loud speakers that Wynn hated are barely visible in front of the center field bleachers, just to the right of the new "Dawg Pound" seats constructed on the upper cinder track.

I began the season with the home opening day, working weekends, but finding time for weeknight games while studying and preparing for finals at JCU, as I had done the previous year.

In 1966, additional seats for Cleveland Browns football were constructed on the upper cinder track area of the center field bleachers—the area later known as the Browns' "Dawg Pound." The bullpens were moved from behind the fence to the foul lines, with the Tribe's bullpen in right field. No more looking for lop-sided balls after home runs. Just scuffed-up ones after foul ground balls.

The move made Early Wynn ecstatic, or as ecstatic as Gus could get. Not only didn't he like the horns on horn night, he also hated the oversized loud speakers for the PA system that were to our left in the bullpen seating area. Between innings, or for announcements, the giant speakers blared too loudly for Gus's sensitive ears. It's a good thing that Gus isn't still around to hear the music that's played during batting practice now blaring over the loudspeaker systems! The move made it more difficult to study surreptitiously while classes were still in session in the spring and early September.

With three catchers on the roster, I would not travel with the club once again, relegated to part-time 'penmanship. After classes ended in the spring, I was able to get a well-paying day job on the loading docks of the New York Central Railroad, starting at 7 AM, finishing at 3 PM. This allowed me to work, eat an early dinner at my grandmother's house on E. 57th Street, then make it to the stadium for batting practice and bullpen duties. My two daily game passes came in extra-handy, though. After late night games, my supervisor at the RR would occasionally find assignments for me behind the boxcars, out of sight, where I could take a brief nap, and then in return said supervisor might somehow occasionally find two tickets waiting for him in will call. When the team was in town, after late night games I would frequently sleep over at my aunt's house at E. 55th St. and Luther Ave., making the early ride to the railyards 25 minutes closer than from my home in Parma. My aunt's house was on the fringe of the Hough area, and it was a bit hairy to drive into her neighborhood late after night games during the Hough riots of July 18–23.

I was sure excited about the prospect of a great season, with the Indians' stock rising from '64 to '65 in both pitching and hitting. The promise was diminished, however, by the lack of a dependable bullpen. In '65, McMahon and Gary Bell had been inconsistent. Birdie decided Sam would pitch every fourth day, no matter what.

During spring training, Sonny developed a shoulder problem that he attributed to working out in his basement, which had a low ceiling contributing to an altered pitching motion. Then in spring training he injured a finger playing catch with Tom Kelley March 16, and that injury held back his progress by about three weeks. By spring training's end he was pitching an inning or two every other day, and had become viewed as a potential bullpen ace, despite his excellent '65 as a starter. Hargan would start in the 'pen, but was still an unknown quantity. Birdie had decided to move his veteran Gary Bell back to the starting rotation.

The '66 season would certainly have numerous highlights, and gratefully, most occurred in Cleveland where I had the opportunity to participate in the fun. In the season opener April 11 in Washington's DC Stadium, McDowell would pitch eight innings, with nine strikeouts, and allow four hits and two runs. The Tribe won 5–2, scoring four runs in the ninth inning. Siebert would get the save in an early season relief appearance necessitated by poor weather, days off, and game cancellations.

That opening day game in the nation's capitol also marked the first game umpired by a black man in the history of major league baseball. Emmett Ashford, who had umpired 15 years in the minors, was at third base that day. I would see him in Cleveland later in the season, with his entertaining flashy style, smooth moves, and exaggerated gestures and calls. "Emmmeeetttt!" would be the call from the 'pen whenever he made a particularly notable, sweet gesture or move.

Due to an off day, a rainout, then another off day, Tebbetts also started Sam in the second game of the season in the Cleveland home opener against the Red Sox four days later. Sam struck out ten in 5 2/3 innings, with five walks, leaving with no decision and the team behind 4–0. The team would come from behind again and win in 12 innings, with six pitchers striking out 17 batters in the four-hour, 41-minute game. When else has the same pitcher started the first two games of the season?

Gary Bell would start the third game of the season April 16, getting his first start since the mid-64 season, striking out 13 in 7 1/3 innings, with lefty reliever Bob Allen striking out 3 in 2 2/3 and getting the win. Although it may be difficult to fathom, Bob was the first true lefty reliever in the bullpen in my three seasons with the club. In the first two home games, the Tribe staff set a major league record by striking out 33 Red Sox in two consecutive games.

The Tribe would continue to win, tying the AL record for wins at the start of a season at nine when Tiant shut out Kansas City 4–0, his second shutout of the young season, striking out 12 (11 swinging). The Tribe would tie the major league record of ten games in a row, allowing only 17 runs, with three shutouts. They would then lose to Chicago 4–1, then win the next four, three of them shutouts as well. McDowell was 4–0, Tiant 3–0, Siebert and newcomer John O'Donaghue 2–0 in the first 15 games. This is what Cleveland had been waiting for since 1954! The clubhouse is a great place to be when you're winning. Ten of those first 15 games were at home, and expectations for a great season grew sky high. Pennant fever around town was rampant!

Interwoven in that initial winning streak and home stand was another of the season's (and the franchise's) all-time individual highlights: two consecutive Sudden Sam 1-hit shutout wins. Sam is one of only six pitchers to accomplish this feat since 1900. He struck out eight vs. KC April 26 in a 2–0 win, and 10 vs. Chicago and Tommy John May 1 in a 1–0 win. Interestingly, Bill Haller was the behind-the-plate umpire for both games. I suppose that's a record, too, but it's difficult to find information about umpire records. Jose Tartabull got KC's only hit in the sixth inning April 26. He took two strikes, barely fouled off the third pitch, then hit an 0–2 sidearm curveball on his fists, arching the ball lazily over the infield into short right center. The one-hitter against KC also is a record for consecutive one-hitters against the same team, insofar as the last hit he gave up to KC was the single by Dick Green in a one-hitter 8-31-65.

In the May Day fray, Don Buford got the only hit, a blooper over first base in the third inning while being jammed by an inside fastball. Sam gave great credit to the old veteran catcher Del Crandall for his part in the accomplishment, as did Bill Haller, the home plate umpire. Hal Lebovitz, Sports Editor of the *Cleveland Plain Dealer,* wrote that Haller pointed out that it's tough for umpires to call games for pitchers with poor control who are all over the place, when catchers are usually jumping up and down, making strikes look like balls, bobbing up into the umpires view. Crandall just coolly stayed in his crouch, let the curve balls come to him, stayed down on the fastballs, and stayed true to his advice in the SI "Book on Baseball." Del would not have a passed ball in 49 games in '66.

Sam would develop arm trouble in his next starts, and would not win another game until June 11. With Bell in the rotation, the team would trade Don McMahon and Lee Stange to the Red Sox for "The Monster" Dick Radatz June 2. The "Monster" tag came from his size, listed at 6' 5", 235 pounds he was an imposing figure. He clearly weighed more that 235 when he joined the Tribe. It seems like builds like that are dime-a-dozen today. But the prospect of catching "The Monster" was exciting. He had led the AL in saves in '62 (24) and '64 (29), was second in '63 (25), was an All-Star in '63 and '64, but his performance began to slip in '65. Dick still threw very hard, but had been having trouble finding the plate in Boston, with his walks/9 innings ballooning up to 5.2 before the trade. The plate remained only 17" wide in Cleveland also, and he had control trouble there as well. The "Monster" would be one of the most feared relievers in history, with a wide, sweeping, side-arm delivery, and would strike out 9.7 batters/9 innings over a seven-year career. Dick would get ten saves for the Tribe the rest of the year after the trade.

Losing Mac, my locker mate to my left, was sad: he had been my 'pen pal the longest of any Indian at 2 ½ years. He was the consummate pro. When the call came, his eyes would steel over, his jaw would firm, and he was ready to go. Mac would get nine saves during the remainder of the season for the Sox after the trade. On July 7 he would win both games of a doubleheader, the only reliever to do so over the encompassing four-year period. He would pitch another eight years with a number of clubs, including the '68 Tigers' World Series team. He retired to coach the Giants' staff in '72. One of his pupils? Sudden Sam, who lockered next to him a decade earlier, was traded to the Giants in the off-season, virtually burned out as a flame-thrower. Don was reactivated in '73 with the Giants at age 43, and finished his career pitching 30 innings in 28 games, with six saves and a 4–0 record. Mac would pitch in 874 games in his career, until that time more than any pitcher except Cy Young, and relievers Lindy McDaniel and Hoyt Wilhelm. Even today, Mac is 98th in the career strikeouts/9 innings category at 6.89, and 18th in hits/9 innings category at 7.23. He would later coach for a number of clubs, returning to the Indians as pitching coach in 1983–84. He suffered a heart attack and died in July 1987, while pitching batting practice for his home-town hero Dodgers.

With Sam on the shelf with shoulder trouble, the disappointment of his two near-misses at no-hitters was about to be temporarily erased. Sonny Siebert had been 4–3 prior to June 10, losing his previous two starts, including giving up three home runs to Minnesota. In his last start, the Angels were stealing his pitches. He subsequently made a few adjustments with Gus, planning to throw more breaking pitches than usual. In his next start on Friday June 10, he pitched a no-hitter against the Senators in Cleveland, allowing base runners on a walk and an error. The ending was not without excitement, as the second batter in the ninth, Bob Saverine, took a ball and then fouled off two. He took the next pitch at the letters, as Sonny started off the mound and the fans went wild. Umpire Jim Honochick called it a ball, and Birdie threw his cap out of the dugout, with the fans booing. Savarine flied out on the next pitch, to end the game.

I warmed Sonny up before the game, when Tebbetts asked his usual question, as he was descending, and I was ascending, the clubhouse steps, I answered, "Yeah, he has it tonight." There's a lot of excitement surrounding any no-hitter, more so here the way the Tribe was playing and leading the league. I have a photo of the fun on the field: Sonny, laughing with his hat off, his catcher Joe Azcue in the foreground, Duke Sims with his right arm around Sonny in a big bear hug, the injured Sam McDowell with his right arm outstretched to shake Sonny's hand, trying to reach down from above. Other newspaper photos highlight Gary Bell's big grin. We were hurrying in from the 'pen when those pictures were taken, looking forward to congratulating Sonny as well. In the clubhouse, I couldn't get close to my locker, located as it was next to Sonny's in the crowded far left corner. Sonny would have another great photo on the front cover of *The Sporting News* June 25 in honor of his no-no.

The Tribe was 34–18 after that weekend of Siebert's no-hitter, Sam's fifth win on June 11, and Gary Bell's 6–2 win on June 12, taking over first place in the AL. From that high point, however, the season disintegrated and raced rapidly downhill: defused, derailed.

The team would fall six games behind the Orioles by July 1 when Sam would win his sixth game, and 15 by August 2, when Sam would start and face 17 batters in his third comeback of the season. McDowell wouldn't win No. 7 until August 18 when he would shut out the White Sox. Believe it or not, Del Crandall broke a ring finger while catching batting practice in Kansas City June 2 and was out three weeks. Duke Sims went on the disabled list June 24 with a herniated disc, and was replaced on the roster by Buddy Booker, who would play in 18 games. The team would not have a winning month after May, and would finish 81–81, 18 games behind. The club finished 40–41 at home, and 41–40 on the road. It was no consolation that the Tribe was the only club to hold a season series advantage over the AL-champion Orioles, ten wins to eight.

The disappointing season would end on a tempting high note, engendering hope, perhaps, for the '67 season: another league record on September 18, when the Indians struck out 21 batters in an 11-inning win in Detroit. The Tribe struck out a record 19 in the first nine innings. Sam struck out 14 in six innings, and when he complained of some arm trouble to George Strickland, Sam was yanked, and

Tiant struck out five in 2 2/3 innings in getting the win. With Sam's arm trouble early in the season, one wonders if starting the first two games of the season, while completing two 1-hitters in the first 15 games, might not have contributed mightily. Sam always threw a lot of pitches, what with his Ks and BBs. Pitch counts were recorded, and Sam was known to hit 120 by the sixth inning, but pitch limits were not necessarily closely watched until some years later.

Despite that phenomenal start, with the arm trouble he would finish the season 9–8 (after four wins in the first 15 games!) with a 2.87 ERA. He would lead the league striking out 225 in 194 innings (10.4/9 innings), despite missing about ten starts. He tied Tiant (and Tommy John!) for the league lead in shutouts with five, in hits/9 innings with 6.0. How do you win only nine games in 28 starts with those stats? Poor Sam would subsequently also be hampered by arm trouble in '67.

On the other hand, Sonny continued his great pitching of '65, going 16–8 for the second straight year, with a 2.80 ERA, striking out 163, walking 62, in 241 innings. He didn't pitch the last three weeks of the season due to a recurrence of his spring-training shoulder problem, missing the opportunity for a 20-win season. The afterthought hurler, working diligently to continually improve himself every day, at age 29 had become one of the league's top pitchers, making the All-Star team in '66. He worked to stay in shape, didn't smoke, didn't drink, was a good family man. His work was being rewarded. He was named the Indians' Man of the Year by the Cleveland Chapter of the Baseball Writers of America.

Tiant appeared in 46 games in '66, with 16 starts, and seven complete games, including five shutouts. He attributed his fast start to losing 20 pounds in the off-season, and coming to spring training in top shape. But his quick 3–0 start stalled as well, and he finished the season with 12 wins again and ten losses. But he pitched well, and struck out 145 in 155 innings (8.4/9 innings), with a 2.79 ERA. He pitched a one-hitter against the Senators on June 16, with Woodie Held (a Tribe member in '64), singling to left to lead off the seventh. It was always puzzling to me that Looie was not just sent out every fourth or fifth day in regular rotation, but Birdie seemed to get down on him a bit after a poor performance early in the year against Baltimore, putting Luis in limbo between starting and the 'pen. His swingman status between starting and relieving was in part dictated by doubleheaders, more rainouts, and off days, which didn't fit the strict four- or five-man rotation. But the lack of a dependable bullpen, unfortunately, dictated that an effective solution be found, and Luis was the sometime solution. Luis would occasionally show disgust when he was called to warm up, but pretty much kept it to himself, muttering some Spanish beyond my comprehension as we walked down from the bullpen bench to the warm-up area.

Birdie's practice of occasionally using his starting pitchers in relief must be acknowledged. The Big Three relieved 30 times out of 122 appearances in '65, and 39 of 115 in '66. Some of those relief appearances were injury-related workouts prior to return to the rotation. Others were brief work-out appearances between starts. Tebbetts's moving Bell to the rotation, and decreasing Looie's starts, is still puzzling, especially since Ding Dong had pitched relatively well in relief in '65. Moving Bell to the rotation left the Tribe with an unproven, less dependable 'pen in '66.

Birdie moved Bell back into the rotation in '66, with 37 starts, 14 wins, 15 losses, 3.22 ERA, and 194 Ks—fifth in the league. Gary actually was second in strikeouts on the Staff in '66. The starting trio of McDowell, Bell, and Siebert led the league in strikeouts by three starters (582), as did the starting four of McDowell, Bell, Siebert, and Tiant (727). Steve Hargan would win 13 games in his first full season, and have the third lowest ERA in the league at 2.48, while striking out 132. Five starting pitchers with over 100 strikeouts in the top 20 in the AL!

The staff would be third in ERA (3.23) and hits, second in complete games and shutouts, but jump to fifth in HRs allowed (but just five behind third place), and ninth in saves with 28. Of course, if you have a lot of complete games, you'll tend to have fewer saves. Overall, they would have their lowest strikeout total of this five-year record period at 1111, but still led the AL as they struck out over 1100 for the third consecutive year. Their strikeouts/9 innings dropped to 6.8, also league-leading, and the only season they would be below 7/9 innings in the '65–68 period. Had Sam pitched anywhere near his usual number of innings, the staff might have surpassed 1200 strikeouts in 1966. However, effective bullpen or not, losing Sam and Sonny to arm trouble for considerable chunks of the season might have been too much to overcome, anyway.

## Cleveland Pitching Staff Statistics 1966

| 1966 | IP | GS | ERA | K | K/9 | BB/9 | HR/9 | CG | SO |
|---|---|---|---|---|---|---|---|---|---|
| McDowell | 194.1 | 28 | 2.87 | 225 | 10.4 (1) | 4.7(31) | 0.6 (5) | 8(13) | 5 (1) |
| Bell | 254.1 | 37 | 3.22 | 194 | 6.9 (5) | 2.8(17) | 0.7(10) | 12(4) | 0 |
| Siebert | 241.1 | 32 | 2.8 | 163 | 6.1(16) | 2.3 (7) | 0.9(14) | 11(5) | 1 (25) |
| Tiant | 155 | 16 | 2.79 | 145 | 8.4 (3) | 2.9 | 0.9(14) | 7(18) | 5 (1) |
| Hargan | 192 | 21 | 2.48 | 132 | 6.2(14) | 2.1 (5) | 0.4 (1) | 7(18) | 3 (7) |
| Kelley | 95 | 7 | 4.34 | 64 | 6.0 | 4.0 | 1.3 | 1 | 0 |
| O'Donoghue | 108 | 13 | 3.83 | 49 | 4.1 | 1.9 | 1.1 | 2 | 0 |
| Radatz | 56.2 | 0 | 4.61 | 49 | 7.8 | 5.4 | 1.0 | 0 | 0 |
| Allen | 51.1 | 0 | 4.21 | 33 | 5.8 | 2.3 | 0.4 | 0 | 0 |
| Kralick | 68.1 | 4 | 3.82 | 31 | 4.1 | 2.6 | 1.2 | 0 | 0 |
| Stange | 16 | 2 | 2.81 | 8 | 4.5 | 1.7 | 0.6 | 1 | 0 |
| Heffner | 13 | 1 | 3.46 | 7 | 4.8 | 2.1 | 0.7 | 0 | 0 |
| Culver | 9.2 | 1 | 8.38 | 6 | 5.6 | 6.5 | 0.9 | 0 | 0 |
| McMahon | 12.1 | 0 | 2.92 | 5 | 3.6 | 4.4 | 0.7 | 0 | 0 |
| Team Total | 1467.1 | 162 | 3.23 | 1111 | 6.8 (1) | 3.0 (5) | 0.8 (3) | 49(2) | 14(2) |

Innings pitched, strikeouts, strikeouts/9 innings, complete games, and shutouts for the 1966 Staff. IP: Innings pitched; K: Strikeouts; ERA: Earned run average; GS: Games started; CG: Complete Games; SO: Shutouts. Individual K, BB, HR / 9 innings rank (parentheses) based on minimum of 1 IP/team game.

After being in 45 1-run games in '64 and 44 in '65, the Tribe was involved in 60 in '66, winning half. It was a team in need of expert relief, with none other in sight. Birdie had also convinced Mr. Paul to get Radatz from the Red Sox for McMahon and Stange. Radatz failed early. The lack of a lights-out bullpen eventually led, in part, to Birdie's resigning August 19. After Birdie resigned, ironically Dick found himself, giving up no runs in 8 innings. Dick credited Early Wynn in this reclamation, calling him "positively the greatest pitching coach I have ever worked with."

Far better than average pitching in '66 was offset by worse than average batting and fielding. They would be 5th in BA and HR, but 10th in doubles, 4th in HR, 8th in OBP and runs, and 8th in fielding. Wagner was 6th in the league in BA at .279, and Colavito 6th in HR with 30. The Rock did set an AL record for most consecutive games without an error (195) on April 26, the night of McDowell's first 1-hitter, that would extend to 207 games before a fly ball by the White Sox' Bruce Howard bounced off his glove. Dick Howser fell off badly at the plate in '66, with only 150 AB's, sidelined for a while with a thumb injury. The little guy had a big heart and a great talent. He was one of many great guys not only on that ball club, but in baseball and life. Gary Bell called me "Meat"; Dick always called me "Doctor." I would be saddened in 1987 to learn he had died of a malignant brain tumor, an area of medicine I worked in daily.

# Chapter 16—Time to Quit?

Somewhere along the line, the intent to give up playing baseball confronted the potential reality of not getting into medical school. I had applied for early admission (after only three years of undergraduate work) to two schools that had records of admitting about 5-10% of their students after just three years of college. I was rejected by one, and was on a wait list at the other.

The prospect of a fourth year as bullpen catcher next year in '67 was indeed a reality. I even considered the possibility I might get into coaching through my bullpen work, with the help of the friends I had made in the front office. Bullpen coaches weren't yet universally used, and I didn't yet envision what kind of coaching I might do. But it seemed I was in a good spot to begin the process. I had really made some good friends with the team's front office, and I think there was a genuine "like" for me there. Perhaps I might actually try to play ball somewhere at a low instructional-league level. Of course, Paul O'Dea had told me I was better off pursuing medicine, because "glove men are a dime a dozen." Yet he knew a fire still smoldered in my heart, somehow hoping to play the game.

Early Wynn came to me one day during the '66 season and asked me to pitch some BP. I didn't think much of it, and, of course, agreed to try, knowing the hitters would be merciless to pretenders who couldn't get the ball over the plate. I hadn't pitched regularly in years, obviously. I had pitched a few innings in high school and in the *Plain Dealer* League with some success. In '65, after I found out I would no longer travel, I dressed for one game with my old Lyon Tailors team. On the bench, I talked our manager into letting me pitch one inning of mop-up relief, striking out two, walking none. My mechanics of throwing from the crouch hardly lent itself to a smooth delivery now, but I would try nonetheless. I did have good release point control from the crouch, and when standing and throwing. The continuous, directly-overhand forward motion of the catcher's throw, directed straight toward the target, with arm follow through in the same direction, differs from the pitcher's motion of a wider arm sweep, and follow through across the body. I don't think I had a dozen erratic or poor returns to the pitcher in my three years in the 'pen: balls that were too high so that pitchers had to jump, or too low so as they had to bend, or too far right or left, so that they had to lean too far one way or the other. I usually returned the ball with some velocity, seldom just lobbing it back—it was too much fun to try to throw it back as fast as the pitcher had thrown it to me.

It was an experience being on top of that high mound, throwing downhill. I never asked anyone how high it was. I assumed it was 15 inches; it could have been more, but I doubt it. I never thought to ask if the mound was the same height in every ballpark. Somehow, I assumed it was, and I don't remember any discussion to the contrary. I could foresee really getting additional velocity going from this height advantage, however.

The mound was certainly higher than the one in front of the dugout, and the one in the bullpen along the right-field foul line. Thank God, because it would have been doubly dangerous for fielders chasing foul balls if those mounds were as high. I did have a bit of trouble keeping good balance while curbing my enthusiasm on the mound, however, and Duke Sims gave me some grief when I let up just a bit to maintain equilibrium as I fell off the rubber as I threw one pitch. Batters want consistency: same delivery, same speed, no breaking stuff, right down the middle at 65-70 mph. Although my mechanics must have left a lot to be desired, I was able to throw strikes pretty consistently, just as I could consistently return pitches back to pitchers at their chest height from a crouch.

Afterward, Gus came up to me and told me I did OK, and asked me if I wanted to continue to work on my pitching. And he didn't mean for pitching BP! A Hall of Famer, a phenomenal competitor, a guy who once told me he "could pitch to the inside and the outside of an ant's ass," asked me if I wanted to work with him! Of course I said yes. No matter what the future would hold, the worst that could happen might be a brief switch from behind the plate to the pitching mound for batting practice. The best? Who knows, maybe my arm, not my glove, certainly not my bat, would be my future! I had a strong arm. Velocity? I don't know. Radar guns weren't common yardsticks in 1966. Measuring velocity via the

Doppler ultrasound principle had just been invented in the 50s. No one was reproducing Bob Feller's measuring his fastball by throwing just as a motorcycle was racing by at 99 mph. Only a few years later McDowell was said to be throwing 100 mph.

So Gus and I worked on a smooth delivery on the sidelines before BP: a horizontal figure-of-eight motion, ball in glove, right hand disconnecting from the glove on the backswing, with the forward swing of the arc of the arm wider, and not as directly overhand and forward, as the catcher's throw. He taught me what he considered the proper grip and delivery for the curve ball: the classic pull-the-lamp-shade-down, forward-wrist-ulnar-rotation movement. I'm not sure he really thought his pupil would ever make it, but he seemed genuinely interested in the experiment, and OK with my progress.

Where was it headed? It was clearly directed toward the possibility of a career in pitching. At whose direction? I think Paul O'Dea sensed my love for the game, and was willing to create an opportunity to let me prove or disprove that I could play. My love for possibly playing the game was rekindled. It was no longer just a great job that I enjoyed immensely, but a potential pathway to professional baseball.

Then it came: a letter from St. Louis University School of Medicine, announcing I had been accepted to begin medical school in September 1966. It was exactly what I had been hoping for, and I could hardly contain my enthusiasm waiting to go out that night with my girlfriend Judy to celebrate. But the pitching experiment had, in effect, created a conflict: maybe both things *were* now possible. I had had my swing at baseball once, and I missed. Would I take a second swing?

Gus and I continued to work on the delivery on the sidelines, but the urgency of progress in preparation for a fling at a minor league opportunity had now been defused by the acceptance letter. I continued my duties as bullpen and batting practice catcher, as always, knowing the landscape and the road ahead had changed dramatically. Medical school would come soon, and maybe pitching and playing ball, or another year in the 'pen, would follow next spring and summer, when I would have a three-month vacation. On the other hand, the experiment may well be over. Only time would tell.

With this news I realized I would indeed be leaving the team soon, and probably forever. Gus had one more surprise in store for me in mid-August, however. In the clubhouse one day prior to going out for batting practice, Gus called me over, and asked me to stand by Rocky Colavito. Gus pulled out his 35 mm camera with flash, and he took our picture. He gave the camera to Colavito, and asked him to take a picture of Gus and me.

Right Fielder Rocky Colavito

Then Gus and I went around the clubhouse to the starting players, who had not yet gone out onto the field: Leon Wagner, Chuck Hinton, Chico Salmon, Jim Gentile. Gus and I went out onto the field, and he called the pitchers one-by-one during their early BP: Sonny Siebert, Sam McDowell, Steve Hargan, Dick Radatz, John O'Donaghue, Bob Allen, Tom Kelley. Luis Tiant was starting that night, and was in the trainer's room while this was happening—unfortunately, I have no picture with him. Gus took pix of a few more position of the "irregulars," non-starting players: Dick Howser, Joe Azcue, Jim Landis. Then coaches George Strickland and Reggie Otero on the bench. Then I put on my gear and got behind the plate.

The next Saturday, Gus brought in a manila envelope, with the photo prints he had taken and developed himself enclosed. I couldn't believe the gift: the gruff old Gus showing a gesture of generosity, warmth, and kindness, a behavior that many stories about him would belie. I took the pics and asked the players to autograph them, and to a one they complied; the pictures and the messages remain treasures to this day. A few of the pictures didn't turn out, either blurred out of focus, or taken with me or the player with our eyes closed in that pre-digital age. I'm surprised as many turned out as well as they did. Some of the pictures are included here. They were a great parting gift from Gus, who would be leaving, too, replaced when Joe Adcock would be named as manager for the '67 season.

I had accumulated a number of additional autographed pictures of team members no longer with the team over the three-year period, or just not around while Gus was snapping the photos, as well: Vern Fuller, The Blade: "To a great roomie, who sure learns fast." Lee Stange: "To my favorite catcher." "Best Wishes" from Dick Donovan, Ted Abernathy, Larry Brown, Max Alvis, Jack Kralick. I have signed baseballs form the '64 and '66 teams; signed team pix as well. A Hall of Famer. All Stars. Record breakers. A bunch of all-around great guys who never felt compelled to remind me of my status, but rather treated me like a member of the team.

Pitching Coach, Hall of Famer "Burly" Early Wynn (aka Gus)

I have no picture with Birdie Tebbetts, sad to say. He stayed in his office before games, and usually came out to the field just before the first pitch, so there were few casual moments to take advantage of. Perhaps with pressure from Mr. Paul, in great part related to the relief-pitcher issue and the trade for Dick Radatz, Tebbetts resigned Friday night August 19.

The clubhouse was a somber, quiet place after Birdie announced to us that he was stepping down. Ballplayers sometimes need to whistle, sing, strut, and joke during a long season to make disappointment bearable. His announcement removed the thin veneer that separates the outward appearance that they "feeeellyy goooodd" from the inner reality that we are all just a disappointment away from allowing the reality of failure to set in.

Tebbetts had spent 11 years in the majors as a player, and 12 as a manager. I would be resigning in two days after three seasons in the bullpen. The irony of the weekend wasn't lost on me. The clubhouse was a somber, quiet place after Birdie announced to us that he was stepping down. I think players felt bad for Birdie, and it merely served to remind them of an unraveled season.

Left-hand Pitcher, strikeout leader "Sudden Sam" McDowell

Best friend on the '64–66 teams, right-hand no-hit pitcher, Sonny Siebert

# Chapter 17—Star of the Game

Well, the final day had come: August 21, presumably the end of my career as batting practice and bullpen catcher. It was a day like many in the past three years, a beautiful Cleveland summer Sunday. It would be a sad, but cheerful, end to my season (and career?), although the team still had six weeks to play.

There were three catchers on the roster, and minor leaguers would soon come up to fill the 40-man roster, so I was dispensable once again. I would leave for St. Louis next week, and embark upon my new career. I was resigned to the likelihood I was walking out of the clubhouse and slipping into baseball obscurity, duffle-bag in hand, baseball career behind me.

But one final unexpected surprise awaited me, one usually reserved for the guy who had thrown the shutout, saved the game, or knocked in the winning run. Jimmy Dudley and Bob Neal, the Indians' play-by-play announcers on WERE radio, asked me to be interviewed as "Star of the Game." The Tribe had just lost, the team was in the doldrums, Radatz had struck out four in two innings of losing relief, so there was no real star to focus on.

How many times over the years had I listened to Dudley and Neal on the radio on summer nights, sitting on the porch with my grandparents, Aunt Helen, and Uncle Joe, turning the radio dial occasionally to Cincinnati's 50,000-watt WLW to hear what the Reds and the National League were doing? (WLW is still alive and well, and still broadcasting the Reds as "The Nation's Station.") How many pictures had Jimmy and Bob painted in my mind of the action on the field? They were great announcers: Jimmy, with his southern Virginia drawl but a bit more excitement in his style, contrasting with Bob's more restrained delivery. Jimmy was identified most readily by his signature sign-off, "So long, and lots of good luck, ya heah!" (that's "you hear" in Virginia-ese). Jimmy had been the Tribe's radio voice since '48; Neal was the Tribe's radio voice from 1957–61, and then '65

–66. Jimmy would be named to the Broadcaster's Hall of Fame years later. Bob's chief claim to fame was being in the right place at the right time: he announced the network broadcast of Don Larsen's perfect game in the '56 World Series.

The TV announcers Harry Jones and Herb Score, the '64 rookie announcer with the Massachusetts accent, were a great team as well, and they too frequented the locker room. No TV interviews for the bullpen catcher, though. I guess I had a face for radio. But they kindly downplayed those occasional occurrences in '66 when bullpen balls would occasionally get loose and onto the field, causing play to stop.

The press staffs, too, had always been friendly on their almost-daily stops in the clubhouse. The newspaper beat writers and senior columnists were a pleasant enough group when in the clubhouse, if not at their typewriters (you catch more bees with honey than with vinegar). They always acknowledged my presence, as well. Hal Lebowitz of the morning *Plain Dealer* actually included me in his "Ask Hal" or his "Notes Off the Cuff" columns six times; when I was named to the job in June, '64; when he outlined the travel room assignments July 15, '64; mentioning that Sam McDowell had borrowed my Louisville Slugger, Mickey Mantle-model bat to get a few hits in '64. He noted when I was accepted to medical school in '66, and when I graduated in '70. He also wrote about a friend of his, former Major League catcher Mickey Cochrane, then a sheriff in Springfield, Mo., telling him of his visit to the Cleveland Police Department, and seeing a picture of a catcher on my father's office desk.

Russell Schneider was a rookie on the *Plain Dealer* staff in 1964, and eventually wrote the excellent daily "Batting Around" column. Russell had played minor league ball as a catcher, and I knew him from the Class A *Plain Dealer* league. Russell would become the historian of the Indians, and write a number of encyclopedic books on a variety of team topics, many of which I've referenced in this book. Regis McCauley, Chuck Heaton and Bob Sudyk of the now-defunct afternoon *Cleveland Press*, to my knowledge, never included me in any notes. The *Press* did publish two pieces on the bullpen, one with no by-line, with a number of photos and a full-page spread on batting practice on June 17, 1965.[75] The other was a piece on my taking the position.[76]

Now Jimmy and Bob wanted to interview me—who was supposed to be seen but not heard. I was going to be heard, but not seen! Of course, I would be glad to: I would love to let the fans in on the deepest, darkest secrets of the bullpen catcher job, the inside stories of the clubhouse. I had learned a lot: the men of iron, in many instances, had feet of clay. Gruff "old" men could be teddy bears at heart. Grown men can act like kids, even to hot heads and fights about TV programs, hot feet, and hot dog simulations.

The interview was quick, perhaps mechanical and perfunctory. No probing questions, no digging up dirt left behind by a promising season gone haywire. The interview represented another kind gesture from those I had met in the course of my work: no embarrassing disclosures, just acknowledgements of feelings for the individuals whom I had befriended, who had shown kindness beyond expectation, who made it more than just a job. I had met many wonderful people who were always great to me.

But maybe I was the story, after all. I was leaving the wigwam early, deserting the teepee and the reservation, moving forward to look for a new hunting ground, a new adventure, at the end of a season gone bad. I was doing something out of the ordinary hum-drum of turning on that microphone, or putting on that uniform, or washing those sanitary socks, day after day, week after week, taking a few months off in the winter, then starting all over again. It's time spent frequently in frustration, with one game blending into the next, only a small fraction of which become individually memorable, but whose sum, hopefully, but all too infrequently for the Tribe, turns into a successful season.

I had a tape of the interview that I hadn't listened to in the years that have passed. I had left it at my mother's house, believing she might enjoy listening to it from time to time, certain I would have no need for it in the future. In writing this chapter, I tried to find the tape there, but couldn't. Thinking about it now, I believe not making sure to preserve that recording was a failure to assign significance to some of the events of that time, taking too many of them for granted, and not preserving that bit of history. Some things only declare their value over time, upon deeper reflection and consideration, be they a radio tape, a photograph, a catcher's mitt, or a letter from the front office. Or strikeout record.

I would quit that day and soon travel to St. Louis to start school. For the time being, I had to put baseball out of my mind: a second swing at baseball, so to speak, but . . . . more like a foul ball. *Strike Two!*

It turns out I wasn't quite out, yet.

# Chapter 18—The Final Break

My first week in St. Louis was an orientation, and I went with some friends to the brand new Busch Stadium to see a game. Busch had just opened in May '66: one of the new, symmetric, cookie-cutter stadiums on natural grass. Of course, I noted where the 'pens were: immediately behind the wall in right-center and left-center fields, parallel to the field. I would go to a few games in St. Louis, and certainly would marvel at Bob Gibson's performance during the '68 season, and the World Series against the Tigers. Little did I know lefty Jon Warden in the Tigers' pen and I would coach together some 20 years later.

Not unexpectedly, my first year of medical school proved to be tough, but I was doing fine. I didn't lead the league in any areas. Won a few, lost a few; some hits, some misses, in class. November brought an unexpected surprise: a check representing a portion of the Indians' share of World Series receipts. It was for $75—a one-third share! It didn't even cover my monthly room and board of $100.65 at Phi Beta Pi medical fraternity rooming house on Lafayette Avenue. The check did serve to keep baseball on my mind, however.

Pre-holiday semester finals provided an event that caused me to reflect deeply on my commitment to medicine as a career. One of my two roommates had been having a bit of trouble academically, enough perhaps that his career was in jeopardy. He was a great guy—dry, sly humor, and a John-Belushi-like elevation of his eyebrow at times of knowing recognition. He was a put-on artist, who was now being put-upon.

We left our room and began walking five minutes to our classroom on Grand Avenue for a test. He exclaimed with surprised concern, "I've got to go back; I've forgotten my pencils!" We offered him a few of ours, but didn't think much of it when he turned us down, just told him to hurry up. He never showed up for the test. His bag was gone when we returned hours later. Some belongings were still there, for which he would return over the holiday vacation after we had all left for home. It was merely a matter of months before he found himself in Korea near the DMZ. He had been drafted by the Army in 1966, but a student deferment allowed him to go to school. Once he dropped out, he lost the deferment and was subject to induction.

I would be drafted four years later in 1970, too, but the Vietnam war was winding down, and few medical draftees were being sent to Vietnam. I was stationed for two years at Ft. Leonard Wood, Missouri, 140 miles southwest from St. Louis. I wanted to be drafted, but by the Indians or Yankees, not by the Army. My fractured clubhouse Spanish (*caliente? doloro?)* helped me get by in troop clinic each morning at 6:30 with the many Puerto Rican soldiers who had enlisted in the Army during the war.

I realized how lucky I was to be able to be successful at what I was doing. How could I possibly choose baseball, when my friend Sonny Siebert (a great all-around athlete), also converted from position player to pitcher, and then took four full years to make the major leagues? I had limited, unproven ability.

Furthermore, I had already been in the Bigs. Shined shoes and laundered uniforms; no long bus trips, just chartered flights. The finest hotels in the country's greatest cities. Meal money on the road to enjoy steaks in great restaurants. Did I really want long bus trips and McDonald's hamburgers?

Paul O'Dea wrote me a letter on Feb. 28, 1967, pointing out he was now Minor League Administrator. He told me to bear down, keep plugging, don't just go through the motions, get in shape, and either rejoin the team, or he'd find a spot for me to find out if I can play ball.

In retrospect, I understand Paul's unique perspective on baseball, and his firm grip on the reality that many are called to play baseball, but few are chosen in the major leagues. He was a promising ballplayer himself, a native Cleveland West-sider who had signed a contract with the Indians at age 17 in 1937. Two years later, while bending over to pick up a ball in the batting cage during batting practice, he was hit by a ball in the face, causing him to lose vision in his right eye. He overcame the disability and played for the Tribe during the war, but lost his position when the top players came home.[77] He knew that I had an opportunity few young men could have—but in medicine, not necessarily baseball.

With his letter, I envisioned that, at worst, I would have a summer job. At best, maybe something would work out and I would even possibly still combine these two careers. I had the best intention to try to get in shape, do some running, enough throwing to strengthen my arm. I played some handball and a little basketball. Classes, however, were pretty demanding. I was doing well academically, which required a great deal of time. When spring came, finals were close behind. I really wasn't able to get into any semblance of the condition to which I was accustomed, or which would be required to compete effectively.

I got a letter from Hank Peters, Vice-President of Player Personnel and the Farm System, on May 18, explaining the team would have a team in Sarasota of the Gulf Coast Instructional League, asking me to report June 15. There would be no salary for the first 2 weeks, then $500 for a six-week season.

I would finish school and get home to Cleveland in early June. It remained to be seen I could be successful among high school and college players who had just finished their seasons. I would have to take time at home to get into shape. The Indians were keeping three catchers, so if had I rejoined the club, there would be no travel, and I would have time to play sandlot ball. I decided to play in the *Plain Dealer* Class A league again, perhaps catching and doing some pitching after my arm was back in shape, or maybe to work my way back into the bullpen. Paul O'Dea was OK with that—*let's see what happens.* Somehow I think I my brain had long known it was over; but my heart wanted to go to the Instructional League to see what I could do; my body couldn't quite let go.

I got a well-paying job as a roofer by day. The pay lent itself better to the tuition needs of a student than did a six-week $500 salary that was subject to loss by injury or failure. At night and on weekends, I could play ball or work in the bullpen, and *see what happens,* as Paul O'Dea said. My first games back with the LaRiche Ford team (successors to my now-defunct old Lyon Tailors team) at Edgewater Park were a bit awkward. After all, I hadn't really played in a game for three years, with the exception of pitching one inning and one at-bat. In the second game back on July 2nd, I was catching, and experienced a sequence of embarrassing moments behind the plate. First, a foul ball came off the lower half of the bat, downward and backward into the dirt, and up into my crotch. All guys wince at the prospect, and the vision of catcher-as-hero quickly dissolves with the discomfort that defies description, with not much else to do but fall to your knees, bend over forward, and pray for time to pass quickly. You then walk it off, take a few tosses, and get back to your crouch for the next pitch.

In this case, the next pitch was hardly more forgiving. *What happened?* Another foul ball, back and slightly, up, and into my thoughtlessly unprotected throwing hand, fracturing my middle finger at the proximal joint.

This meant my career as a roofer was over: I went to work with a splint-cast the next day, but the nature of the labor really didn't lend itself to working with only one good hand. But more importantly, my career in baseball was over as well. Recalling that Del Crandall had broken his finger in BP the previous summer was little consolation. I couldn't catch confidently or throw accurately, and certainly couldn't pitch. The location and nature of the fracture would require four weeks to heal well, then "rehab." That would take us almost to August, too late to worry about the '67 season.

In August I would go back to St. Louis for my second year of med school. There would be no "maybe next summer." The third year of medical school began July 1, with full-time clinical duties, and no summer vacation to try professional baseball. It was a foul ball, but it was Strike Three, my final swing at baseball, no more to wonder if, where, when, or how. My future as a sports hero, as the field-general catcher standing tall, strong, and unnerved, dressed in battle gear, or as the pitcher hurling his lightning bolts down from on the high of the hill, had finally given way to a career saving lives, not games. An ignominious end to a glorious "career." The truth is, I probably would not have had a successful professional career, anyway.

That, then, ends the tale that could never be written today, with the intensity and single-minded purpose required by young athletes pursuing their dream. Limited or focused talent would never achieve today what it almost, or might have, accomplished then. A "see what will happen" approach would likely never be entertained by management either, where the business of baseball demands a higher expectation, dedication, and level of performance. The generosity and kindness exhibited by many individuals around the ballclub, both in the clubhouse, on the field, and in the front office, will never be repeated.

I would finish the second year of school, come home and be married that July to my darling Judy. Sonny and his wife Carol, and Cy and his wife Mary were at the wedding. Sonny was in the midst of a record-setting season with the rest of the staff.

Cy would work as equipment manager until 2006, when he retired after 45 years in the clubhouse. He most deservedly won the Cleveland Baseball Writers' Good-Guy Award in 1977 and 1993. Cy may have been small in stature, but he bench pressed some giant egos. I dropped by the clubhouse every year for a while to say hello to Cy and a few of the players who were still around, and to keep a thin connection to the game. The last time I stopped in to see Cy was around '81 or '82, and Cy got Len Barker, the author of a perfect game in '81, to autograph two balls for Lisa and Scott. (Len had led the AL in strikeouts/9 innings in 1980 at 6.8. Sam, Sonny, and Looie averaged 8.44 from '64-68!) Cy's career included a bit part in an NBC movie on Babe Ruth in 1991, where he was cast as the Yankees' batboy. The part wasn't so much due to his height of 4' 6", but the fact ball clubs actually did use adults as batboys in the 20s.[78] My baseball connection has dissolved, however, and now I'm just another fan, but one with a few great memories and, perhaps, a few stories to tell.

I would finish school, and move to Cincinnati to begin my medical internship July 1970. Judy and I went to a Reds' game against Willie Mays, Willie McCovey, Juan Marichal, and Bobby Bonds, at old Crosley Field on an earlier April trip to look for an apartment. The only detail of the evening I remember is leaving the lights on on my Malibu in the downtown Holiday Inn parking lot, then having a dead battery in the morning, and getting off to a slow start finding a place to live. Crosley Field would soon be replaced by Riverfront Stadium on June 30, 1970.

I have been at the University of Cincinnati since that time: no trades, holdouts, strikes, or arbitrations. A few road trips. A professor's academic salary remains less than Mickey Mantle made in 1964.

I didn't go to many ballgames for a number of years: I had seen plenty. But I would get this funny, restless feeling every year, seemingly coinciding with the announcement that pitchers and catchers were reporting to spring training in February, indicating that it was time to go out and play ball again. The feeling was satisfied for a while by coaching my son Scott's teams, but then it slowly diminished. In reality, it has yet to completely disappear. I do like to go to a few Reds' games every summer, preferably with my family, and listen for the ball to explode into the catcher's mitt, thinking occasionally about the most prolific combination of strikeout pitchers in the history of the game, the guys that used to really make the Popper explode.

# Chapter 19—The Season: 1967

While the story of the bullpen catcher's connection to the Tribe had ended, the saga of the Tribe pitching staff would continue, as they persisted in setting individual, group, and team records. Many of the individual records and accomplishments of the Big Three of the Tribe staff occurred primarily in the '64-'66 years, as I've recounted. The old guard was changing, however. Joe Adcock, who had no managerial experience at any level, took over as manager and kept George Strickland as a coach. Early Wynn was replaced as pitching coach by Clay Bryant. That means Gus and I had enjoyed the same tenure with the club: 1964–66.

1967 Indians. Front: Brown, Davalillo, Clay Bryant, Del Rice, Joe Adcock, Pat Mullin, Strickland, Ed Connolly, Gus Gil, Salmon. Middle: Alvis, Azcue, Tiant, Sims, Gonzalez, Steve Bailey, Whitfield, Orlando Pena, George Culver, Bock. Rear: Wagner, Colavito, Hinton, Don Demeter, McDowell, Horton, Lee Maye, Hargan, Siebert, O'Donoghue, Allen

Gary Bell was traded to the Red Sox after nine appearances in '67, later going 12–8 with a 3.16 ERA , naturally helping lead *them* to the pennant. He would strike out over 100 for Boston again that season, and again in '68. "Ding-Dong" would finish a 12-year career, pitch in 519 games, with 121 wins, 51 saves, with a career 3.68 ERA, striking out 6.2 batters, walking 3.8 batters, and allowing 0.9 home runs per nine innings. Jack Kralick appeared in two games in '67, then was traded to the Mets, never to pitch in the majors again.

But 1967 would be *the* highlight strikeout year for the Tribe's staff, again setting new AL (and major league) team record of 1189, and setting a club record for innings pitched at 1,478. But the strikeouts/9 innings was still a new record of 7.2 strikeouts/9 innings . This AL single-season team record would remain in place for 30 years, until 1997 when Seattle would strike out 1,207 batters, with Randy Johnson contributing 291. Seattle's single-season record was later broken by the Indians with 1213 in '00, by the Yankees with 1266 in '01. Tampa Bay struck out 1194 in '07 (40 years later, and only five strikeouts more than the Tribe).

McDowell would have some of the same arm trouble he had had in '66 and falter in '67, with a 13–15 record, ERA of 3.85, yet still striking out 236 in 236 innings (9.0/9 innings), second in the league to the Red Sox' Jim Lonborg's 246, despite Sam's relatively few innings pitched. Perhaps contributing to Sam's reversal was the release of his private catcher, Del Crandall, in October after the '66 season. Del then retired and began a coaching and managerial career.

Tiant went 12-9 in '67, with 9.2 strikeouts and 2.8 BB/9 innings, with a 2.74 ERA. Luis and Sam were once only the second starters in AL history to average one strikeout an inning. Mac and Sonny were the starting duo that had done it first in '65, and none other would do it again until Nolan Ryan and Bobby Witt in 1990.

In '67, Sonny would win 12, with a 2.97 ERA, with 6.6 strikeouts, 2.6 BB, and 6.6 hits per nine innings. The Big Three would average 8.29 strikeouts/9 innings, striking out 601 in 634 innings. The next closest trio, Mickey Lolich, Denny McLain, and Earl Wilson of the Tigers, would average 6.70. However, the Big Three wouldn't strike out the most batters overall, with Dean Chance, Ken Boswell, and Jim Kaat of the Twins striking out 635 in 768 innings, but only 6.38/9 innings, almost two less than the Tribe!

## Cleveland Pitching Staff Statistics 1967

| 1967 | IP | GS | ERA | K | K/9 | BB/9 | HR/9 | CG | SO |
|---|---|---|---|---|---|---|---|---|---|
| McDowell | 236.1 | 37 | 3.85 | 236 (2) | 9.0(2) | 4.7 (30) | 0.8 (27) | 10 (13) | 1 |
| Tiant | 213.2 | 29 | 2.74 | 119(4) | 9.2(1) | 2.8 (16) | 1 (30) | 9(17) | 1 |
| Hargan | 223 | 29 | 2.62 | 141 (20) | 5.7(24) | 2.9 (20) | 0.4 (1) | 15 (2) | 6 (1) |
| Siebert | 185.1 | 26 | 2.38 | 136 (22) | 6.6(13) | 2.6 (11) | 0.8 (21) | 7(22) | 1 |
| O'Donoghue | 130.2 | 17 | 3.24 | 81 (44) | 5.6 | 2.3 | 0.7 | 5 | 2 |
| Williams | 79 | 8 | 2.62 | 75 | 8.5 | 2.7 | 0.7 | 2 | 1 |
| Pena | 88.1 | 1 | 3.36 | 72 | 7.3 | 2.2 | 0.8 | 0 | 0 |
| Allen | 54.1 | 0 | 2.98 | 50 | 8.3 | 4.1 | 0.7 | 0 | 0 |
| Bailey | 64.2 | 1 | 3.90 | 46 | 6.4 | 5.8 | 0.7 | 0 | 0 |
| Connolly | 49.1 | 4 | 7.48 | 45 | 8.2 | 6.2 | 1.1 | 0 | 0 |
| Culver | 75 | 1 | 3.96 | 41 | 4.9 | 3.7 | 0.2 | 0 | 0 |
| Bell | 60.2 | 9 | 3.71 | 39 | 5.8 | 3.6 | 1 | 1 | 0 |
| Tiefenauer | 11.1 | 0 | 0.79 | 6 | 4.8 | 2.4 | 0 | 0 | 0 |
| Kralick | 2.0 | 0 | 9 | 1 | 4.5 | 4.5 | 0 | 0 | 0 |
| Radatz | 3 | 0 | 6 | 1 | 3.0 | 6.0 | 310 | 0 | 0 |
| Team Total | 1477.2 | 162 | 3.25 (6) | 1189* | 7.2*(1) | 3.4(8) | 0.7 (2) | 49 (2) | 12 (8) |

Innings pitched, strikeouts, strikeouts / 9 innings, complete games, and shutouts for the 1967 Staff. IP: Innings pitched; K: Strikeouts; ERA: Earned run average; CG: Complete Games; SO: Shutouts. Individual K, BB, HR/9 innings rank (parentheses) based on minimum of 1 IP/team game. * indicates single-season AL record.)

The Big Three would each pitch only one shutout. Steve Hargan became the fourth starter, constituting a new "Big Four," and he struck out 141 (5.7/9 inn.), leading the team with 15 complete games (second in the AL), including six shutouts (first in AL), and giving up 0.4 HR/9 innings once again (first in AL). But the four starters would win only 49 games during the season, while setting a new AL strikeout record. The staff did not lead the league in any other individual pitching statistics, not even wild pitches. Stan Williams, whom I caught briefly in '65, rejoined the club and contributed 8.5 strikeouts/9 innings to the Tribe totals while starting and relieving. "Lurch," as Gary Bell called Stan after the popular Addams Family man-servant character due to his tall, gangling stature, would contribute mightily again in '68. Orlando Pena was the main bullpen addition, with eight of the club's 27 saves.

By comparison with the previous three years, the strikeout line looks more impressive, yet it didn't lead to wins on the field. The Big Three would suffer from poor offensive support, however, giving up 15% more runs than the team scored. In addition to leading the league in strikeouts once again, they were second in complete games, fifth in ERA and hits allowed, sixth in shutouts, and eighth in saves.

It was grayer than usual on the shores of Lake Erie in Cleveland that summer. There were few other highlights. No Tribe one-hitters, no-hitters, or ten-game winning streaks to start the season. Municipal Stadium would be the site of a no-hitter Aug. 25, but it was thrown by my TV co-star Dean Chance of the Minnesota Twins against Sonny Siebert. The Indians jumped on top with a run in the bottom of the first on two walks, an infield error, and a wild pitch, for a 1–0 lead. The Twins tied it in the top of the second, then went ahead in the sixth when the winning run scored on Sonny's only balk of the season. It was that kind of year.

The Tribe attracted 26,133 opening day, but wouldn't draw over 9,000 at home in their next 18 games, going 17–18. They wouldn't be more than two games over .500 the entire year. They finished 75–87, eighth in the AL. The attendance would fall off dramatically to 662,980, last in the league. The Rock would be traded to Chicago July 29, slowed by a back problem, after hitting only five home runs. Daddy Wags would hit 15. Max Alvis would lead the club with 21. My old roomie, "The Blade" Vern Fuller, would return to the Bigs and become the starter at second base. The only team highlight were the new AL records for total strikeouts and strikeouts/9 innings by the pitching staff.

It was a dismal season for the team, a disappointing season for me, but my season was mercifully shorter than the Tribe's. Manager Joe Adcock would be replaced after only one season by Alvin Dark, who had had no previous managerial experience himself for his first manager's post with San Francisco in 1961. Dark would name his former Giants teammate Jack Sanford as his pitching coach for the '68 season, which will always be remembered as the Year of the Pitcher.

# Chapter: 20—The Season: 1968

Compared to the previous disappointing season, 1968 would provide a dramatic reversal of fortune for the club, the Tribe would go 86–75, finishing in third place, but 17.5 games behind the Tigers. Sam would come back strongly in '68 with a 15–14 record, with a 1.81 ERA (second only to Looie in the AL), striking out 9.5/9 innings to lead the league again, while walking 3.7/9, the second best of his career. Sam would break an AL record for most strikeouts in two consecutive games, as well as for three consecutive games, twice. He struck out 16 Oakland A's on May 1, then 14 Twins on May 5, for a total of 30 in two games, followed by ten versus Baltimore for a total of 40 in three games. Then he would strike out 40 in three consecutive starts in July, including 11 Twins July 1, 14 Angels July 6, 15 A's July 12. There's something about the green and gold of Charley Finley's A's that brought out some of Sam's best games over the years. What an Irishman!

Tiant's career-best year would be 1968, with 21 wins, 9 losses, 9.2 strikeouts and 2.5 BB/9 innings, with a league-leading ERA of 1.60 (the lowest since Walter Johnson in 1919), 19 complete games and 9 shutouts. He threw four consecutive shutouts (41 innings) in the spring, one short of setting the AL record set 98 years previous. His 5.295 hits/9 innings was a new major-league record, and remains second only to Nolan Ryan's 5.261 of 1972.78[79] He struck out 19 Twins in a 1–0 victory on July 3 in ten innings. In that game, he had 16 strikeouts after nine innings, then struck out the side in the 10th, with battery mate Joe Azcue singling in the winning run in the bottom of the inning. The game lowered his ERA to a microscopic 1.11 at the time. He pitched the second one-hitter of his career Sept. 25 in New York, striking out 11, with the Mick singling to center in the first inning. His performance earned him a spot on the '68 All-Star team.

Sam and Looie once again each both struck out over 1 batter/inning, the first and only duo in history, with a reasonable number of innings pitched, to do that twice. No two teammates have duplicated that feat since. In '68, Sonny would go 10–12, but with a 2.38 ERA, with 6.4 Ks, 3.8 BB, and 6.3 hits per nine innings. Great stats, with little to show for it in wins compared to his 16–8 record in both '65 and '66. Sonny threw a one-hitter on May 19, with Curt Bleffary getting the only hit, a double to left-center.

Steve Hargan, who had shown yearly improvement as the fourth starter, developed arm trouble himself, and ballooned up to a 4.15 ERA, winning eight, losing 15, striking out 78. Stan Williams would step in and start 24 games and strike out 147 (6.8/9 innings). Of interest, Stan Williams may be considered the one pitcher to pitch on the top strikeout staff in the history of both the American and National Leagues, having struck out 7.7/9 innings alongside Koufax and Drysdale when they were the first staff to strike out 1100 in '60 and '61.

The staff would lead the league in lowest ERA (2.66), hits/9 innings (6.7), and fewest home runs/9 innings (0.6), but be tied at eighth for most BB/9 innings (3.3). In addition to leading the league again in strikeouts with 1157 total (32 short of another all-time high) and 7.1/9 innings, they were the first staff in history to strike out more batters than hits allowed. They were first in shutouts and fewest hits allowed, second in ERA, and fourth in complete games, and second in saves. The team had four starters in the top 17 strikeout pitchers in the AL.

The '68 Big Three set several records that still stand: fewest hits/9 innings by three starters on the same team: 5.83. In addition, the Big Three would strike out 693 batters in '68, more than any other AL trio in history. The pennant-winning Tigers' Mickey Lolich, Denny McLain, and Earl Wilson fanned 645 that same year. No other group of three starters has ever struck out more batters in a single season in modern history than did the Tribe's Big Three. By comparison, during the subsequent single-season record-breaking years of the Mariners (1997), the Indians (2000), and the Yankees (2001), their top starters struck out far fewer hitters. Seattle would break the Tribe's season staff record with 1207 strikeouts, 18 more than the Tribe's top season. Their top three starters (Randy Johnson, Jeff Fassero, and Jamie Moyer) would fan 593. In 2000, Cleveland would strike out a record 1213 batters. Their three top starters (Bartolo Colon, Dave Burba, and Chuck Finley) struck out 581 batters. In 2001, the Yankees' Roger Clemens, Mike Mussina, and Andy Pettitte struck out 631 on their way to the new all-time high of 1266. In the post-steroid era, the Tampa Bay Devils struck out 1194, in 2007, five more than the 1964–68 staff's top season mark. Their top three starters, Scott Kazmir, James Shields, and Edwin Jackson, struck out 551 batters.

### Cleveland Pitching Staff Statistics 1968

| 1968 | IP | GS | ERA | K | K/9 | BB/9 | HR/9 | CG | SO |
|---|---|---|---|---|---|---|---|---|---|
| McDowell | 269 | 37 | 1.81 | 283 (1) | 9.5 (1) | 3.7 (30) | 0.4 (2) | 11 (9) | 3 (13) |
| Tiant | 258.1 | 32 | 1.60 | 264 (3) | 9.2 (2) | 2.5 (14) | 0.6 (11) | 19 (2) | 9 (1) |
| Williams | 194.1 | 24 | 2.5 | 147 (16) | 6.8 (9) | 2.4 (12) | 0.6 (11) | 6 (29) | 2 (18) |
| Siebert | 206 | 30 | 2.97 | 146 (17) | 6.4 (16) | 3.8 (31) | 0.5 (6) | 8 (21) | 4 (9) |
| Paul | 91.2 | 7 | 3.93 | 87 | 8.5 | 3.4 | 1.1 | 0 | 0 |
| Hargan | 158.1 | 27 | 4.15 | 78 | 4.4 | 4.6 | 0.6 | 4 | 2 |
| Romo | 83.1 | 1 | 1.62 | 54 | 5.8 | 3.5 | 0.5 | 0 | 0 |
| Fisher | 94.2 | 0 | 2.85 | 42 | 4.0 | 1.6 | 0.8 | 0 | 0 |
| Pina | 31.1 | 3 | 1.72 | 24 | 6.9 | 4.3 | 0.0 | 0 | 0 |
| Kurtz | 38 | 0 | 5.21 | 16 | 3.8 | 3.6 | 0.5 | 0 | 0 |
| Gardner | 2.2 | 0 | 6.75 | 6 | 20.3 | 6.8 | 0.0 | 0 | 0 |
| Rohr | 18.1 | 0 | 6.87 | 5 | 2.5 | 4.9 | 2.5 | 0 | 0 |
| Sutherland | 3.1 | 0 | 8.10 | 2 | 5.4 | 10.8 | 9.0 | 0 | 0 |
| Gramley | 3.1 | 0 | 2.70 | 1 | 2.7 | 5.4 | 0.0 | 0 | 0 |
| Smith | 5 | 0 | 0.00 | 1 | 1.8 | 1.8 | 0.0 | 0 | 0 |
| Bailey | 5 | 1 | 3.60 | 1 | 1.8 | 3.6 | 1.8 | 0 | 0 |
| Hedlund | 1.2 | 0 | 10.8 | 0 | 0 | 10.8 | 0.0 | 0 | 0 |
| Team Total | 1462 | 162 | 2.66 (2) | 1157 | 7.1 (1) | 3.3(8) | 0.6 (1) | 48(4) | 20(1) |

Innings pitched, strikeouts, strikeouts/9 innings, complete games, and shutouts for the 1968 Staff. IP: Innings pitched; K: Strikeouts; ERA: Earned run average; CG: Complete Games; SO: Shutouts. Individual K, BB, HR / 9 innings league rank (parentheses) based on minimum of 1 IP/team game.

Unfortunately, these individual and staff strikeout records that I've recounted did not translate into team wins during 1968 and the previous four years. Why didn't the team win more games with an outstanding strikeout staff? The two single-season strikeout records of '64 and '67 coincided with seventh- and eighth-place finishes for The Tribe.

In 2000, Voros McCracken identified some pitching data that are generally reproducible from year to year, and that translate into individual pitching success. These factors are under control of the pitcher, and are defense-independent factors. Strikeouts, BB, and HR allowed are under the pitcher's control. Once the ball is otherwise put in play, and beyond the pitcher's control, anything can happen.[80] Some of the parameters he emphasized are detailed below: strikeouts, home runs allowed, base on balls given up, hits allowed per 9 innings, and ERA. The figures demonstrate that the Tribe's best pitching years were '65 and '68, where their league ranking averaged 2.4 in these five areas, contributing to fifth- and third-place finishes, respectively. The other three years suggest no direct correlation between these pitching statistics and final finish. After '64, which were partial seasons as starters for the Big Three, the Staff was well above average in all parameters except BB.

### Indians' pitching staff record for years '64-'68

| | 1964 | 1965 | 1966 | 1967 | 1968 |
|---|---|---|---|---|---|
| Strikeouts | 1161 (1) | 1156 (1) | 1111 (1) | 1189 (1) | 1157 (1) |
| Base on Balls/9 Inn. | 3.4 (8) | 3.1 (2 T) | 3.0 (5) | 3.4 (8) | 3.3 (8 T) |
| Home Runs /9 Inn. | 0.9 (5) | 0.7 (2) | 0.8 (3 T) | 0.7 (2 T) | 0.6 (1 T) |
| Hits / 9 Inn. | 8.7 (7) | 7.7 (1) | 7.7 (2) | 7.7 (3 T) | 6.7 (1) |
| ERA | 3.75 (6) | 3.30 (6) | 3.23 (3) | 3.25 (5) | 2.66 (1 T) |
| Finish in AL | 7 | 5 | 5 | 8 | 3 |

The Staff's pitching rankings were generally well above average, except for bases on balls over the period. Their AL finishes were middle of the pack. (AL rank in parentheses.) (T = tie)

It is intuitive that, to achieve team success in terms of wins, good pitching performance needs to be accompanied by adequate offensive production, and satisfactory fielding of balls hit into the field of play. The table below outlines eight major offensive statistics from '64–68 demonstrating the Tribe's AL offensive rank was consistently lower than the pitching ranking, including the best offensive year of 1965, when they finished fifth in the AL pennant race, despite being fourth or higher in 10 of 12 key pitching and batting statistics, as well as being first in fielding percentage. On the other hand, the best finish ('68) was marked by their worst offensive, but best pitching, statistics. They came close in '68, but the lack of power and ability to score runs , in the year of great pitching performances throughout the league, only allowed them to finish third.

**Offensive Statistics 1964–1968**

| | 1964 | 1965 | 1966 | 1967 | 1968 |
|---|---|---|---|---|---|
| 2B | 208 (6) | 198 (6) | 156 (10) | 213 (4) | 210 (2) |
| AB/HR | 34.2 (4) | 35.1 (3) | 35.3 (4) | 41.7 (6) | 72.2 (9) |
| AVE | 247 (7) | .250 (3) | 237 (5) | 235 (6) | 234 (5) |
| HR | 164 (4) | 156 (3) | 155 (4) | 131 (4) | 75 (9) |
| OBP | 312 (7) | 315 (4) | 297 (8) | 293 (8) | 293 (6) |
| OPS | 693 (6) | 695 (3) | 657 (6) | 652 (5) | 620 (7) |
| R | 689 (4) | 663 (4) | 574 (8) | 599 (6) | 516 (8) |
| Strikeouts | 1063 (9) | 857 (1) | 914 (4) | 984 (3) | 858 (2) |
| Field Ave. | 981 (4) | 981 (1) | 977 (8) | 981 (2) | 979 (4) |
| Finish in AL | 7 | 5 | 5 | 8 | 3 |

Seven key offensive statistics, fielding average, and AL finish for '64–'68 Indians. Their poor finishes are generally parallel to a low on-base percentage (League rank in parentheses).

It is likely that the Staff and Big Three are not better remembered for their accomplishments specifically because the team was not a winning ball club. On the other hand, one might argue that the memory of Nolan Ryan hasn't been diminished, despite the fact he never won a Cy Young award, and that his personal winning percentage was only .520, barely higher than McDowell's. The longevity of his career and total numbers of strikeouts certainly dictates his place in history. In addition, it became easier to ultimately dismiss the Staff when their individual and composite records were eventually broken by others near the turn of the century, in another era.

But just as Ruth, Maris, and Aaron maintain a revered position in baseball circles for their prior-day season and career home-run-hitting accomplishments, perhaps the Big Three should be regarded in a similar light as well for their strikeout dominance from 1964 to 1968, the last year the Big Three was together and leading the Indians to new strikeout records.

# Chapter 21—The Seasons: 1964–1968

Appendix 3 lists the numerous records the Tribe Staff set, many of which persist to this day. The Tribe's five-year league-leading strikeout average of 1155, the four-year ('65 –'68) league-leading average of 1153, and the three-year ('66–'68) league-leading average of 1152 remain records, and all were achieved averaging over a record 7.0 strikeouts/9 innings.

The California Angels would eventually lead the league in strikeouts eight consecutive years, from '72–79, but average only 955/ year, and 5.9/9 innings in doing so! Where superb performance might be judged by comparison to performance by the rest of the AL teams, the Staff's average of 1155 was significantly higher than the average of 953 for the remainder of AL teams over that five-year period.

If we compare the Tribe's staff's five-year record compared to the records of the four teams that broke their single-season record of 1189 (Seattle with 1207 in 1997, Cleveland with 1213 in 2000, New York with 1266 in 2001, and Tampa Bay with 1184 in 2007), the Staff struck out 202 more batters than the league average, a 21.2% difference. Those four clubs also struck out 202 more batters, on average, than the rest of the AL, a 19.8% difference, indicating the staff was more dominant, on average, in comparison to the rest of the league in '64–68 than were subsequent staffs in their single record-breaking years.

Only five staffs have averaged more strike outs/9 innings over five seasons than the Tribe's 7.04: Boston '99–03 (7.2), Seattle '94–'98 (7.12), Anaheim '04–08 (7.1), Cleveland '98–02 (7.06), and New York '99–03 (7.06). Perhaps superiority should not be based on raw numbers of strikeouts or strikeouts/9 innings alone, but rather upon relative numbers compared to strikeouts in the rest of the league. A "highest" number means less if all the league's teams are performing at a high level as well, with a smaller difference from the highest to the average. For teams with seven or more average strikeouts/9 innings, the Tribe is the only staff in history to average more than one strikeout per inning greater than the league average for any consecutive five-year period. And, the difference between the Tribe's league-comparison and the other six staffs' is highly significant. Their differential is 11.5% higher than the next highest staff, the Red Sox of '99–'03. When we consider that all the other teams' results were obtained over 30 years later, the feat becomes all the more remarkable, all other contributing factors, to be discussed in Chapters 22 and 23, notwithstanding.

The '64–68 Indians were the only team to average greater than 1 strikeout/9 innings greater than the league average for 5 years, for teams striking out greater than 7 batters / 9 innings over the same period.

| | Difference from League Ave. | SO/9 Inn | % Difference from League |
|---|---|---|---|
| Cleveland 64–68 | 1.02 | 7.04 | 14.5 |
| Boston 99–03 | 0.94 | 7.2 | 13.0 |
| Seattle 94–98 | 0.88 | 7.12 | 12.3 |
| New York 99–03 | 0.8 | 7.06 | 11.3 |
| Cleveland 98–02 | 0.74 | 7.06 | 10.4 |
| Anaheim 04–08 | 0.66 | 7.1 | 9.3 |
| Boston 05–09 | 0.54 | 7.0 | 7.7 |

Sam, Sonny, and Luis were the only three pitchers to be with the Tribe for all five of the '64–68 seasons. They would average together 582 strikeouts per year over that period, with Sam averaging 249, Luis 177, and Sonny 156. From '64–'68, The Big Three averaged 8.44 strikeouts/9 innings, an all-time record.

They also allowed only 3.42 BBs, and 6.83 hits per 9 innings. No AL trio playing together five consecutive years matches the Big Three in career strikeouts per nine innings: 7.13. In career strikeouts/9 innings for non-relievers pitching ten years or more, McDowell is 8$^{th}$ (8.86), Siebert 119$^{th}$ (6.32) and Tiant 128$^{th}$ (6.24). In hits/ innings, McDowell is 10$^{th}$ (7.03), Tiant 101$^{st}$ (7.93), Siebert 119$^{th}$ (8.03). The three allowed 0.69 HR/9 innings pitched, when the league average was 0.92 from 1964-2008.

To get some additional legitimate comparison of the records of the Tribe's staff vs. the staffs that later broke their records, we can compare the records of the Big Three versus the others' top starters. The top three starters on those staffs averaged only 32 appearances over their record-setting seasons, all starts except for one appearance in relief. They averaged 209 innings, and 196 strikeouts, or 8.4 strikeouts per nine innings. In addition, they averaged .eight HR/9 innings. If we examine the average for the Tribe's Big Three for their four consecutive complete seasons of '65–68, we find the Big Three had more average appearances, starting only 2.3 fewer games on average, but pitching 5.2 more innings, on average. They struck out more batters, had a similar strikeout/9 inning ratio, and gave up fewer HRs. The Big Three's average season compared favorably to best of other staffs.

**Individual and average statistics for the top three starters of staffs that set the AL record for strikeouts that broke the Tribe's record of 1967.**

| | G | GS | IP | SO | SO/9 | HR/9 |
|---|---|---|---|---|---|---|
| Johnson (Sea '97) | 30 | 29 | 213 | 291 | 12.3 | 0.8 |
| Fassaro (Sea '97) | 35 | 35 | 234.1 | 189 | 7.3 | 0.8 |
| Moyer (Sea '97) | 30 | 30 | 188.2 | 113 | 5.4 | 1 |
| Finley (Cle '00) | 34 | 34 | 218 | 189 | 7.8 | 0.9 |
| Burba (Cle '00) | 32 | 32 | 191.1 | 180 | 8.5 | 0.9 |
| Colon ('00) | 30 | 30 | 188 | 212 | 10.1 | 1 |
| Mussina (NYY '01) | 34 | 34 | 228 | 214 | 8.4 | 0.8 |
| Clemens (NYY '01) | 33 | 33 | 220.1 | 213 | 8.7 | 0.8 |
| Pettitte (NYY '01) | 31 | 31 | 200.2 | 164 | 7.4 | 0.6 |
| Average | 32.1 | 32.0 | 209.0 | 196.1 | 8.4 | 0.8 |

If we look at the Big Three's stats for the '64 season, where they were together only after July 19, and where Siebert and Tiant were starters only in the second half of the season, as a group they averaged 7.8 strikeouts/9 innings in 385.8 innings as starters, and 8.2 in 160.4 innings of relief. The strikeouts as starters would represent the highest seasonal numbers recorded.

## Big Three Statistics, 1965–1968

| | G | GS | IP | SO | SO/9 | HR/9 |
|---|---|---|---|---|---|---|
| McDowell '65 | 42 | 35 | 273 | 325 | 10.7 | 0.3 |
| Siebert '65 | 39 | 27 | 188.2 | 191 | 9.1 | 0.7 |
| Tiant '65 | 41 | 30 | 196.1 | 152 | 7 | 0.9 |
| McDowell '66 | 35 | 28 | 194 | 225 | 10.4 | 0.6 |
| Siebert '66 | 34 | 32 | 241 | 163 | 6.1 | 0.9 |
| Tiant '66 | 46 | 16 | 155 | 145 | 8.4 | 0.9 |
| McDowell '67 | 37 | 37 | 236.1 | 236 | 9 | 0.8 |
| Siebert '67 | 34 | 26 | 185.1 | 136 | 6.6 | 0.8 |
| Tiant '67 | 33 | 29 | 213.2 | 219 | 9.2 | 1 |
| McDowell '68 | 38 | 37 | 269 | 283 | 9.5 | 0.4 |
| Siebert '68 | 31 | 30 | 206 | 146 | 6.4 | 0.5 |
| Tiant '68 | 34 | 32 | 258.1 | 264 | 9.2 | 0.6 |
| Average | 37.3 | 29.7 | 214.2 | 201.9 | 8.4 | 0.7 |

Individual and average statistics for the Big Three in their 4 complete seasons (excluding 1964), including the record breaking season of 1967.

McDowell and Siebert were the first duo to strike out 9 batters/9 innings, in 1965 No other duo has struck out 9 batters/9 innings twice as did McDowell and Tiant in '67 and '68. No other duo would strike out 9 batters/9 innings until Nolan Ryan and Bobby Witt in 1990. Martinez and Nomo would do it in 2001, with Martinez pitching only 116 innings, however.

The Big Three averaged 8.94 strikeouts/9 innings in 1965 (McDowell 10.7, Siebert 9.1, Tiant 7.0). No AL trio with more than 125 innings pitched or more than 20 starts has struck out more.

**Top Strikeout Starting Trios AL History (minimum 125 Innings, 15 Starts)**

| Year | Pitchers (Strikeouts/9 Innings) | Average Strikeouts/9 Innings |
|---|---|---|
| 1964 | McDowell (9.2), Siebert (8.3), Tiant (7.4) | 8.3 |
| 1965 | McDowell (10.7), Siebert (9.1), Tiant (7.0) | 8.9 |
| 1966 | McDowell (10.4), Tiant (8.4), Siebert (6.1) | 8.3 |
| 1967 | Tiant (9.3), McDowell (9), Siebert (6.6) | 8.3 |
| 1968 | McDowell (9.5), Tiant (9.2), Siebert (6.4) | 8.4 |
| 1972 | Ryan (10.4), Messersmith (7.5), May (7.4) | 8.4 |
| 1973 | Ryan (10.6), Singer (6.9), May (6.5) | 8.0 |
| 1987 | Higueroa (8.3), Bosio (7.9), Nieves (7.5) | 7.9 |
| 1990 | Ryan (10.2), Witt (9.0), Hough (4.7) | 7.9 |
| 1997 | Johnson (12.3), Fassaro (7.3), Moyer (5.4) | 8.3 |
| 2000 | Colon (10.1), Burba (8.5), Finley (7.8) | 8.80 |
| 2001 | Clemmens (8.7), Mussina (8.4), Lilly (8.4) | 8.5 |
| 2001 | Nomo (10.0), Wakefield (7.9), Cone (7.6) | 8.83 |
| 2007 | Kazmir (10.4), Shields (7.7), Jackson (7.2) | 8.4 |

The Big Three are also the top teammate trio when their career SWHIP (which considers strikeouts, walks, hits, hit batters per 9 innings) for both leagues are analyzed. Where SWHIP = (walks + hits + hit batters – strikeouts/innings pitched), Sam is 15th on the list (0.347), Luis is 56th (0.520) and Sonny is 61st (0.536). They are the highest ranking three teammates of any duration on the list, which includes some current pitchers as well as hurlers from both leagues, insofar as trades and free-agency moves have currently clouded the distinction of designating many pitchers as AL or NL pitchers.[81]

The numbers and comparisons I've just put forward seem to speak for themselves. The Tribe's staff and the Big Three are in a class by themselves, objectively, setting numerous records during those years, some of which still stand (Appendix 3). But can or should they be judged on a different basis than staffs that preceded or followed them? The following chapters will further address that question.

# Chapter 22—End of the Era (?)

The next year, 1969, brought Woodstock, the Surgeon General's warning label on cigarette packaging, Neil Armstrong and Apollo 11 landing on the moon, Bobby Kennedy's assassination, and the official 100th Anniversary of Major League Baseball.

That year also brought major changes in rules designed to diminish the impact of pitching. This was due to the pitching dominance throughout baseball in '68, when the lowest batting average in major league history (.237) was reached, and when pitchers' ERAs also hit new lows. Carl Yastrzemski led the AL in batting average at .301. The season came to be known as the "Year of the Pitcher." The maxim that "good pitching beats good hitting" was never truer.

But the pitching dominance was not based on power pitching and increased strikeouts. Of note, strikeouts/9 innings had already been trending downward league-wide in the five years prior to 1969 (see chart next page), despite the Tribe's uptrend with record-setting numbers, after a steady increase in the post-war years. If pitchers' strikeouts are the measure, it would be erroneous to suggest the larger strike zone introduced in 1963 was fully accomplishing the original intent of its proponents. The change was actually failing to help the other nine AL pitching staffs in relation to strikeouts, on average.

The Tribe had clearly been the tail wagging the strikeout dog before the 1969 shrinking. Owners experimented with a new, livelier baseball in spring training in 1969. Five teams moved their fences in to promote homerun production. More importantly, major league baseball responded and not only lowered the pitching mound from 15 inches (the maximum height since 1903), but also shrunk the strike zone for the 1969 season.[82] Before the change, mound heights were said to vary throughout baseball, rumored as high as 25 inches in Dodger Stadium.

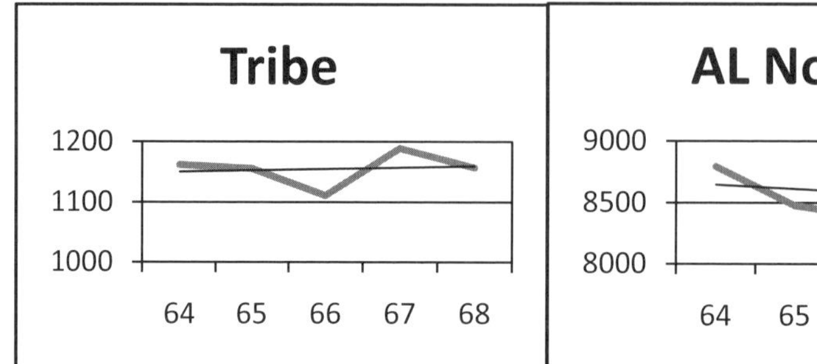


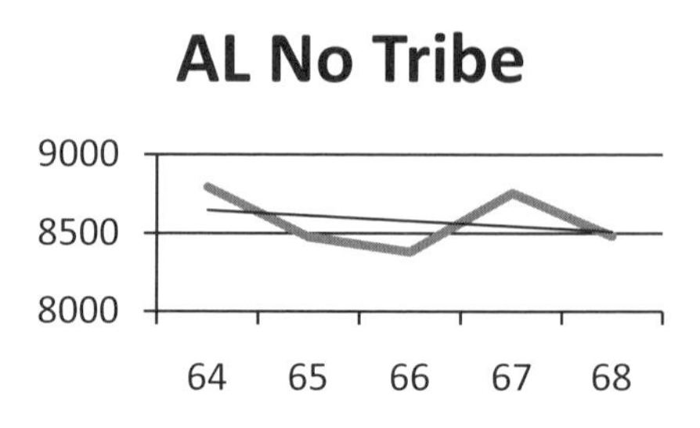


Left: Graph of total strikeouts for the remaining 9 AL staffs for the same time period, excluding the Indians, with a downward trendline. Right:. Graph of Tribe strikeouts '64–68 with upward trendline.

The exact height of the mound in Cleveland is not known, and there is some sentiment the Indians built their mound higher than the rules allowed from the 1940s onward.[83] The Indians' groundskeepers, Emil Bossard and his sons Harold and Marshall, had a reputation for "cheating" by doctoring ballfields to gain advantage for the home team, or to reduce advantage for visitors. They were known to increase the slope of the infield foul lines toward foul territory when a good bunting team or player was coming to town, so that his bunts might have a greater tendency to roll foul. Conversely, they were said to decrease that slope when the Tribe had a particularly adept bunters. It was rumored the Bossards would hose down the infield when sinker ball pitchers were starting, so as to slow down ground balls and make them more playable. They would shorten the infield grass, or allow it to lengthen, to suit the team's purpose. It was said they wet down the base paths near first base when a top base stealer would be visiting, so as to slow down his first steps as if he were running in quicksand. Despite these well-publicized methods of doctoring the field, elevating the pitching mound was not a generally well-publicized accusation. The Bossards acknowledged being at the maximum allowed.[84]

In addition to variable height, mounds may have greater or lesser slopes, despite their height. The fact is, with 10 or 12 pitchers on a team, there would be just as many preferences for height, slope, and firmness, and dissatisfaction with these characteristics would certainly have generated more complaints than I ever heard. In discussing this mound height issue with my engineer father-in-law, Chester, he immediately asked me, "What about a sidearmer, who throws from down below the belt line, or a submariner whose knuckles sometimes come perilously close to scraping the mound on delivery?" Does he benefit from a mound height of 15 inches or one of 10 inches? In reality, the Phillies did keep their mound low pre-'69 because their staff was mostly sidearm and three-quarter motion pitchers.[85] I have a picture of sidearmer Dean Chance delivering from a low mound in 1967, before the official league-wide reduction of mound height. It made me wonder if the '57 and '58 Washington Senators, who had three submarine-sidearmers (Ted Abernathy, Tex Clevenger, and Dick Hyde) clandestinely lower their mound height below regulation, to take advantage of the unorthodox deliveries. Sam's direct overhand delivery lent itself to success with a high mound, as opposed to Abbey's. I guess the mound height issue could be a relative one!

I have analyzed a number of photographs of the pitcher's mound at Cleveland Municipal Stadium from the '64–'68 period. A mound can be made to look taller than it is, but not shorter, if the photographer's vantage point is above ground level. If he is at ground level, the mound could appear shorter then it is, but not taller. And mound height alone may be deceptive—well within regulation height at the mound itself—but it must be compared to the level of home plate, not just the edge of the mound itself. Entire infields may have an elevation, or a "crown," designed to improve field drainage, that might secondarily elevate the mound in relation to home plate.

My estimates are based on three photos from belt-buckle level or below, and I believe the mound in Cleveland was definitely not more than 15 inches high, and probably at the maximum allowed. Admittedly, the photos I analyzed do not allow adjustment for the crown effect, wherein the effective height of the mound compared to home plate could be greater. I recently asked Vern Fuller what he thought of the height of the mound at Municipal Stadium, and he said he thought it was high, but many mounds were high around the league. He did single out the Angels' Chavez Ravine as particularly high, however.

Under the new rule, the mound could be no taller than ten inches. The strike zone was shrunk to its pre-1963 dimensions, in effect trying to recreate the pre-1963 live-ball era that prompted shrinking of the strike zone in the first place. As

George Will has said, "Baseball knows on which side its bread is buttered—the side of offense."[86]

It could be argued that the Tribe's pitchers were the last to benefit from any strikeout advantage afforded by a higher mound and larger strike zone (where they averaged almost three Ks/9 innings more than the league average) and that subsequently other staffs might have broken the Tribe's records earlier than 1997, had the former had a similar benefit.

The mound and strike zone changes of 1969 did correspond to a lower strikeout number for the Big Three over time, although they continued to trend well above the league average for the remainder of their AL careers. Whereas the average AL strikeout/9 innings up until 1973—the last year at least two of the three pitched in the AL simultaneously—was 5.7, the Big Three's average was: McDowell 9.3, Tiant 7.2, and Siebert 6.6. The Big Three failed to be at or above the AL average only twice (Looie in '70 and Sonny in '71) in these 28 pitcher-seasons. It is not unexpected that players will exhibit a steady increase in performance parameters early in their careers, followed by a peak in their fifth year in the majors at about age 27, and then a rapid decline after age 30 until they are no longer capable of competing at the major league level.[87] [88] Any decrease in strikeouts and performance the Big Three were experiencing may have been merely a general manifestation of a typical career pattern, as opposed to any negative effect elicited by changes in the rules of the game.

Contrary to supposition that these rule changes could have only negative effects for pitchers, one might also consider that McDowell's BB and HR/9 innings dropped to the lowest levels of his entire career the season after the mound was lowered and the strike zone was contracted in 1969. With such devastating stuff, it is entirely possible that a lower mound might have improved his sometimes erratic control early in his career, thereby decreasing his BB and even increasing his strikeouts, improving his overall performance secondarily. Under that circumstance, his entire career might have taken a different turn, and some of the psychological problems he battled may never have come to the foreground.

In addition, following these rule changes Sonny Siebert's SO/9 innings were the third-highest of his career in '69. A number of factors have been suggested as responsible for Tiant's poor performance in '69, including difficulty accommodating to the new mound height and strike zone.

**Big Three Statistics, 1965-1968**

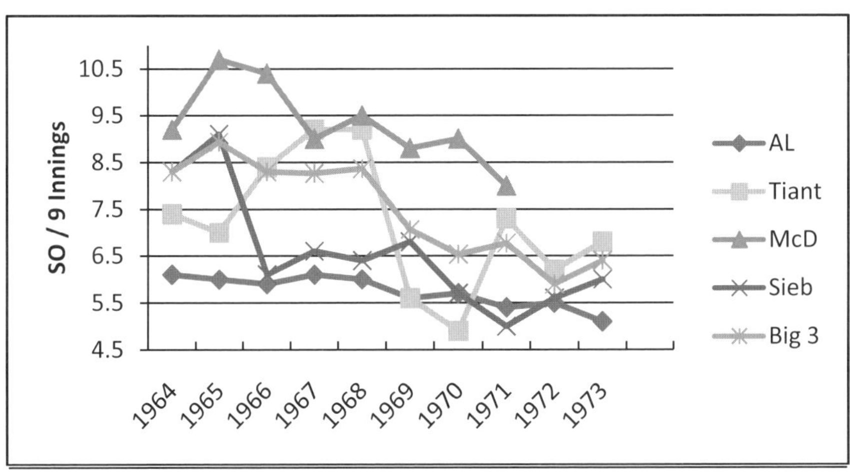


Strikeouts/ 9 innings for the Big Three individually, as a group, vs. AL average. The Big Three continued above the AL average after the mound was lowered, and the strike zone contracted, for the'69 season.

The end of the Tribe's staff's Record Strikeout Era went generally unnoticed, triggered by Sieb's trade to Boston in April, 1969, along with Joe Azcue. Sonny would average 15 wins and nine losses for the next three years, and be an All Star again in '71. His career would last 12 years prior to his retiring in '75, at age 39, having won 140 (one fewer than McDowell), losing 114, with a career ERA 3.21, 0.70 K/inning, 0.32 BB/inning. Had he not started his pitching career late, we can only guess what he might have accomplished.

Tiant's performance fell off badly to 9–20 in '69. There's considerable opinion that it was in great part due to injuries. After his phenomenal season in '68, he skipped winter ball for the first time, then at the start of the next season, he developed arm soreness that supposedly took two years to improve. He still started 37 games and pitched 249 innings in 1969. His BB/9 innings ballooned up to 4.7, leading the league in BB and HR allowed, while his strikeout/9 innings dropped almost 40% to 5.6, suggesting that if he weren't injured, he certainly was having trouble accommodating to the new mound height and a tightened strike zone. It's difficult to believe the man who could throw pitches from any angle couldn't adjust. He was subsequently traded to the Twins.

But his career would be resurrected with the '72–'78 Red Sox, where he would win 122 and lose 81. Luis would have a 19-year career, winning 229, losing 172, with 187 complete games, striking out 0.69 and walking 0.32 batters per inning. He threw 49 shutouts, and is tied for 21st on the all time list with three Hall of Famers: Don Drysdale, Fergie Jenkins, and his first major league pitching coach, Early Wynn. El Tiante's career stats are comparable to a number of Hall of Famers, including Catfish Hunter's and Don Drysdale's. Ironically, he waits with Tommy John, with whom he traded roster spots in '64, for a call from the Hall's Veterans' Committee.

McDowell remained an enigma, covered in a puzzle, wrapped in a question mark. He could bring it: pitcher's mound smoke signaled Sam's pitching today. Bill James named Sam the hardest-throwing pitcher of the 60s.[89] The saga of Sudden Sam has been well-synopsized by Terry Pluto, with disclosure and analysis of Sam's idiosyncrasies, contradictions, and confabulations.[90]

Sam's inestimable talent may have been short-circuited by his need to be more than just a blazing fastball pitcher, by the need to work those change-up curve balls into his pitch rotation. It remains hard to believe that someone as talented, with the 100 mph fastball and devastating curve ball, of whom so much was anticipated, who was in the major leagues by age 20, would win less than 10 games per year. To be sure, his talent may have been wasted on a light-hitting team, with spotty relief pitching from 1965–67.

Therein lay Sam's problem: his personal ongoing inner conflict for failure to live up to expectation, which contributed greatly to an off-the-field problem with alcohol. Years later Sam admitted to developing an alcohol addiction early in his career, which by his own admission affected his performance. It becomes more amazing that he accomplished what he did with excessive use of a performance-diminishing substance.

A six-time All Star, Sudden Sam would have a 15-year career, striking out 0.98 but walking 0.53 batters per inning, winning 141 games, losing 134 (winning pct. 513) , allowing 0.78 hits/innings pitched, with a career ERA of 3.17. He would lead the league in strikeouts five times, the major-league strikeouts/9 innings list six times and be second twice. He is still tenth on the major league strikeout/9 inning list at 8.86, and tenth in fewest hits/9 innings at 7.03. He would throw two more one-hitters in his career. He would also lead the league in BB five times, and wild pitches three times. He was traded to the Giants after the '71 season for Gaylord Perry.

By Sam's own admission, his addiction derailed a career that "should have" ended in the Hall of Fame. To his great credit, Sudden Sam went on to earn degrees in psychology and addiction, and became a sports addiction counselor after retiring.

In Sonny's absence, the staff dropped to second place in strikeouts in '69 with 1000, 32 fewer than the Tigers' 1032. The Indians would lead the AL again in '70, with 1076 and 6.7/9 innings. In essence, they were those 32 Ks short of matching the Angels' record of leading the league eight consecutive years from 1972–79. The Tribe would strike out 1000 or more batters from '63–70, or eight consecutive years. California would do so only twice in their eight league-leading years. Only the Yankees ('96–04) and Oakland ('01–09) have struck out 1000 each for nine consecutive years, but while leading the league only once over the nine-year periods.

# Chapter 23—Between the Eras

In arguing the case for the Tribe's staff's position as the top strikeout staff in AL history, and to contrast the Tribe's strikeout performance to latter-day staffs and statistics, a number comparisons must be drawn. The Tribe's staff accomplished their records at a time when batters tried their best to avoid strikeouts. Today, there is no stigma to the strikeout. We must also consider the climate in which the strikeout numbers in both eras were attained. Preexisting trends in strikeout occurrence must be examined to understand the evolutionary process of the Tribe's performance in comparison to what had come before. Ongoing trends demonstrated below show that there had been a steady increase in strikeouts prior to any changes in baseball of the early 60s.

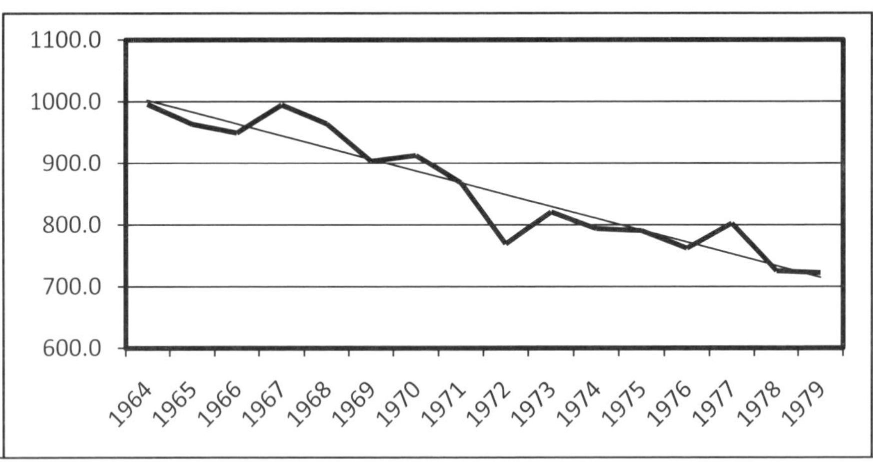


Average team strikeouts, 1964-79. An AL-wide increase in strikeouts from 1946-1963 became a decrease in strikeouts beginning in 1964, continuing through not only the change in the strike zone and mound height in '69, but also the introduction of the DH in '73, through 1979.

Clearly, the trends for strikeouts over the years, and the external factors that might have impacted those numbers and trends subsequently will have to be analyzed here, as they have been in other presentations elsewhere.

Roger Angel discussed some of the factors as early as 1978, but did not focus on strikeouts themselves, without benefit of foresight and comparison to events to come.[91] Comparing strikeout data to not only other pitching performance parameters but also contemporaneous and historical hitting parameters will give insight into external global trends that may not be intuitive. Some of these factors are:

1. Expansion in the AL from 8 to 10 teams in 1961, from 10 teams to 12 teams in 1969, and from 12 to 14 in 1977
2. Effect of strike zone and mound-height rule changes on pitching statistics
3. The designated hitter
4. Interleague play
5. Ballpark effects
6. Relief pitching effects
7. Base on balls and pitcher control
8. Day/night games, doubleheaders, Astroturf
9. Discrepancy between a High-SO Low-HR ('64 –68) , and High-SO High-HR period ('94-04)
10. Effects of performance-enhancing drugs.

Could dilution of hitting talent created with two new expansion teams added in 1961 artificially inflate the number of strikeouts by the Tribe staff? The chart on the last page demonstrates a slight increase in strikeouts, and a plateau in HR, following expansion in '61. More strikeouts might be explained by dilution of hitting talent. But the increase was barely above the preexisting upward trend. On the other hand, any increase in HRs might be explained by the dilution of pitching talent in the expansion. A small percentage increase in HRs might be seen if previous hitters on the eight clubs then had a small number of games against pitchers of lesser talent who might otherwise not be in the majors. No early increase in HRs is identified, however.

But if a slight increase in strikeouts and HRs are attributed to expansion from eight to ten teams with an accompanying dilution in talent, the effect was to inflate the Tribe's strikeout numbers in relation to previous staffs, with no direct bearing on comparison to later staffs also diluted by expansion effects. By the same rationale, expansion from 10 teams to 12 teams in 1969, and from 12 to 14 in 1977, should have led to a sustained increase in strikeouts as well. At any rate, an increase in Ks, as might have been related to expansion from '61–63, was not seen immediately in either instance, further clouding the effect of expansion on strikeouts.

Dilution of talent theoretically also occurred in the NL one year later in 1962. No effect of expansion on the strikeout data is suggested in the NL statistics. But, in commenting on the effects of expansion in relation to his 1961 season where he led the NL in HR and RBI, Orlando Cepeda recently pointed out it was his greatest season, because there were only eight teams, and each team had four good pitchers, and he faced good pitching every day.

Intuitively, dilution of talent had an effect on quality of the teams and of the game. Yet, in and of itself, it is likely not the explanation for the Tribe's continuous '64–68 five-year strikeout peak while the rest of the AL was experiencing a simultaneous decrease in strikeouts. Bill James calls expansion effects a wash when it comes to increases in offensive production in the 90s, affecting hitters and pitchers equally. It is reasonable to believe it was a wash in the 60s as well, when comparing effects on hitters and pitchers during the same year(s).[92] Yet comparison of the two eras based on expansion and dilution of talent, in its most general terms, can only suggest the latter years may have benefitted numerically by expansion more than the former.

If a larger number of pitchers doing the same job defines dilution of pitching, then it has certainly occurred over the years. The Tribe used 38 pitchers from '64–'68 to set the records I've described. The 2000 Indians and 2001 Yankees used 53 pitchers in just those two record seasons, and the 2009 Indians used 29. But numbers alone do not define quality of performance. There were approximately 100 pitchers in the ten-member AL in '64, compared to approximately 200 pitchers in the latter years. Increase of pitchers does not necessarily mean dilution of talent, however. An increase in numbers of hitters occurring simultaneously might balance effects on home runs or strikeouts.

After the rules changes regarding strike zone and mound height of 1969, the ongoing decline in strikeouts league-wide continued until 1979, as might be expected. The strike zone was sufficiently small that Vern Fuller compared it to "hitting off a tee." Knockdown pitches disappeared, the inside part of the plate was taken away.

The AL had been successful in reversing that inexorable trend of increasing strikeouts from 1948–63. Two years of increasing batting averages and HRs in '69 and '70 were followed by two equivalent declines in '71 and 72, netting essentially no change in major hitting stats four years after the strike zone was enlarged and the mound height was reduced. Reduced? Have mounds remained inviolately ten inches high since 1969? Disputes about mound heights are still raised from time to time. MLB measures mound height in stadiums once per year, and trimming height in some parks has indeed been directed by the league over the years.[93]

An upswing in offense then did finally begin in the AL, and both HR allowed and strikeouts began an upward trend after 1980 until 1987. Both again decreased in parallel until 1992, followed by the final upswing in both strikeouts and HR that carried into the new century. It is difficult to attribute each and every of these reversals and trends to identifiable factors, at least until the final upswing. Postulates of dead balls or live balls have been made, but it's difficult to see how a dead or live-ball affects strikeouts in parallel with HRs. [94]

The following chart illustrates the AL leader in pitching strikeouts (with a focus on the Cleveland peak from '64–68), and the AL average team home run totals since 1960. The Tribe's strikeout peak was associated with a simultaneous decrease in average HR. A negative correlation rate between home runs and contact rate is expected, as has been pointed out.[95] If you don't hit the ball, you can't hit a HR. Of course, strike-zone size effects could account for both observations. But bear in mind the rest the league was undergoing a decrease in strikeouts in the same time.

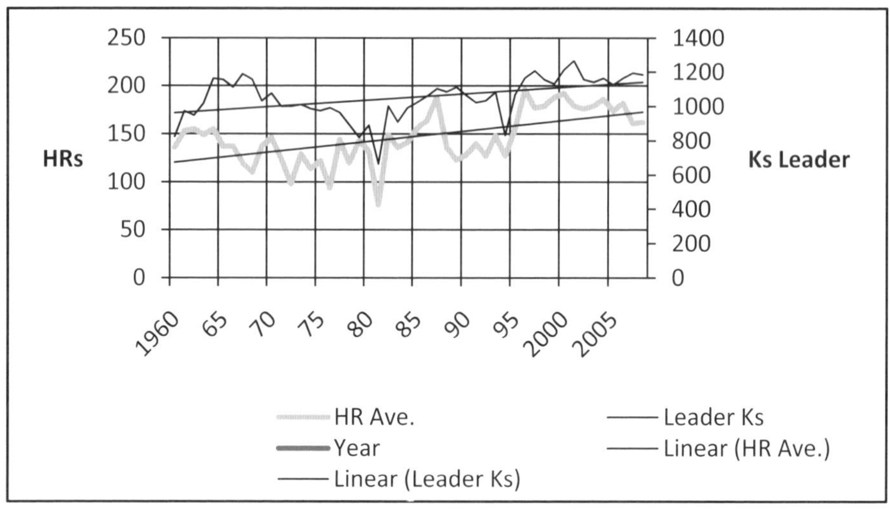


AL Team HR (average) & AL strikeout (K) leader, 1960-2008. Note the increase Ks with decrease HR from '64–'68 (when the Tribe led the league in strikeouts), but new peaks for both from 1997-2004. (1981 and 1995 dips are due to strike-shortened season). The peak strikeout trendline courses at a rate of 2.3 strikeouts per year. (1981 and 1995 dips are due to strike-shortened season).

In addition to a decrease in HR from '64–68, there was a decrease in batting average also, commonly attributed to the larger strike zone as well. The chart shows that batting averages (BA) in both the AL and NL had been declining in the post-war era. The most dramatic decline occurred in the American League between '64–'68, after which an upswing in BA began.

The previously highlighted decrease in HR, with this decrease in BA, seems to indicate that not only can't you hit home runs if you don't make contact, but you can't get base hits, either. The trends for both leagues are generally parallel until 1964, at which time the largest historical difference between the two leagues notably occurred. Not only is it the largest difference, but it's also a reversal of the previous circumstance of the NL lagging the AL in BA. The nadir in AL BA occurred in '68 with the last year of the Tribe's strikeout supremacy. A reversal then occurred in 1973, with the designated hitter, where the AL batting average surpassed the NL, where it has remained since.

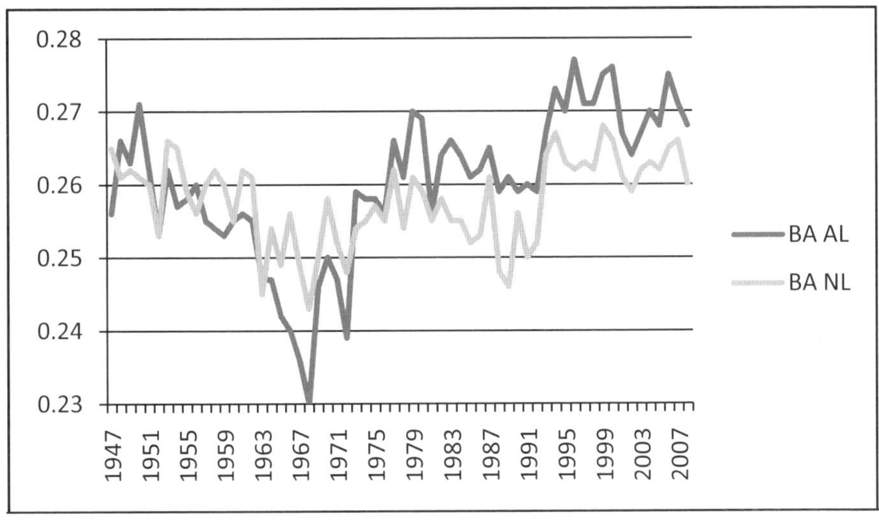


AL and NL batting averages (BA) from 1947-2008. The low point of AL averages in 1968 represents a .013 difference with the NL that year.

What other factors might affect the strikeout rate and HR numbers between the Tribe's record years and the later era of new strikeout records? Use of the designated hitter in the AL began in 1973, not long after the Tribe's staff pitching records. Every trivia buff knows who the first designated hitter in a major league game was, right? Ron Blomberg of the Yankees, on April 6, 1973, of course. It's more than ironic, considering the issue under discussion, that the pitcher who pitched to Blomberg was none other than Luis Tiant. Blomberg walked, had two hits in the game, and didn't strike out.

One might expect the DH rule to decrease strikeouts and increase HR by allowing better hitters into the game, if the designated hitters strike out less than the pitchers did previously. A trend for decrease in strikeouts indeed occurred, but it was statistically no different than a continuation of a downhill trend that had been in place league-wide since 1964. The average HR/9 innings was 1.0 in '65 and 0.8 in '83, with a horizontal saw-tooth line between the two points. From 1983 through 2004, a slight uptrend occurred, though not in direct fashion. The trendline for homeruns/9 innings and strikeouts/9 innings has shown a slight, parallel yearly increase since 1964, but only after reversing downward trends that began prior to the designated hitter and continued for 10 years after the designated hitter was introduced.[96]

To further analyze the effect of the designated hitter, one could compare the AL and NL, where pitchers continued to bat, for possible effects of the designated hitter on home runs and strikeouts. The chart below demonstrates a divergence between the leagues in strikeout/9 innings from post-DH 1973 through 1985, with a lower number in the AL, as might be expected if the designated hitter is striking out less commonly than the pitcher he is replacing. The NL has averaged 0.4 more strikeouts than the AL for the entire DH period since 1973.

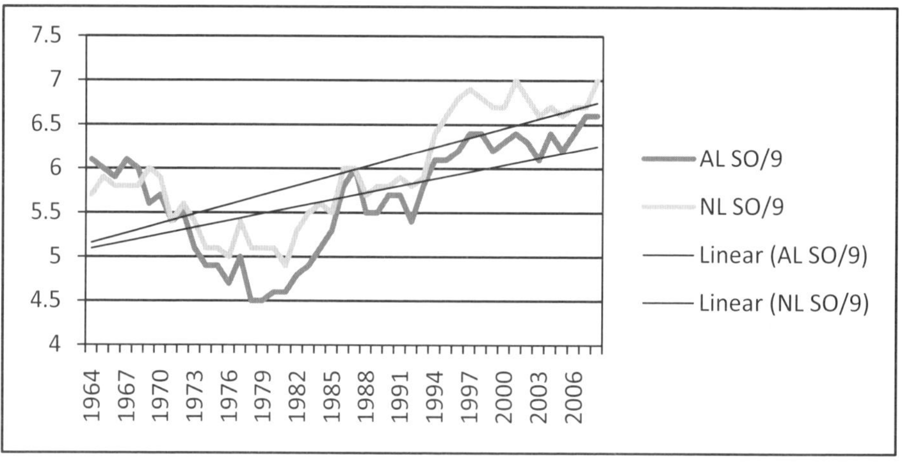


Average strikeout (SO)/ 9 innings from 1964-2008. Strikeout/ 9 innings in the AL decreased after the DH was introduced in 1972, although it had been decreasing prior to that time. It is not clear that use of the DH alone contributed to the decrease.

If we examine the curve prior to 1973 more closely, we find the AL strikeout/9 innings generally lagged the NL curve as well in the entire post-war, pre-1964 era. Any superiority of the NL over the AL post-DH can't easily be ascribed to the DH itself. It may merely be a manifestation of an otherwise inexplicable counter-intuitive historical advantage of the NL over the AL. The only period the American League has superseded the NL is the Big Three Era of '64–68. The Indians and the Big Three led the league with record numbers of strikeouts throughout that period, reversing the long-term trends of NL superiority prior to their time. The Tribe's staff's impact is emphasized by the reversal after their time, in comparison to the effect of any other individual, trio, staff, or external factor on strikeouts in the AL. The same five-year period also coincided with the largest difference in batting averages between the two leagues, as shown below.

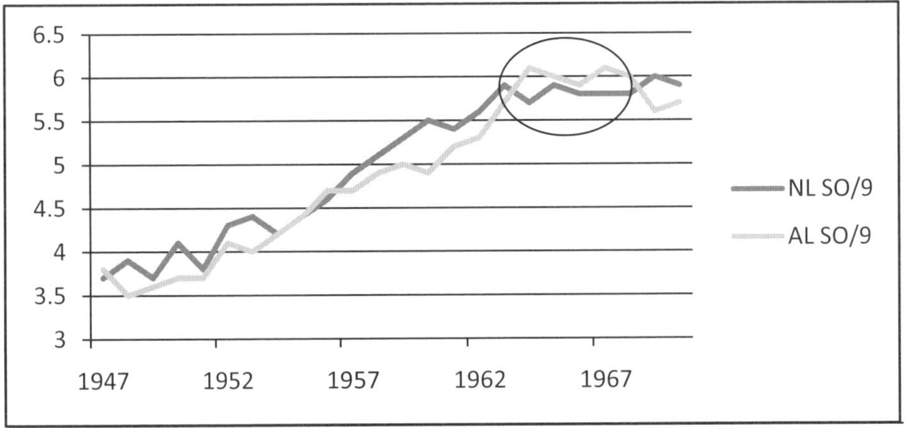


Average strikeout SO/ 9 innings from 1947-1970. The two cross-over points, where AL and NL numbers become reversed, are 1964 and 1969, after Siebert was traded.

The DH was not the only difference between the leagues. The strike zone rules were to be equally applied in both leagues. De facto differences probably continued to exist between the leagues, however. The NL was known as a low-strike league, where low pitches were more likely to be called strikes than in the AL. The traditional explanation has to do with umpires' chest protector differences between the leagues. The NL umpires wore more flexible wrap-around foam protectors under their shirts, allowing them to bend more deeply, even to the point of positioning themselves over either of the catcher's shoulders, and getting a better look at the low pitch. On the other hand, the AL umpires wore stiffer, inflexible exterior protectors, that limited their ability to bend, and dictating they take a higher position above the catcher's head, and thereby not getting the same view of the low pitch as the NL umpires. It is interesting that the largest differences in strikeouts of 0.6 and 0.7/9 innings per season were in 1978 and 1979. When the chest protectors were standardized between the leagues in 1980, with the AL adopting the NL variety, the differences in strikeouts between the leagues began to decrease, with the AL striking out proportionally more batters, until they equalized in 1987. The differences later increased once again, averaging 0.5 or greater from 1995 to 2003.

In discussion of the designated hitter, consideration for interleague play must be taken into account as well. Interleague play has been a reality since mid-summer 1997, the year Seattle broke the Tribe's season strikeout record. If we examine strikeout data from interleague play for the three teams that broke the Tribe's '67 record, the teams (Seattle '97, Cleveland '00, New York '01) played 52 interleague games. There were 333 strikeouts in the 24 AL home-city games, and 415 in the 28 away NL city games. The home and away teams were essentially equal in their strikeouts. The difference of 0.95 more strikeouts per game (or 0.425 per team per game) in NL cities where no DH was used is notable, but not statistically significant. It is unlikely that interleague play has contributed in any meaningful way to differences in numbers of strikeouts between the two leagues in the designated hitter/interleague-play era.

The impact of the designated hitter on differences in pitching strikeouts between leagues or between eras might also be estimated by examining differences in strikeouts between pitchers batting and by designated hitters batting in their place. From 1964 to '66, the Indians staff struck out an average of 1.07 opposing pitchers per game, which does not include pinch hitters batting for pitchers. Designated hitters averaged one strikeout every five at bats, or just under one per game, in 1997, the year Seattle broke the Tribe's single-season strikeout record.

It is also reasonable to argue that strikeouts might increase overall in proportion to the use of relief pitchers, when starters do not necessarily have to "pace" themselves, with strong-armed set-up men and closers available, frequently good strikeout pitchers themselves. It's been suggested pitchers in the 60s could afford to coast sometimes because every team has some weak spots in their batting order, whereas today pitchers must bear down harder because everyone in the batting order can hit it into the seats.[97] If so, more strikeouts yet might have occurred in the 60s if only the starting pitchers had bore down a bit harder, with relief only an arm wag away.

But the trend for fewer complete games has been occurring very slowly over a very long time, decreasing from 40% in 1947 to 3% in 2008, or about 0.6%/year.

Study of the rate of yearly change of CG demonstrates a relatively flat curve, with a -4% average decrease in complete games year-to-year, albeit with occasional large bidirectional spikes from year to year. In addition to the complete game metric, the number of pitchers per game has dramatically increased over the years. The strikeout curve has had large peaks and valleys, but the trendline in the percentage yearly change CG curve does not support the hypothesis that it is a primary determinant in peaks in strikeout occurrences.

A slight flattening of the curve from 1997 to 2008, suggests that the increase was not in any great part due to increase in use of relief pitchers. 1964-'68 actually demonstrated a flattening or slight reversal of the downward trend in CG that had been occurring prior to those years, somewhat comparable to the upward trend in strikeouts the Tribe's staff created.

Pitcher control, as might be measured by BBs or even wild pitches, may have an effect on both strikeouts and HRs. Strike-zone size certainly would impact BB, strikeouts, and HRs. The larger strike zone of '64-'68 should make BBs less likely, strikeouts more likely, probably decreasing HRs. The low peak team average of 3.2 BB/9 innings may have been, at least in part, due to a larger strike zone.[98] But the league average for strikeouts had decreased over the time, with the exception of the Tribe.

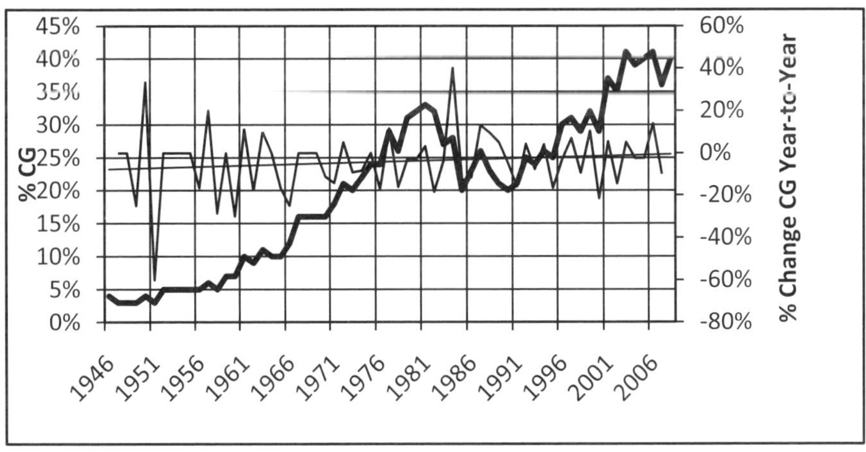

AL Average for % complete games (CG), and % change year-to-year in CG (dash line) from 1948–2008. Solid trendline indicates an average decrease of 4%/yr. in % CG year to year.

A smaller strike zone of '69 and thereafter makes BBs more likely, strikeouts less likely, and would likely increase HRs, as batters look for better strikes to hit. The smaller strike zone, better pitcher control, or reluctance to pitch inside and move batters back after 1969 might have allowed batters to stand in, looking for better pitches to hit, getting more BB, and then hitting more HR, a situation comparable to the American League of the '50s. Comparing the '64–68 era above to 3.4 BB/9 innings for the '99–04 period, does not suggest that there should be any direct relationship between low BBs of the latter period with an increase in strikeouts or HRs, however.

Wild pitches may be a measure of pitcher control, presuming batters will not be swinging at wild pitches. WP averaged 0.31/9 innings in the low-BBs 64–68 period, 0.33, from '94–04, an increase of 5%. It is interesting that BB, WP, and SO curves parallel one another from 1973 through 1994, when SOs increase while WPs and BBs decrease. It would be reasonable to believe a high number of strikeouts, on average, as a measure of pitching excellence, in itself might lead to fewer BBs and HRs, rather than an increase in HRs. It would be tempting to suggest hit batsmen might also be viewed as a metric of pitcher control, although batters currently protected by better wrist or elbow pads might more aggressively attack the strike zone, leading to increased batters hit, but on pitches that would have been avoided decades ago. A peak in hit batsmen in '06 has been followed by a 3-year decrease.[99]

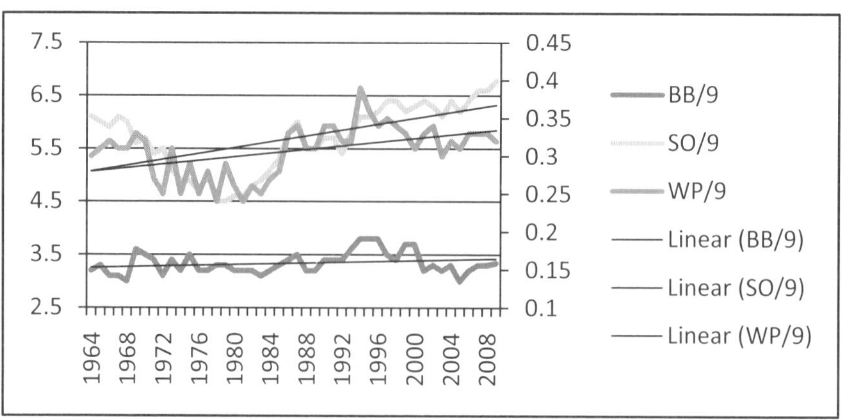

BB/, SO/, and WP/9 innings from 1964 through 2009 demonstrate a decrease in WP and BB from 1994 through 2004, while strikeouts increase.

The more recent trendline of decreasing BBs since 2001 might support either argument: that pitchers have better control, or that batters in the past decade have been less willing to accept a BBs, swinging more freely, then striking out more often. It will be interesting to continue to watch the uptrend of BBs and strikeouts since 2005, the former potentially in part related to taking more pitches (trying to realize the value of the BBs espoused in *Moneyball)* and not swinging, with the attendant potential risk of taking more strikes, with a greater risk of strikeout. The nadir for BB sof 3.0 in 2005 post-dates the androstendione ban, and may be related to a learned behavior of swinging for the fences.

Someone might suggest that new ballparks might lead to increases or decreases in HRs—but it is not so clear how new ballparks, in and of themselves, should affect strikeouts. Whereas differences in mound height in new parks might have an effect on strikeouts, a presumption that league rules are more uniformly applied must be assumed. Park adjustments are difficult to calculate in hitting records. It is not clear that parks affect strikeouts per se, unless a high-strikeout pitching staff, who pitches approximately half of its innings in the same park, gives the appearance that the park alone may be responsible. Both teams pitch from the same mound. It is reasonable that the team pitching half its games from its own mound finds a level of comfort in doing so, whereas visiting teams might have difficulty adjusting to the mound, however advantageous it might theoretically be. From 1964–68, the Tribe's hitters were second in fewest strikeouts in the AL. It would be hard to ascribe pitching strikeout effects to the ballpark under the circumstance that a team's pitchers are striking out the most batters, while the hitters are near the league lead in fewest strikeouts.

From 1964 to '66, the Indians' pitchers struck out more batters in Cleveland than did the opposition: 7.3 to 5.7 per 9 innings. On the road, the Tribe struck out 6.7 and the home team 5.9 per 9 innings. This does suggest some positive Cleveland Municipal Stadium effect on strikeouts by Indians' pitchers, although the opposition also struck out more hitters in their own familiar confines.

Base hits, batting average, and home runs may be more readily associated with individual ballpark factors. But it's not clear that any ballpark-related increases in HR, in and of themselves, should directly lead to the contemporaneous increase in strikeouts seen from '98–04.

New stadiums were introduced in Minneapolis in '82, Toronto in '89, Chicago in '91, Baltimore in '92, Arlington and Cleveland in '94, and Detroit in 2000. So most new parks were online well before the eye-catching mid-late 90s and early 21st century peak in strikeouts and HRs. If we look at HRs by those teams in the ten years before and ten years after new stadium introduction, compared to the league average in all stadiums, there were, on average, only 3.2 more HRs per year in the new stadiums compared to the previous, no different than the general trendline. New ballparks per se are unlikely to account for observed changes of contemporaneous increase in HRs and strikeouts, especially if they hadn't had a greater effect before that time.

But the introduction of new stadiums with Astroturf, some domed, did add a dimension that affected the game indirectly. More doubleheaders forced by rainouts in former years may have led to disparities in strikeouts based on staff pitching schedules: a workout relief appearance may not be approached in the same way a starting assignment might be. The ability to create a rotation of pitchers that would not be interrupted by rainouts and subsequent doubleheaders had an immeasurable positive effect on starting pitching.

The opening of the Astrodome in 1965 was just the start of this trend. Addition of more such stadiums over the years, essentially in the post-Tribe era in the AL, increasingly allowed starters to be starters, and further contributed to cultivation of a larger crop of relievers to continue to decrease the trendline of complete games. The Big Three pitched in an era of more dirt fields, fewer domed stadiums and more rainouts, necessitating more doubleheaders (24 in '64, 18 in '66, 22 in '67, and 15 in '68), compared to no scheduled doubleheaders today. For example, in 1965 opening day was April 13, and then the team played April 15, 17, 18, 21, 23, 24, and 27. Seven games in 15 days due to a few early days off, and a few rainouts critically spaced. Starters can't get into rhythms to carry their spring training regimens into the season under such circumstances. Some starters will need to pitch in relief just to get workouts to keep sharp. I previously noted that Sam started the first two games of 1966 due to these scheduling irregularities. In 1964, of 45 American League pitchers starting 15 games or more, only four did not have a relief appearance. In '65 there were ten, and in '66, five had no relief appearances. In '64 the Big Three had 51 starts in 91 (56%) appearances, even though all three were not yet in their first full major-league season. In '65, they had 92 starts of 122 (75%) appearances; in '66, 76 of 115 (66%).

The size of foul territory in new parks may differ from that in old ones. Less foul territory means more foul balls into the stands, more chances to swing, and has been associated with higher batting averages.98F[100] It's been estimated that Fenway Park with its small foul territory adds five to seven points to batting averages.99F[101] On the other hand, more foul territory means fewer foul balls going into the stands, more foul balls caught for outs, fewer strikes against batters, which theoretically generates fewer strikeouts.

Cleveland Municipal Stadium had more foul territory area than any other park in the AL from 1964–66. Based on estimations of foul territory area from digitized diagrams by Andrew Clem at andrewclem.com, the area was almost twice as much as at Yankee Stadium and Fenway Park (approximately 44,000 feet compared to 23,000 and 22,000 feet, respectively). Comiskey was third in overall area at ~35,000 sq. ft.). There was an inverse correlation between the size of foul territory and strikeouts in the AL for the 1964–68 period. The sum of linear measurements of the distance between home plate and first base to the stands correlates better than the foul area to total strikeouts by the home team from that ball park, however, with Cleveland first and Chicago second. Behind home plate, Comiskey Park was deepest, but quickly narrowed to the dugouts.[102]

Remember, the Tribe's and the White Sox' hitters struck out the least over the five-year period under consideration, giving some support to the theory that increased foul area should decrease batters' strikeouts! Tribe hitters struck out less at home than on the road from '64-'66 by 0.23 strikeouts/9 inning. They struck out less frequently at home than on the road in '67 -68 by 0.4 strikeouts/9 innings. However, they struck out more at home in '64-66 than in '67-68, by 0.24 strikeouts/9 innings. This fails to support the foul territory hypothesis, but may suggest hitters strike out less in more familiar surroundings.

Staffs pitching in stadiums with less foul territory (such as the Red Sox at Fenway Park) may have been helped over the years from a strikeout standpoint by virtue of stadiums with less foul territory. The Chicago Cubs have enjoyed high strikeout figures over the years as well, while playing on a diamond with approximately 20,000 square feet of foul territory, the smallest in the majors. It's interesting to note that Roger Clemens pitched 19 of his 24 years at Fenway Park or Yankee Stadium. He averaged more strikeouts in five seasons in Toronto (~31,700 sq. ft.) and Minute Maid Park in Houston (~24, 500 sq. ft.). An effect of foul territory, indoor play, both, neither, or something else?

| Stadium | Foul Territory Sq.Ft. (Est.) | SO | Rank SO | | Stadium | Distance (Home+ 1st Base) To Stands | Rank SO |
|---|---|---|---|---|---|---|---|
| Cleveland | 44000 | 4676 | 2 | | Cleveland | 143(60+83) | 2 |
| Kansas City | 35500 | 5147 | 9 | | Chicago | 136(83+53) | 1 |
| Chicago | 35000 | 4379 | 1 | | Kansas City | 133(69+64*) | 9 |
| Minnesota | 34000 | 4774 | 4 | | New York | 127(80+47) | 3 |
| Detroit | 33500 | 4809 | 5 | | Baltimore | 124(57+67) | 6 |
| Baltimore | 32000 | 4873 | 6 | | Detroit | 123(61+62) | 5 |
| Washington | 29000 | 5319 | 10 | | Minnesota | 120(60+60) | 4 |
| California (LA) | 25000 | 5056 | 8 | | Washington | 115(53+62) | 10 |
| Yankee | 23500 | 4745 | 3 | | Boston | 108(60+48) | 7 |
| Boston | 22000 | 4895 | 7 | | California | 105(60+45) | 8 |

On the left, estimated foul territory area (square feet) for AL ball parks from 1964–66, total strikeouts, their rank in fewest total strikeouts. On the right, the ballparks are listed according to the sum of the linear measurement from home plate and from first base to the stands, with their rank in fewest total strikeouts by the home team.

The Tribe's staff may actually have been disadvantaged, then, compared to their contemporaries from a strikeout perspective by the wide foul territory at Municipal Stadium from 1964 to 1966. The foul territory at Municipal Stadium was decreased in 1967 by addition of several thousand new box seats, making first base 26 feet closer to the stands. This decrease dropped the Stadium from the largest in area to the third largest at 34,500 sq. ft., but to seventh largest in linear dimension. Indeed, the Tribe staff averaged 30 more strikeouts overall in '67 and '68, but actually averaged 20 fewer at home than they did from '64–66. Similarly, the Tribe hitters struck out less in '67–68 as well, contradicting the statistical data and compelling logic presented earlier that decreased foul territory correlates to increased strikeouts. Either some other unidentified factors were operative, or the numbers of foul balls hit that might affect strikeout opportunities are actually negligible. Nevertheless, any differences between the staff's strikeout performance and that of the rest of the league might actually still be an underestimation of what the Tribe may have accomplished pitching elsewhere.

Having said all that, how many foul balls are hit into the stands in an average game? I've read an estimate of 30.[103] It's not immediately possible to identify how many of those foul balls in small parks might have been catchable, although some analysis of strikes and foul balls on different counts has been accumulated.[104] But only two or three foul balls into the first few rows at critical junctures of a game (with one or two strikes on a batter) could immediately increase strikeout opportunities. Pitchers such as the Big Three striking out one of three outs per game could gain an extra strikeout per game on a home field with less foul territory

Other factors may have affected strikeout numbers, such as an increase in night games over the years, where strikeouts might be increased secondarily post-1990 in comparison to the 60s. There were no Saturday or Sunday night games in the '60s, which probably reduced strikeout numbers of the staff compared to modern pitchers. Field lighting during night games may have had an effect on Indians' strikeout figures—there was some sentiment that Municipal Stadium was not well lit. In 1967, 920 newer, brighter lights were also added to the light poles, and the Tribe did strike out 20 fewer batters yearly during the '67-'68 years compared to '64–66. So the experiment of decreasing foul territory dimensions was confounded by the simultaneous improvement in lighting conditions. Again, new lights may have decreased the numbers the pitchers would have put up or may have offset the numbers they might have gained with reduced foul territory in the later years. Better lighting may also explain, at least in part, the decrease of Indian hitters' strikeouts as well.

Again, new lights may have decreased the numbers they would have otherwise put up, or may have offset the numerous potential variables discussed above, which might account for, or coincide with, the strikeout peak the Tribe staff enjoyed in a high SO/low HR period, or an increase in strikeouts and new season strikeout records in the high-SO/high-HR post-90s period, might be studied in complicated multivariate statistical analyses. A reasonable mathematical evaluation of the multiple factors that might be affecting pitchers' strikeouts might be derived. On the other hand, where strikeouts and home runs are not normally distributed variables, it is difficult to envision that a single definitive mathematically-derived solution to the question of "Who was the best strikeout Staff?" will ever be determined.

# Chapter 24—What About the NL?

We have identified the reversal of the customary pattern of NL strikeout advantage over the AL between 1964 and 1968 as an atypical deviation from the pattern of NL strikeout superiority. What was going on in the NL during these years while the Indians were the dominant strikeout Staff in the AL? Was there a lull in NL strikeouts that allowed the Tribe to appear superior by comparison?

The leading strikeout staff in the NL from '64–68 was the Cincinnati Reds. They struck out 1122, 1113, 1043, 1065, and 963 for the five seasons, an average of 1061 per season. The Dodgers were second at 1037 per year. The Reds were first, first, second, first, and fifth in the league for those five years. The Reds' average was still far below the Tribe's five-year average of 1154 for the same period. Cincinnati's 6.51 strikeouts/9 innings for the five years were almost ½ per 9 innings fewer than the Tribe's of 7.04.

The '64 Reds remarkably had six pitchers striking out over 100 hitters. The Reds were led in strikeouts by Jim Maloney for four of the five years. After striking out 9.6/9 innings in '63, he averaged 8.27/9 innings for the next five years.

Maloney was the only starter on the club for the entire '64–68 period under consideration. The Reds did have their own successful Big Four of Maloney, O'Toole, Jay, and Nuxhall for six years from '61–66. It's interesting that while 1968 was the "year of the pitcher" throughout baseball, strikeouts league-wide were historically only the fourth highest before to that year, having been higher in '63, '65, and '67. They would be higher four more times prior to 1990.

**Reds Strikeouts**

| | 1964 | 1965 | 1966 | 1967 | 1968 |
|---|---|---|---|---|---|
| Maloney | 214 (31) | 244 (33) | 216 (32) | 153 (29) | 181 (32) |
| Tsitouris | 146 (24) | 91 (20) | --- | --- | 6 (3) |
| O'Toole | 145 (30) | 71 (22) | 96 (24) | --- | --- |
| Jay | 134 (23) | 102 (24) | 44 (10) | --- | --- |
| Purkey | 78 (25) | --- | --- | --- | --- |
| Ellis | 125 (5) | 183 (39) | 154 (36) | 80 (27) | --- |
| Nuxhall | 111 (22) | 117 (16) | 71 (16) | --- | --- |
| McCool | 87 (3) | 120 (2) | 104 (0) | 83 (11) | 30 (4) |
| Pappas | --- | --- | 133 (32) | 129 (32) | 43 (11) |
| Nolan | --- | --- | --- | 206 (32) | 111 (22) |
| Queen | --- | --- | --- | 154 (24) | 20 (4) |
| Culver | --- | --- | --- | --- | 114 (35) |
| Arrigo | --- | --- | --- | --- | 140 (31) |
| Cloninger | --- | --- | --- | --- | 65 (17) |
| Team Total | 1122 | 1113 | 1043 | 1065 | 963 |

Cincinnati Reds Strikeouts 1964–68 for starting pitchers. Games started in parentheses.

Of course, it's a shame that the Reds' management did not have sufficient vision to identify the true promise and ultimate value of the young left-hander across town at the University of Cincinnati, Sandy Koufax. He entered UC in '52, and went 4–0 with 58 strikeouts in 30 innings as a freshman.[105] Then in '54 he went

3–1 with a 2.81 ERA, 51 strikeouts, and 30 walks in 32 innings. He signed with the Dodgers on December 15, 1954 for $20,000. The attraction of playing for his hometown Bums probably was too great for any other team to overcome, insofar as he turned down higher offers to sign with Brooklyn.

As a bonus baby (a free agent signed for more than $4,000), he had to stay on the major-league roster for two years before he could be sent to the minors for seasoning. In his second major league start Aug. 27, 1955, at age 19, he shut out the Reds on two hits, striking out 14 . Had Koufax been a Red, the combination of Maloney and Koufax would have been dominating. Koufax was the hub of the Dodgers staff from '56–66, which included the period of '60–63 that was likely the top strikeout staff in history of the NL.

The Reds signed no bonus baby free agents in '54. In June '55 they signed Al Silvera, an outfielder from University of Southern California. He had a total of seven NL at-bats in '55–56 before being released. Gabe Paul (Indians GM during my tenure) was the Reds' GM at the time of Koufax's and Silvera's signing. I guess Gabe will go down in history for passing, in one form or other, on two of the greatest left-handed pitchers of all time, Sandy Koufax and Tommy John.

The Reds '64 were not the first club to reach the 1100 level, however. The Koufax/Drysdale Dodgers had struck out 1122 in '60, 1105 in '61, with 154-game schedules and an eight-team league, and 1104 in '62 in 165 games. They struck out 1104 in '62 in 165 games, and 1095 in '63 in 163 games. The Dodgers averaged 1100 strikeouts from '59–63, the only NL club to do so for five consecutive years prior to the 90s. The Reds'-Dodgers' record of 1122 strikeouts would be broken by the Astros in 1969. Who was the pitcher that broke it? Jim Bouton struck out the Reds' Tony Perez for #1123, on the way to a new NL team record of 1221 strikeouts, bringing an end to the Indians' and the AL's team strikeout superiority.

The Dodgers led the NL in strikeouts for an unbelievable 16 years, 1948–1963. The string started in Brooklyn for ten years through 1957, and continued in two separate ballparks in Los Angeles for six more years. This is certainly the greatest team-pitching record, probably never to be surpassed. The high strikeouts might be a reflection of the claim that the mound in Los Angeles was over 20 inches high. Vern Fuller told me it was the highest hill he had ever climbed.

# Chapter 25—The Drug Era

None of the foregoing discussion confirms any intrinsic direct correlation between simultaneous high strikeout numbers (high-SO) and high home run numbers (high-HR), as occurred in the period of '99–04. If we study the Boston Red Sox for strikeouts by the staff versus home runs given up by their pitching, the trend for the league-wide simultaneous increase in HRs and strikeouts between '99 and '04 is aborted, with an increase in strikeouts accompanied by a decrease in HRs given up. More importantly, the ratio of strikeouts to HRs given up by Sox pitchers from 1999–2004 mirrors the same curve as the Tribe's 1964–68. While it is true that the AL staffs, on average, experienced decreases in HRs allowed over the '64–68 period, the Tribe's staff's decrease was still 29% greater than the rest of the league, similar to the Red Sox' curve.

If the '99–04 AL-wide simultaneous peak in strikeouts and HRs was due to some external factor, it was one that was overcome by the top strikeout staff in the league, who were able to reduce the league-wide home run trend well beyond its mean. A surge in HRs was occurring in the rest of the league, but the strong Sox staff was able to reverse it. Comparing the high-SO/high-HR '95–04 period to the Tribe's high-SO/low-HR '64–68 period suggests a similar force was contributing to the SO climate in these two instances: exceptional pitching countercurrent to the trend elsewhere in the league.

The simultaneous peak in strikeout leaders and average HRs after 1996, as well as the steady increase in HR/9 innings suggests that this new spike in K's may be due to some similar physical factors to which increases in HRs have been also attributed, including the use of performance-enhancing drugs, such as the steroid androstenedione.

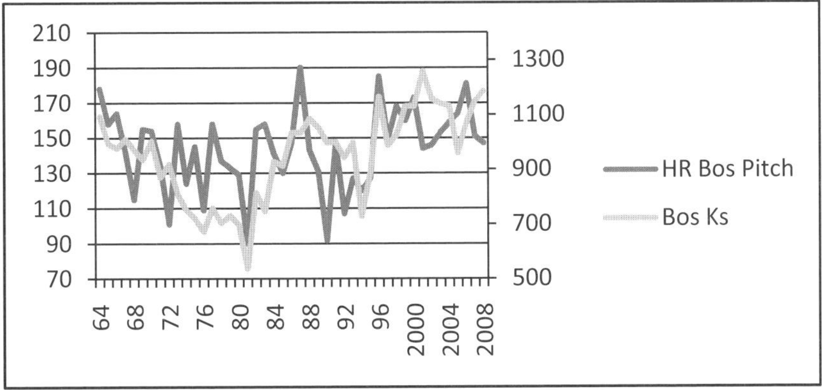


HR given up by Boston pitchers, and strikeouts by Boston pitchers, from 1964 to 2008. A decrease in HR given up by pitchers coincides with their increase in pitchers' Ks from 1999-2004. This is opposite to the effect seen throughout the league, where HR and strikeouts were parallel.

It has been argued that hitters' performance-enhancing drug use might have increased HR output while, at the same time, created a tendency to over swing, causing a parallel increase in strikeouts, totally unrelated to any intrinsic change in pitchers' performance, during the same time period. In doing so, more hits may be home runs rather than singles, doubles, or triples. The chart above examines HR as a percentage of base hits since 1960. Does an increase in the percentage from 1992 to 2000 indicate hitters were swinging for the home run, and converting some percentage of base hits to home runs? Or is this trend a manifestation of bigger, stronger hitters hitting the ball further independent of effort and intent?

In an attempt to debunk HR-drug use link, Arthur Devaney has pointed out that "HR output has moved up and down, declining a bit from late 1970s and early 1980s, and only coming back to the 1961 level in the late 1990s. There is evidence that hitters began 'swinging for the fences' more in 1993. Modern players strike out more, but they are not as efficient in hitting home runs as players of the past." He points out that the number of home runs per strikeout is a bit less now than it was in 1959–1962, conveniently picking that four-year period before the Tribe's record-setting performance, ignoring the fact that home run per strikeout ratio from '64–68 was much lower than '59–62, and lower than recent years.[106] Bill James believes the increased strikeouts post-1990 are simply due to more players who were swinging for the fences, with no mention of possible drug-enhanced relationship.[107] Swinging for the fences does not necessarily correlate with strikeouts, however. Maris struck out 67 times while hitting 61 HRs in '61. Ted Kluszewski struck out 35 times while hitting 49 HR in '54, and 40 times while hitting 47 HR in '55.[108]

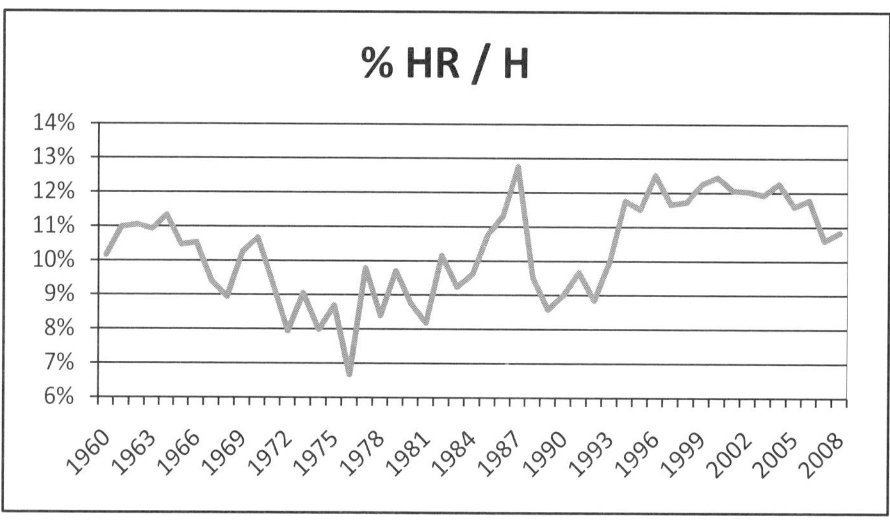


A graph of HR / 9 innings as a % of hits/ 9 inning from 1960–2008. An upward trend existed from 1960 to 1962. After 1963, when the strike zone was enlarged, slight dip occurred, followed by a 24-year peak in 1964. A decrease from '65 to '68 occurred, followed by alternating peaks and valleys until a new peak in 1994, which continued until 2004, followed by four years of decline.

We could look at strikeouts over time by recognized home-run hitters whose names have been associated with steroid use, for analysis of potential effects of steroids upon increased strikeouts in their own careers. The data could be compared to strikeouts/AB for the AL over the same period, even if some of the players were NL hitters. If steroids led to swinging for the fences, perhaps an increase in strikeouts over time with steroid use might be identified for the league in general, the group as a whole, or for individual players, in particular. The curve for the American League from 1986-2005 period is displayed in the chart below, with only a gently rising trendline, with no dramatic increases over the same time period to indicate any initiation of increased strikeouts due to some extraneous factor such as steroid use. The AL average was 17.4%, and ranged from a low of 15.8% in 1992 to 18.7% in 1997.

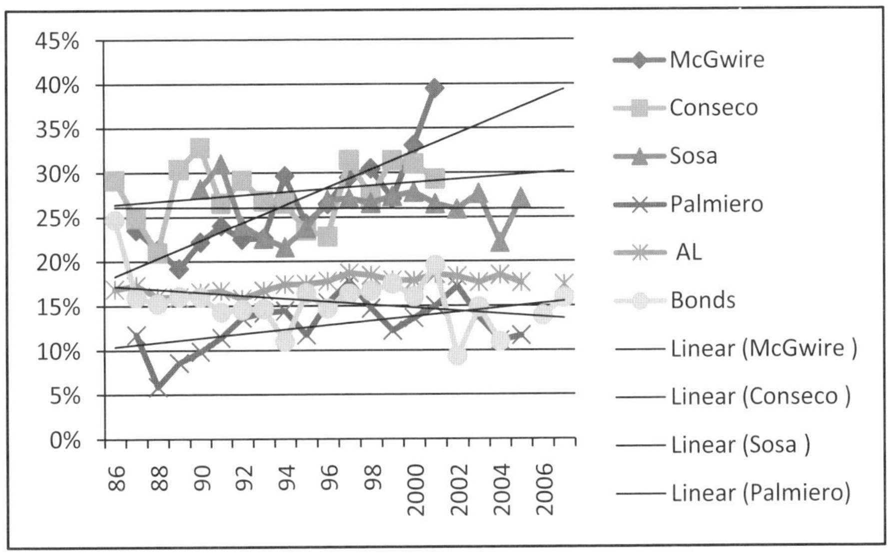


Percentage SO/AB for the AL (1986–2005), Mark McGwire (1987–2001), Jose Conseco (1986–2001), Sammy Sosa (1990–2005), Rafael Palmiero (1986–2005), and Barry Bonds (1986–2007).

Barry Bonds, Jose Conseco, Mark McGwire, Rafael Palmiero, and Sammy Sosa are perhaps the five most notable HR hitters of the era whose name has been associated with performance-enhancing drugs.[109] [110] [111] [112] [113] The above chart examines their SO/AB ratios over their careers, beginning with their first years of at least 150 at bats. Three graph patterns appear. The trendlines of the players are dramatically different.

McGwire exhibits a lower percentage early in his career, with a dramatic increase over time, culminating in a peak in his last two years of play, where, perhaps, swinging for the fences might have contributed to an increase in strikeouts. Conseco exhibits a generally higher percentage early, followed by a relatively small increase from 1991–2001.

As a better contact and average hitter, Palmiero, had the lowest percentage of SO/AB throughout his career, averaging 12.8% per year, with a slight uptrend similar to Conseco's, and only a slightly higher trendline than the league overall.

Sosa exhibits a similar percentage early, but a flat line over the 17-year period (1990–2006), appearing to show his SO/AB was very steady, with no increase in strikeouts over time due to failure to make contact as his career progressed.

Bonds is the only hitter to have a downward trendline over the period in question. His personal strikeouts/at bat average did not increase due to swinging for the fences.

On the other hand, all these trendlines might have been flat or declining even in the absence of steroid use. Examining the data in this fashion does not confirm a cause and effect relationship between drug use and increased strikeouts caused by "swinging for the fences." It does not exclude that it occurred in certain instances. Yet the small upward trend, with no precipitous spikes, for the entire league is in keeping with an increase in strikeouts over time, just as has been seen well before manipulation of the strike zone and mound height, the DH, or steroids came on the scene.

This leaves room for the theory that steroids and other performance-enhancing drugs might have had a more direct effect on increased strikeouts by pitchers. A wider analysis would be required to identify variations from these hitters' data points. But it is interesting to observe the decrease of both HR and the percentage of homeruns/hits after the steroid ban in 2004, while the strikeout peak continued. If strikeouts were a measure of swinging for the fences from '99–04, it must become an ingrained behavior, difficult to suppress post-androstenedione.

Baseball rates poorly regarding "antidoping" policies according to a recent panel that compared policies of 22 sports or governing bodies based on the presence of a policy, its accessibility to the public, severity of sanctions for policy violators, and administration of the code itself, ranking just behind the Professional Golf Association.[114]

Whereas not much has been made of performance-enhancing drugs in golf, it's been reported that a Canadian doctor, Anthony Gallea, visited Tiger Woods four times between February and March, 2008, to provide platelet-rich plasma. Gallea's assistant was stopped at the US–Canadian border, and HGH and Actovegin, a drug extracted from calf's blood, were found in Gallea's bag in the car.[115] Hardly a ringing indictment, but we'll just have to weigh Woods's words claiming he built himself up through rigorous weight-lifting work from skinny college golfer to NFL-safety type body.

Whereas the performance-enhancing drug issue in baseball has been directed primarily at hitters and increase in HR numbers, it remains possible, or even likely, that it had some, if not a similar, direct effect on pitching performance and statistics as well. As recently as July 30, 2009 Bronson Arroyo of the Reds admitted to use androstenedione and other performance-enhancing drugs from 1998–2002, before their ban in 2003, and to feeling "like a monster."[116] [117] I wonder if Arroyo, a guitar-playing singer and sometime-local performer himself, knows the tune and words to "Act Naturally."

John Rocker admitted to using steroids in the same period, and attributed some of his aggressive behavior to that use.[118] Steroids weren't the only performance-enhancing drugs alleged to be used by pitchers in recent years. Human growth hormone (HGH), which is believed to prevent injury and help recovery via stimulation of connective tissue component synthesis, has also been implicated. The combination of HGH with steroids may prevent injuries attributed to steroid use, and therefore their effect may be additive. There is some difference of opinion, however, about the anticipated beneficial effects of HGH, and it certainly has side effects with prolonged use. Arroyo also admitted freely to using other approved performance-enhancing drugs, even to that day. His admission did not prevent him from winning the Reds' Joe Nuxhall Good Guy Award.

Any peaks in strikeouts from '97–04, when steroid use was formally banned, must be questioned as potentially related to the same factors leading to contemporaneous peaks in HRs, such as steroid or other drug use. We don't know how much earlier drugs may have been having an effect. Jack Armstrong, another pitcher for the Reds, estimated more than 30% of players in 1988–1994 were using at least maintenance doses of steroids.[119] If maintenance doses were used in '88, how much earlier had their use been introduced? According to the LA Times in 1995, Tony Gwynn estimated 30% of players were using steroids. The

Padres GM, Randy Smith, said "We all know there is steroid use."[120] Steroids were "the secret we're not supposed to talk about." This tacit approval did for baseball what a smaller strike zone, lower mound, and designated hitter could not do.

The *Report to the Commissioner of Baseball of an Independent Investigation into the Illegal Use of Steroids and Other Performance Enhancing Substances by Players in Major League Baseball*, of December 13, 2007, also known as the "Mitchell Report" after Senator George Mitchell, identified and named a number of players implicated in the use of such substances.

Luis Perez, a Montreal bullpen catcher in 1992, admitted that he supplied steroids to players 1998–2001 while he was bullpen catcher for the Florida Marlins. He told baseball officials "that virtually every player on the Marlins was 'doing something'...and he also claimed that every pitcher in Montreal's bullpen was on some form of steroid."[121] Roger Clemens and Andy Pettitte of the record-setting '01 Yankee club are implicated in the Report based on testimony of Brian McNamee, former Yankee bullpen catcher, and Clemens' former trainer. But no pitchers of the record-breaking Seattle Mariners of 1997 or Cleveland Indians of 2000 are on the list of players in the Report.

The report points out that use of these substances was not limited to the players identified in the report. On Nov. 13, 2003 Major League Baseball announced 5-7 % of 1428 tests were positive for performance-enhancing drugs during the 2003 season.[122] It strains incredulity to believe performance-enhancing drugs did not have some role in the strikeout records of the Indians' Staff being broken.

Whether strikeout increases and new records are due to hitters swinging for the fences, or due to pitchers taking drugs throwing harder, more aggressively, or more effectively, some combination of both of these factors, or some other yet-unidentified indirect effect, the results are the same: increased strikeouts. Records achieved in that setting are tarnished compared to those records that have been surpassed, just as new home run records are now considered to be. "Act Naturally" in the 60s was more than a hit song: casual joking about "greenies" or "bennies" went on, but I never heard serious discussion of, or saw, such drug use at that time. And being there, I would surely have seen it. I had been known to take some No-Doz, with caffeine as its stimulant component, while studying for tests in '64, but I usually fell asleep anyway.

Bouton wrote of his teammates taking stimulants. Jim Brosnan wrote of Jim Maloney taking a "bomber," or dexedrine (an amphetamine) stimulant prior to pitching in 1961, making him feel "real *strong!*" [123] He also wrote of taking a "bomber" himself on a post-series plane ride from Chicago to LA so that he could stay awake to play bridge.[124] He did not tell the reader if the drug enhanced his bridge game, though. Even Doc Bauman,, the venerable and respected trainer for the Cardinals and St. Louis University for many years, whom I met while working out at the St. Louis University gym in 1966, had a supply of "Boom Booms" on the shelf in 1959, according to Brosnan.[125]

There has been a recent estimate that 50–80% of ball players have used amphetamines before their addition to the list of drugs banned in baseball. Ralph Kiner, slugger of the '50s, said "all the trainers in all the ballparks had them then."[126] But "feeling real strong" is far from adding muscle, bulk, strength, and stamina, however. Plenty of pitchers have gone out on to the mound and "felt strong," but then got boom-boomed themselves.

Amphetamines are now on baseball's list of banned drugs, and testing for them has been done since 2006. Although it would not surprise my wife that I wouldn't see unapproved drug use that was right under my nose, I just didn't see players' use of drugs, or behavior that might be ascribed to it. The only drug use I recall occurred when the whole team took antibiotics as a precautionary measure when third baseman Max Alvis contracted meningitis in late June 1964. It was written in the *Plain Dealer* that, after his no-hitter, Sonny Siebert did speak of maybe needing a sleeping pill to fall asleep. That's about as much as I saw or heard.

There are two sides to the strikeouts story: the man striking out, and the pitcher throwing the strikeout. The hitter's side gets the most attention. There is more attention cast on Mark Reynolds and Ryan Howard striking out over 200 times in a season than on a pitcher throwing 200 Ks.[127] [128] Numerous treatises on "Are strikeouts overrated?" focus on the batter. Both sides of the story should get equal consideration when it comes to the effects of performance-enhancing substances.

# Chapter 26—The New Era

Both HR and the percentage of home runs/hits decreased after the steroid ban in 2004, while the strikeout peak continues. If strikeouts were a measure of swinging for the fences from '97–04, it must have become an ingrained behavior, difficult to suppress post-androstenedione.

The new post-steroid era allows us to reflect on our discussion of strikeout performance over the years, remembering that drugs like HGH may still be in use, with no testing mechanism to detect them until recently. A British rugby league player, Terry Newton, has become the first athlete suspended for use of HGH based on results from a new test kit. He subsequently admitted using the drug.[129] Bud Selig, Commissioner of Major League Baseball, has announced that MLB anticipates using the test in the immediate future, beginning at the minor-league level. But it's unclear whether the players' association will agree to its use.[130]

Does the disconnection of the peak levels of home runs with strikeouts from 2004 to 2008 suggest hitters may soon be in need of league intervention once again? Or does an upward trend in HRs and strikeouts indicate a new trend in home run production? Only continued, ongoing monitoring of future trends in both will provide the answers. Has a new level of performance arrived, whether or not based upon drug use, for which tests can't be currently performed?

As George Will has pointed out, pitchers can get bigger and stronger and more easily elevate their performance on a pure physical basis than can hitters. Whereas hitters can increase their strength as well, they still have to make contact before the strength bears result. The laws of eye-hand coordination and ball contact cannot be suspended by adding muscle mass and strength.

Team pitching records, including team strikeout records, receive short shrift in the SABR Baseball List & Record Book.[131] Multi-year team records such as staff strikeout records highlighted here may not be viewed as worthy of notice, or as a modern-day measure of effectiveness. But yearly and year-to-year consistency should be a goal of any team endeavor, in every aspect of play, to the extent it may contribute to team success. The Yankees are generally remembered by many fans as the leading home run hitting club of the 50s and early 60s, but they never led the league more than two years in a row! (In fact, the Tribe actually led the league in HRs five consecutive years from '50–54!)

Free agency, first granted in 1975, virtually guarantees that few players today will now stay with the same club for five consecutive years to contribute to team records over a protracted period. But we must remember that the Big Three's records were accomplished within the *first* five years of their continuous major league careers, a time when limitations to player movement by free agency rules currently do exist. Players are currently tied to teams for the first six years of major league service on the team's 40-man roster.[132] Limitations to movement under free agency does allow that other talented trios should have had the opportunity to match or surpass Sam, Sonny, and Looie's records, provided they were talented enough to do so.

*Based on the information in this book, it is irrefutable that the Indians' '64–68 pitching staff, anchored by the Big Three of Sam McDowell, Sonny Siebert, and Luis Tiant, with the major contributions of Gary Bell, Jack Kralick, Steve Hargan, Stan Williams, Don McMahon, and others, were the top strikeout staff in the history of the American League in terms of raw numbers, differential, and duration.*

They were the first staff to reach 7.0 strikeouts/9 innings, and 1100 strikeouts/season. They led the league with record numbers of strikeouts five years in a row, a record not since matched. Averaging more than one strikeout greater than the league over the same prolonged period is an internal barometer that diminishes the importance of any external effects, such as mound height, strike zone size, and, yes, even performance-enhancing drugs, on strikeout numbers. They reversed the usual circumstance of the NL leading the AL in strikeouts, and surpassed the NL leading Reds by ½ strikeout/9 innings. Yes, their single-year staff record of 1967 has been broken subsequently, but not for 30 years, and then only in an era of drug-enhanced performance.

No nucleus of three AL starting pitchers has matched the strikeout levels of the Big Three for single years or for as protracted a period of time, most notably accomplished within the first five uninterrupted years of their careers in the major leagues. This fortuitous contemporaneous convergence, alignment, and illumination of these three stars is unprecedented in the AL universe.

Every year since 1968 staffs have had the opportunity to match the Big Three's productivity, but it has yet to occur in 41 seasons.

The big questions naturally follow from the foregoing discussion: Well, could they do it now? Would the Tribe's staff, and the Big Three, enjoy the same success today they enjoyed then? Would they have struck out as many hitters and set records in the '95–09 era, as they did from'64–68?

The eras were indeed different, but the differences could have exerted their effects in both directions. No DH? No set-up men and closers. Larger strike zone? Bigger bodies. Expansion with worse hitters? Expansion with worse pitchers? Higher mound for mechanical advantage? No steroids or HGH for muscular advantage. Fewer night games? Fewer rainouts and doubleheaders.

The questions of making legitimate comparisons between eras parallel the questions asked regarding record home run hitters of different eras as well: who would hit more home runs today: Ruth, Maris, Aaron, McGwire, or Bonds? Ruth and Gehrig, Maris and Mantle, Snider and Hodges, Aaron and Mathews, Mays and Cepeda, McGwire and Conseco? Are homerun statistics achieved in an era where starters also relieved, and relief pitching wasn't as specialized as we see today, truly comparable? I suspect there will be no unanimity on the answers to these questions. But McGwire's garnering only 25% of the sportswriters' votes required for Hall-of-Fame entry certainly confirms that milestones achieved by a rule-breaker are not viewed as qualifying the record-breaker for the ultimate in baseball recognition.

It is pure speculation to attempt to predict the staff's performance in a later era. Would Sonny have succumbed to pressures to improve his performance through chemistry, and would it accomplish its goal? Would Sam's fatal flaw still derail the promise of his Hall-of-Fame career, or would it be neutralized by drug enhancement, improved preparation and training methods, and commitment and devotion to purpose? Would Looie combine his 95 mph velocity, with the craftiness, cunning, and precise control at every speed and from every angle, as the Cuban Cutie learned to do successfully later in his career? Would performance-enhancing drugs have reduced the considerable time they lost to injuries over the years, and allowed them to perform at even higher levels than they were otherwise able? Whatever the opinions on their ability to do so, the fact remains: they did it once; no one can say that they wouldn't do even better if given the opportunity to do it again.

This book has raised as many new questions as questions answered. It leaves room for new discovery and confirmation or refutation of some of the question raised. Does the loss of the stigma of the strikeout essentially nullify the records discussed here? Does the number of strikeouts differ at night, when there is poorer field lighting? Does foul-territory area actually have a correlation to strikeouts? Does the ninth spot in the batting order usually filled by the pitcher contribute to significantly more strikeouts than the spot filled by the DH? Do batters strike out more on the road, or at home?

Should strikeout superiority be recorded, when so many factors can relatively affect the numbers? I suspect few would say no to the latter question. If yes, then, how should individual and team strikeout superiority be measured? Most strikeouts in an inning? Most strikeouts in a 9-inning game? Most strikeouts in an extra-inning game? Most strikeouts in a season? Highest strikeouts/9 innings in a season? Greatest strikeout differential between a staff and the rest of the league? Certainly all of these measures are legitimate yardsticks, and each of these measures identify an individual level of excellence.

By direct extension, it is reasonable to extend analysis over longer periods such as the '64–68 period described here, and give appropriate recognition to the unparalleled performance of the Big Three together for all five of those years, and to the remainder of the staff. They should be remembered and viewed in this new light for not only their team records, but for their individual ones as well, records reinforced by the passage of time, many not since duplicated, and not yet overshadowed by the subsequent later events.

# Appendix 1: Indians bullpen catchers and coaches 1946–2010

| | Bullpen Coach | Bullpen Catcher | Pitching Coach |
|---|---|---|---|
| 1646-51 | n/a | Bill Lobe | Mel Harder (1948) |
| 1951-56 | Bill Lobe | n/a | “ |
| 1957-61 | n/a | n/a | “ |
| 1962 | n/a | Enrique Izquierdo | “ |
| 1964-66 | Early Wynn* | Tom Tomsick | Early Wynn |
| 1967 | n/a | Frank Keeney | Clay Bryant |
| 1968 | “ | “ | Jack Sanford |
| 1969 | “ | Don Smith | “ |
| 1970-1 | “ | “ | Cot Deal |
| 1972-3 | “ | “ | Warren Spahn |
| 1974 | “ | “ | Clay Bryant |
| 1975-6 | Jeff Torborg | “ | Harvey Haddix |
| 1977 | none | “ | “ |
| 1978 | Dave Duncan | “ | “ |
| 1979 | Dennis Sommers | “ | Chuck Hartenstein |
| 1980-1 | “ | “ | Dave Duncan |
| 1982 | “ | | Mel Queen |
| 1983-85 | “ | “ | Don McMahon |
| 1986 | Doc Edwards | “ | Jack Aker |
| 1987 | Luis Isaac | “ | “ |
| 1988-91 | “ | “ | Mark Wiley |
| 1992-3 | “ | Dan Williams | Rick Adair |
| 1994 | “ | “ | Phil Regan |
| 1995-8 | “ | “ | Mark Wiley |
| 1999 | “ | “ | Phil Regan |
| 2000-01 | “ | “ | Dick Pole |
| 2002 | “ | “ | Mike Brown |
| 2003 | “ | “ | Carl Willis |
| 2008 | “ | Wiliams, Dennis Malaave | “ |
| 2009 | Dan Williams | David Wallace | “ |
| 2010 | Scott Radzinsky | David Wallace | Tim Belcher |

# Appendix 2: Ballpark dugout and bullpen locations in 2009

| | Field Location On Field; Behind Fence | Position (Perpendicular /Parallel to Field; Side to Side; End-to-End) | Bullpen Field Location (Left, Center, Right)<br><br>Web site Images | Home Dugout<br><br>1st or 3rd Base Side | Visitors' Dugout<br><br>1st or 3rd Base Side |
|---|---|---|---|---|---|
| Atlanta Braves Turner Field | Behind Outfield Fence | Perpendicular | Braves: Right Field Visitors Left Field Corner http://yickit.com/wp-content/uploads/PhotosFourthofJuly1_EFAC/DSC02968.jpg | 1st Base | 3rd Base |
| Arizona Diamondbacks; Chase Field | Behind Outfield Fence | 45° Angle to Fence, parallel to Field Pitcher's Mound-Home Plate Direction | 'Backs: Left Field Corner at Foul Pole Visitors: Left Field Corner at Foul Pole http://www.ballparksof baseball.com/nl/chase08901.jpg | 3rd Base | 1st Base |
| Baltimore Orioles Camden Yards | Behind Outfield Fence | Home, visitor's parallel to fence, adjacent | Both Left-center<br><br>http://www.ballparksof baseball.com/nl/chase08901.jpg | 1st Base | 3rd Base |
| Boston Red Sox Fenway Park | Behind Outfield Fence | Home, visitors parallel to fence adjacent end-to-end | Both Right Field<br><br>http://www.flickr.com/photos/brentmid/3733972584/ | 1st Base | 3rd Base |
| Chicago Cubs Wrigley Field | On Field, Foul Territory | | Cubs: Left Field Visitors: Right Field<br><br>http://en.wikipedia.org/wiki/File:20070616_Chri | 3rd Base | 1st Base |

| | | | | | |
|---|---|---|---|---|---|
| | | | s_Young_visits_Wrigley_(4)-edit3.jpg | | |
| Chicago White Sox US Cellular Field | Behind Outfield Fence | Parallel, Adjacent to Fence | White Sox: Left Field Visitors: Right Field<br>http://www.baseball-fever.com/showthread.php?t=69308 | 3rd Base | 1st Base |
| Cincinnati Reds Great American Ballpark | Behind Outfield Fence | Perpendicular to Fence | Reds: Left Center FieldVisitors: Right Field | 1st Base | 3rd Base |
| Cleveland Indians Progressive Field | Behind Outfield Fence | Perpendicular to Fence | Indians: Center Visitors: Right Field http//en.wikipedia.org/wiki/Bullpen | 3rd Base | 1st Base |
| Colorado Rockies Coors Field | Behind Outfield Fence | Parallel to Field<br>Home, visitors adjacent, end-to-end | Both Right Field<br>http://www.flickr.com/photos/jjacobsen/3634926240 | 1st Base | 3rd Base |
| Detroit Tigers Comerica Park | Behind Outfield Fence | Parallel to Fence<br>Home, visitor's parallel, adjacent | Both Left Field<br>http://www.flickr.com/photos/jillsphotosrock/175009720/ | 3rd Base | 1st Base |
| Florida Marlins Land Shark Stadium | Behind Outfield Fence | Parallel to Foul Lines | Marlins: Right Field Foul Line Visitors: Left Field Foul Line http://www.teresco.org/pics/fromabq-20040523-0602/0529/game.html | Ist Base | 3rd base |

| Houston Astros Minute Maid Park | Behind Outfield Fence | Astros: Parallel to Fence | Astros: Right-Center Visitors: Enclosed beyond Left Field Wall, indoors | Ist Base | 3rd base |
|---|---|---|---|---|---|
| Kansas City Royals Kaufman Stadium | Behind Outfield Fence | Parallel to Fence | Royals: Right Field Visitors: Left Field | Ist Base | 3rd base |
| Los Angeles Dodgers Dodger Stadium | Behind Outfield Fence | Perpendicular to Fence | Dodgers : Left Field Visitors: Right Field<br><br>http://www.insidesocal.com/tomhoffarth/archives/2009/07/more-scenes-fro.html | 3rd Base | 1st Base |
| Los Angeles Angels; Angels Stadium Anaheim | Behind Outfield Fence | Parallel to Fence, side-to-side, home adjacent to fence | Both: Left Field<br><br>http://pages.sbcglobal.net/halofan/_images/2008/Bullpen.jpg | 3rd Base | 1st Base |
| Milwaukee Brewers Miller Park | Behind Outfield Fence | Parallel to Fence | Brewers: Left-Center Visitors www.expressmilwaukee.com/article-2316-hanging-in-the-bullpen.html | 1st Base | 3Rd Base |
| Minnesota Twins Metrodome | On Field, Foul Territory | Parallel to Foul Lines | Twins: Left Field Visitors: Right Field | 3rd Base | 1st Base |
| New York Mets; Citi Field | Behind Outfield Fence | Parallel to Fence, Side-to-side, home field adjacent to fence, Visitors at higher level | Mets: Right Field Visitors: Right Field<br><br>www.panoramio.com/photo/18303715 | 1st Base | 3Rd Base |
| New York Yankees; | Behind Outfield | Parallel to Fence; Adjacent to | Yankees: Center-left Visitors: Center-right | 3rd Base | 1st Base |

| Yankee Stadium | Fence | Monument Park | http://snaggingbaseballs.mlblogs.com/assets_c/2009/07/13_yankee_bullpen_from_above-thumb-550x408-1301611.jpg | | |
|---|---|---|---|---|---|
| Oakland Athletics;<br>Oakland A's | On Field, Foul Territory | Parallel to Foul Lines | A's: Left Field<br>Visitors: Right Field<br>flickr.com/photos/lodolce/3515889353/ | 3rd base | 1st base |
| Philadelphia Phillies ; Citizens Bank Park | Behind Outfield Fence | Parallel to Fenc e Side to side Phillies adjacent to Fence | Both Center-left<br>http://z.about.com/d/philadelphia/1/0/T/_/1/cbp_022.JPG | 1st Base | 3rd Base |
| Pittsburgh Pirates; PNC Park | Behind Outfield Fence | Parallel to fence, end-to-end | Pirates: Center-Left Visitors: Center-Left<br>www.sports.webshots.com/photo/1034646137035359372cdePuk | 3rd Base | 1st Base |
| San Diego Padres Petco Park | Padres: Behind Outfield Fence<br>Visitors: On Field, Foul Territory | Padres: Parallel to fence<br>Visitors: Parallel to foul line | Padres: Left-center Field<br>Visitors: Right Field<br>http://www.ebaseballparks.com/images/DSC_2016.JPG<br>http://www.ballparksof baseball.com/nl/PetcoPark.htm | 1st Base | 3rd Base |
| San Francisco Giants; ATT Ballpark | On Field, Foul Territory | Giants: Parallel to foul line<br>Visitors: Parallel to foul line | Giants: Left Field<br>Visitors: Right Field<br>http://www.ballparksofbaseball.com/nl/AT&TPark.htm | 3rd base | 1st base |

| | | | | | |
|---|---|---|---|---|---|
| Seattle Mariners Safeco Field | Behind Outfield Fence | Parallel to fence, end to end, mound s adjacent | Both Left Field http://www.baseball-fever.com/showthread.php?t=74756&page=5 | $1^{st}$ Base | $3^{rd}$ Base |
| St. Louis Cardinals; Busch Stadium | Behind Outfield Fence | Parallel to Fence<br>Left and Right Field | Cards: Right Field Visitors: Left Field | $1^{st}$ Base | $3^{rd}$ Base |
| Tampa Bay Devil Rays Tropicana Park | On Field, Foul Territory | Parallel to fence | Rays: Right Field Visitors: Left Field http://blogs.tampabay.com/photos/uncategorized/2008/10/14/ot_296011_cass_rays_1c.jpg | $1^{st}$ Base | $3^{rd}$ Base |
| Texas Rangers Ballpark | Behind Outfield Fence | Rangers: Parallel to Fence Visitors: | Rangers: Right Center Visitors: Left Center www.ebaseballparks.com/ballpark.html | $1^{st}$ Base | $3^{rd}$ Base |
| Toronto Blue Jays Rodgers Center | Behind Outfield Fence | Parallel to Field | Blue Jays: Left Field Visitors: Right Field | $3^{rd}$ Base | $1^{st}$ Base |
| Washington Nationals; Nationals Park | Behind Outfield Fence | Nationals: Parallel to Fence Visitors: Parallel to Fence | Nationals: Right Field Visitors: Left-center Field http://www.ballparksof baseball.com/natsballparkseat.gif http://www.ballparksof baseball.com/nl/NationalsPark.htm | $1^{st}$ Base | $3^{rd}$ Base |

## Appendix 3. American League Records of 1964–1968 Indians' Pitching Staff:

**Staff:**

Most consecutive years leading the AL with 1100 strikeouts or more (5: 1964–68).

Most strikeouts in season (1189): 1967

Broken by Seattle Mariners (1207), 1997

Most strikeouts/9 innings in a season (7.2):

Broken by Seattle Mariners (7.5), 1997

Most years holding single-year record for most strikeouts (32 years: 1967—1999).

Highest average strikeouts, leading league, for 3 (1152.3), 4 (1153.2), and 5 (1155) consecutive years.

Most strikeouts vs. same opponent, 2 consecutive games (33) vs Boston Red Sox, April 16, 1966.

Most strikeouts in 9 innings (19) vs. Detroit, Sept. 18, 1966.

Greater than 1 strikeout/9 innings greater than AL average for staffs with greater than 7 strikeouts/9 innings or more ('64—68)

First Staff to average 7 strikeouts / 9 innings (1964)

First Staff to strike out more batters (1157) than hits allowed (1087) in 1968

Most consecutive victories to start the season: 10 (1966)

**Big Three (McDowell, Siebert, Tiant):**

Most Strikeouts/9 innings for trio starting pitchers, > 125 innings, 5 consecutive years: 8.44

Most strikeouts/9 innings /year, 3 starting pitchers: 1964: 8.32

Most strikeouts/9 innings /year, 3 starting pitchers: 1965: 8.94

Most strikeouts/9 innings /year, 3 starting pitchers: 1966: 8.31

Most strikeouts/9 innings /year, 3 starting pitchers: 1967: 8.29

Most strikeouts/9 innings /year, 3 starting pitchers: 1968: 8.35

Most strikeouts/season, 3 starting pitchers: 1968: 693

Career strikeouts/9 innings for trio teammates for 4 or 5 consecutive years ( 7.13)

Starting duo with > 9 strikeouts/9 innings: Sam McDowell (10.7) and Sonny Siebert (9.1): 1965

Starting duo, highest total strikeouts/9 innings (19.8): Sam McDowell, Sonny Siebert , 1965

Most years greater than 9 strikeouts/9 innings (2), starting pitchers: McDowell, Tiant 1967 (9.0, 9.1), 1968 (9.5, 9.2)

Fewest hits/9 innings, 3 starters, teammates: 5.83 (1968)

**Sam McDowell:**

10.71 Strikeouts/9 innings (1965); broken by Nolan Ryan (1987): 11.48 Strikeouts/9 innings

Youngest pitcher to strike out 325 batters, age 23 (1965)

First pitcher since 1900 to strike out 300 batters in fewer than 300 innings (1965).

Most strikeouts in 2 consecutive games (30): 16 Oakland A's on May 1; 14 Minnesota Twins on May 5, 1968

Most consecutive one-hit games: 2 . April 26, M ay 1, 1968.

Most strikeouts in 3 consecutive games (40):

1) 16 Oakland A's on May 1, 14 Minnesota Twins on May 5, 10 Baltimore Orioles May 10, 1968.

2) 11 Twins July 1, 14 Angels July 6, 15 A's July 12, 1968.

**Luis Tiant:**

Most strikeouts in 10 inning game (19), 196; tied by Nolan Ryan, June 8, 1977. Broken by Randy Johnson (20 in 9 innings) May 8, 2001.

Fewest hits/9 innings, season (1968): 5.295; broken by Nolan Ryan (5.261), 1972

Most consecutive shutouts (4), tie, 1968.

# Acknowledgements

Statistical data used in tables and charts was obtained and/or derived from:

http://www.baseball-reference.com

http://www.baseball-almanac.com

http://cleveland.indians.mlb.com

http://the baseball cube.com

And thanks to:

Andrew Clem for his stadium layout diagrams at www.andrewclem

Curtis Danburg and the Publicity and Communications Dept., Cleveland Indians Baseball Club

Jane Khoury, Ph. D., for statistical support.

Jon Warden, who played the game, for his insider's opinions

www.thebaseballcube.com

Vern Fuller, for rekindling an old friendship and for his viewpoints from a guy who stood at the plate with not only the old large strike zone and the new contracted strike zone after '68, but also with the old mound height of 15 inches, and the shortened height of 10' after '68.

Russell Schneider, unofficial historian of the Cleveland Indians, for his insights and suggestions

To these Individuals and Major League Clubs for Information regarding their Bullpen Catchers and Coaches:

Rob Butcher, Director of Media Relations, Cincinnati Reds

Scott Wadsworth, Kansas City Royals

Scott Rusiski, Pittsburgh Pirates

Maribel Castro, San Diego Padres

Carey Patas, Baltimore Orioles

Brett Searson, Los Angeles Dodgers

Phil Derick, Boston Red Sox

Bullpen Catchers David Wallace of the Indians and Mike Stefanski of the Reds for sharing some information on *The Job: 2010*

Leo Bradley, for taking time to read the manuscript and weighing in on its merit.

Larry Zajac, who frequently stepped out of the box, and who inspired people to be as good as they could be.

Lucille and Adolph, my first fans.

Cleveland Police Education Foundation

Greater Cleveland Police Scholarship Fund

Bill O'Brien for many helpful suggestions

David Wallace, Cleveland Indians' bullpen catcher

Mike Stefanski, Cincinnati Reds' bullpen catcher

# Index

# References

[1] Associated Press: Jenkins calls out McGwire. Cincinnati Enquirer, January 22, 2010. P. C3

[2] http:www.med.uc.edu/radiology/directory/profile.html?userid=MTQwMg%3D%3D

[3] Bouton J: Ball Four. Dell Books, 1971.

[4] Brosnan J: Pennant Race, Harper & Bros., New York, 1962.

[5] Kucinich D: The courage to survive. Phoenix Books, Los Angeles, CA, 2007, pp. 40-41

[6] Lewis M: Moneyball. W. W. Norton & Company, Inc. ,New York, NY, 2004

[7] Lederer R: Review of *Baseball Abstracts* at http://baseballanalysts.com/archives/2004/07/abstracts_from_12.php.

[8] McCracken V: Pitching and defense. How much control do hurlers have? http://www.baseballprospectus.com/article.php?articleid=878

[9] Gouldsberry E: Is the strikeout overrated? http://www.thisgreatgame.com/opinion5-09.html

[10] Smith C: On Baseball: Numbers tell it all: 1997 was impressive. New York Times, Sept. 29, 1997. www.new yorktimes.com/1997/09/29/sports/on-baseball-numbers-tell-it-all-1997-was-impressive.html

[11] Edes G: Clemens implicated in steroid scandal by trainer. http://www.newser.com/archive-sports-news/1P2-12038055/clemens-implicated-in-steroid-scandal-by-trainer.html

[12] Lewis M: op. cit., p. 81

[13] Wikipedia: http//en.wikipedia.org/wiki/Bullpen

[14] Unsung major league mentors: the coaches. 247baseball.com/web/wp-content/uploads/2009/04/07-ban-bb2008-cr1.pdf

15 Bedingfield G: Bill Lobe. Baseball in wartime. http://www.baseballinwartime.com/player_biographies/lobe_bill.htm

[16] Burick S: Cinderella Catcher. Baseball Digest. 1967; 26:83

[17] McDermott M: Bullpen catchers-how they impact a baseball game and the team. http://www.ezinearticles.com/?BullpenCatchers—How They Impact a Baseball-Game-and-the-Team.html

[18] http://www.stevepinto.com/Baseball_Related/Baseball_Coaching/21963.html

[19] Dodd M. Batting practice: the game before the game. http://usatody.com/sports/baseball/200-08-15-cover-batting-practice_x.htm

[20]http://oakla=.athletics.mlb.com/news/article.jsp?ymd=200608178&content_id=1615561&vkey=news_oak&fext .jsp&c_id=oaknd

[21] Young G: Bullpen catchers. http://www.everyjoe.com/knucklecurve/bullpen-catchers/

[22] Ron Hunt, Ultimate Mets Database. http://www.ultimatemets.com/profile.php?PlayerCode=0053&tabno=7

[23] http:www.usatoday.com/sports/baseball/sbbw5246.html

[24] Schneider R: The Cleveland Indians Encyclopedia , Third Edition. Sports Publishing L.L.C., Champaign, IL, 2004.

[25] Costa, B: New York Mets bullpen catcher is jack of all trades, master of being invisible. http//www.nj.com/mets/index/.ssf/2009/05/new_your_mets_bullpen_catcher.html

[26] Costa B: New York mets bullpen catcher Dave Racaniello is jack of all trades, master of being invisible. http://www.nj.com/mets/index.ssf/2009/05/new_york_mets_bullpen_catcher.html

[27] Maitre M: A's bullpen catcher learns on the move. The Oakland Tribune. http://www.highbeam.com/doc/1P2-7071590.html

[28] www.oaklandyard.com/baseballcenter.htm -

[29] Anonymous. Pierre Arsenault. Baseball-reference.com/bullpen/Pierre_Arsenault

[30] Mandel K. Phils name Gradoville bullpen catcher. http://philadelphia.phillies.mlb.com/news/article.jsp?ymd=20081205&content_id=3703775&vkey=news_phi&fext=.jsp&c_id=phi

[31] Arnold K: 14 innings is no easy day for the bullpen catcher, either. http://www.heraldnet.com/article/20090918/BLOG05/909189976

[32] Anonymous. Rick Stelmazek. http://en.wikipedia/Rick_Stelmaszek

[33] Hoynes P: Cleveland Indians spring-training chatter: Grady Sizemore hits first homer at Goodyear Ballpark http://www.cleveland.com/tribe/index.ssf/2009/02/cleveland_indians_springtraini_1.html

[34] http://www.baseball-reference.com/minors/player.cgi?id=salas-002mar

[35] http://www.baseball-reference.com/players/m/mercaor01.shtml

[36] Lassen D: Soliz finds home in Angels' bullpen. Ventura County Star. Aug. 15, 2009 http://www.venturacountystar.com/news/2009/aug/15/soliz-finds-home-in-angels-bullpen/

[37] http://www.baseball-reference.com/minors/player.cgi?id=deck--001ron

[38] http://www.baseball-reference.com/minors/player.cgi?id=duplis001wil

[39] Marshall M: A day in the life of the bullpen catcher. http://hamptonroads.com/node/97661

[40] Sherman J: Former Yankees staffer: "no way alex was on juice." New York Post. http://www.nypost.com/p/sports/yankees/former_yankees_staffer_no_way_alex_8J7rcbbf2jozLa2JS6JpnJ

[41] http://www.baseball-reference.com/minors/player.cgi?id=borzel001mic

[42] http://en.wikipedia.org/wiki/John_Gibbons

[43] Lewis F: The Cleveland Indians.. Kent State University Press, Kent, OH, 2006. P.95.

[44] http://www.mlive.com/tigers/index.ss...cher_will.html

[45] http://www.thenewsroom.com/details/3748049

[46] Morris P: *Catcher*, Ivan R. Dee, Publisher, Chicago, IL, 2009, p.279.

[47] Brosnan J: The long season. Harper and Row, Publishers, New York, 1960, p. 16.

[48] Crandall D: "Del Crandall on the art of catching." In Sports Illustrated baseball." J. B. Lippincott Co., Philadelphia and New York, 1960, p. 35.

[49] Morris P: Op cit., p. 278.

[50] Neal LF: Bullpen catcher: a masked ball http://www.startribune.com/sports/twins/53256822.html?page=2&c=y

[51] Patterson M: http://newsok.com/redhawks-report-ryan-reddick-catches-nifty-role-as-bullpen-catcher/article/3388227

[52] Grosshandler S, Diamond Docs. Journal of baseball research. 1975; 4:12. At http://research.sabr.org/journals/archive/brj

[53] Lewis F: op cit., P.90.

[54] Halberstam D: October 1964. Random House Publishing Group, New York, 1994, p. 119

[55] Powers AT: The business of baseball. McFarland & Company Publishers, Jefferson, North Carolina, 2003, p.143

[56] James B, Neyer R: The Neyer/James guide to pitchers. Fireside, New York, 2004, p. 38.

57 ACT NATURALLY © Sony/ATV Musoc Publishing LLC. All rights administered by Sony/ATV & Music Square West, Nashville TN 37203. All rights reserved. Used by Permission.

58 Judge M: Stealing home. http://online.wsj.com/article/SB10001424052970204908604574332641476471218.html

59 Anonymous. It's pre-game warm-up time. Cleveland Press, June 17, 1965, p. C 12

60 McCoy H: www.highbeam.com/doc/1P2-1199223.1.html

61 Costa B: New York Mets turn focus back to defense with early infield practice. http://www.nj.com/mets/index.ssf/2009/04/new_york_mets_turn_focus_back.html

62 McCalvey A: Crew takes rare infield practice Tuesday. http://washington.nationals.mlb.com/news/article.jsp?ymd=20090728&content_id=6110300&vkey=news_mil&fext=.jsp&c_id=mil

63 Lewis F: The Cleveland Indians.. Kent State University Press, Kent, OH, 2006. Forward by Russell Schneider, p. xi.

64 Cryns J: Hanging in the bullpen. http//www.expressmilwaukee.com.article-2316-hanging-in-the-bullpen.html

65 The Brushback Report. "Bullpen catcher not sure what to do during bench clearing brawl. http://www.thebrushback.com/Archives/bullpen_full.htm

66 Cafardo N: Bullpen and first are odd jobs. Boston Globe, April 1, 1994. http://www.encyclopedia.com/doc/1P2-8273008.html

67 Hammer T: Seven questions with Rob Flippo, Dodgers' bullpen catcher. http://laist.com/2009/04/24/seven_questions_with_rob_flippo_dod.php

68 James B, Neyer R: op. cit., p. 30.

69 Zumstead D: The cheater's guide to baseball. Houghton Mifflin Co., New York, NY, 2007, p. 145

70 Encyclopedia of Baseball Catcher's Equipment - Mitt http://members.tripod.com/bb_catchers/catchers/equip1.htm

71 Gonzalez B: http://www3.signonsandiego.com/stories/2009/jul/31/1m31digangi001739-joe-digangi-coronadan-told-tales/

72 Ginn TA, Smith AM, Snyder JR, Koman LA, Smith BP, Rushing J: Vascular changes of the hand in professional players with emphasis of digital ischemia in catchers. J Bone Joint Surg Am 2005; 87: 1464-1469.

73 Schneider R: "Howdy doody or Jackie Gleason?." In Tribe memories: the first century. Moonlight Publishing, Hinckley, OH. 2000, p. 123.

74 http://images.ulib.csuohio.edu/cdm4/browse.php?CISOROOT=/press&CISOSTART=1,161

75 Anonymous, It's pre-game warm-up time. Cleveland Press, June 17, 1965, p. C12

76 Royse P: Bull pen scholar helps Indians. Cleveland Press, Aug. 19, 1964, p. A7.

77 Schneider, R : Op cit p. 80.

78 Kurkjian T: Between the lines. Sports Illustrated. June 24, 1991 .http://sportsillustrated.cnn.com/vault/article/magazine/MAG1139902/index.htm

79 Keri J: Forty years later, Gibson's 1.12 ERA remains magic number. http://sports.espn.go.com/espn/blacjhistory2008/columns/story?page=keri/080221

80 Ngo B: Archive for the Voros McCracken category. http://bobngo.com/research/blog/?cat=93

81 Reina C: Unlocking dominant pitchers with SWHIP. http://baseball.realgm.com Jan 15, 2009

82 Leggett W: From mountain to molehill. Sports illustrated, March 24, 1969, pp. 22

83 James B: The new Bill James historical baseball abstract. Simon and Schuster, New York, 2001, p. 250.

84 Zumstead D: Op cit., p. 20

85 Leggett W: Op cit.,., p. 23

86 Will G: Men at work. Harper Perennial, New York, 1990, p. 103.

87 Ibid. p. 804

88 Scully GW: The business of major league baseball. University of Chicago Press, Chicago, 1989, p. 47.

89 Ibid., p. 253

90 Pluto T: The Curse of Rocky Colavito , Simon and Schuster, Inc., New York, NY, 1995, pp. 81-99.

91 Angel R: The summer game. CBS Publications. Pp. 196-200.

92 James B:Op. cit., p. 307.

93 Tuttle D: Leveling the playing field: moaning about pitcher's mounds is in vogue this season. The Sporting News. June 30, 2003. http://findarticles.com/p/articles/mi_m1208/is_26_227/ai_104440066/

94 Tango T: Changes in home run rates during the retrosheet years. Hardball Times. Feb. 15, 2008

95 LW Cinamon. The Tradeoff Between Home Runs and Contact Rate. SSRN: http/ssrn.com/abstract=953409

96 Goff BL, Shughart WF, Tollison RD Economic Inquiry, Vol 36, 1998

97 Barra A: A battle of the bullpens. Wall Street Journal, October 24, 2009, p. W14.

98 Treder S: Eddie, eddie, eddie and the American league walkathon. Hardball Times, Sept. 01, 2004. http://www.hardballtimes.com/main/article/eddie-eddie-eddie-and-the-american-league-walkathon/

99 Miller, S, Plunking parallel: Steroid use and hit batsmen. New York Times, Apr.25, 2010, p. SP 9.

100 http://mlb.imaginesports.com/bball/reference/park_factors/popup

101 http://www.answers.com/topic/fenway-park

102 http://www.andrewclem.com/Baseball/Stadiums_by_class.html

103 http://www.chacha.com/search/foul+balls+per+game

104 Andrechek S: Two strikes, you're out? Could baseball improve the game by altering one of its Fundamentalrules? http://baseballanalysts.com/archives/2009/07/two_strikes_you.php

105 http://www.walteromalley.com/hist_hof_koufax.php

106 Devaney A: Steroids, Home Runs, and the Law of Giants. www.arthur devany.com/webstuff/DeVanyHomeRuns.pdf.

107 James B: Op. cit., p. 306

108 Anonymous, Home runs vs. strikeouts. Baseball Research Journal, 1972; 1:14

109 Galbraith K: Is Mark McGwire on steroids? http://www.slate.com/id/1001967/

110 http://en.wikipedia.org/wiki/mark_mcgwire

111 http://www.baseballssteroidera.com

112 Anonymous. Report: Sosa tested positive for steroids in 2003 http://sportsillustrated.cnn.com/2009/baseball/mlb/06/16/sosa.steroids/index.html

113 Curtis B: The juice and I. http://www.slate.com/id/2113745/

114 Dennis Y: Which sports can you believe in? Wall Street Journal, Nov. 12, 2009, p. D10.

115 Associated Press. Doctor denies drug claims. Cincinnati Enquirer, Dec. 16, 2009. P B6.

116 Groeschen T: Arroyo says he could be on list. Cincinnati Enquirer, July 30, 2009, p. D1.

117 Nightingale B: Risky routine for Arroyo. Cincinnati Enquirer, Aug. 13, 2009, p. C1

118 http://ballhype.com/story/the_associated_press_rocker_rangers_advised_on/

119 Coffey W, Former All-Star Jack Armstrong Hoping to Set the Record Straight on Steroid Era, N.Y. Daily News, Dec. 9, 2007.

120 Time line of baseball's steroid scandal. http://nbcsports.msnbc.com/id/22247395/

121 Mitchell Report. http://files.mlb.com/mitchrpt.pdf, pp. 60-61

122 Ibid., R-2.

123 Brosnan J: op cit., p.130.

124 Ibid, p. 132

125 Brosnan J: The long season. Harper and Row, New York, 1960, P. 26.

126 Frias C: Baseball and amphetamines. http://www.palmbeachpost.com/sports/content/sports/epaper/2006/04/02/PBP_AMPHET_0402.html

127 Regan J: The war against strikeouts. http://bleacherreport.com/articles/261657-the-war-against-strikeouts

128 Bahr C: Hitters' strikeouts are baseball's most overrated stat. http://www.sportingnews.com/mlb/article/2009-09-24/hitters-strikeouts-are-baseballs-most-overrated-stat

129 Anonymous. Rugby star banned in 1st HGH detection. USA Today, Feb. 23, 2010, p 7C.

130 Schmidt, MS: Ripples of English HGH test are being felt across the US. New York Times, Feb. 28, 2010, p. SP 1

131 Spatz L, Ed.: The SABR baseball list and record book. Scribner, New York, 2007.

132 Kendrick S: Free agency primer. http://baseball.about.com/od/majorleaguebasics/a/freeagentprimer.htm

# Biography

Thomas A. Tomsick, M.D. has been a faculty member of the University of Cincinnati College of Medicine since 1976 and Director of Neuroradiology since 1993.

Tomsick achieved the Samuel Kaplan Visionary Award for Research in Cardiovascular Disease from the Cincinnati Division of the American Heart Association in 2005. He was awarded the Harold B. Spitz Resident Teaching Award (2009). He has been named one of the Best Doctors in America 2001–2010. His research has included participation in multiple studies of methods and devices for treatment of aneurysms, vascular malformations, tumors, and stroke.

Tomsick has authored or co-authored over 130 manuscripts and chapters. He co-authored and edited the book *Carotid Cavernous Fistula*, Digital Educational Publishing (1997).

Dr. Tomsick is an alumnus of Saint Ignatius High School of Cleveland, Ohio. He attended John Carroll University and attained a doctorate at Saint Louis University School of Medicine.

Tom is married to his college sweetheart, Judy. They have two children: Lisa, a lawyer living in Los Angeles, and Scott, a Muscukoskeletal Radiologist in Denver. Tom is a grandfather of Jackson and Grace.

Tom is a member of The Society for American Baseball Research (SABR), baseball enthusiasts dedicated to researching all facets of the game.